"In Israel, Cypel effectively argues, force has triumphed over international law." —*KIRKUS REVIEWS*

"An impassioned...critique of Israel's 'rightward drift' since the 1967 Six-Day War that resulted in the occupation of the West Bank and Gaza." —*PUBLISHERS WEEKLY*

"Cypel's book convincingly demonstrates that his conscientious, eminently Jewish, self-criticism, while full of moral outrage and righteous censure, addresses both sides of the homeland–diaspora divide." —*MUSLIM WORLD BOOK REVIEW*

"Cypel offers an unflinching and unrelenting survey of the many ways in which the occupation occupied Israel, and Israel repeatedly chose the occupation over the Jews of the diaspora." —GERSHON SHAFIR, DISTINGUISHED PROFESSOR OF SOCIOLOGY, UNIVERSITY OF CALIFORNIA, SAN DIEGO, AND AUTHOR OF *A HALF CENTURY OF OCCUPATION: ISRAEL, PALESTINE, AND THE WORLD'S MOST INTRACTABLE CONFLICT*

"Alarmed, angry, and appalled, Sylvain Cypel accurately and succinctly describes an Israel that, if it were not Jewish, would have reminded all diaspora Jews of regimes they suffered and fled from." —AMIRA HASS, H/ ...)E OCCUPIED PALESTINIAN TERF

T0182667

"This book often feels like a high-precision scalpel on the skin: its incisiveness may hurt, but it is always put at the service of the reader's betterment. This is one of the most poignant and accurate accounts of the moral demise of a complex society, both brutal and vulnerable. Sylvain Cypel demonstrates in this book why he is one of the most important journalists in France." —EVA ILLOUZ, AUTHOR OF *THE END OF LOVE: A SOCIOLOGY OF NEGATIVE RELATIONS*

"The content of Sylvain Cypel's new book, *The State of Israel vs. the Jews*, is as stunning as the title. A distinguished journalist at the top of his profession, Cypel documents the systematic injustice that Israel perpetrates against Palestinians. Ultimately, he shows that Israel is (in the words of the late Tony Judt) 'bad for the Jews': Jews in Israel and elsewhere in the world. Israel is 'bad for the Jews' precisely to the extent that it is ruinous for the Palestinians. This original angle makes *The State of Israel vs. the Jews* stand out in the vast literature on Israel–Palestine. Cypel, moreover, writes as an insider: a Jew who lived in Israel for twelve years and studied at the Hebrew University of Jerusalem. Holding a mirror up to reality, denouncing injustice, Cypel is an exponent of an ancient Jewish art that began with Amos, Isaiah, Jeremiah, and the other Hebrew prophets: iconoclasts who shattered the false self-images of their contemporaries." —DR. BRIAN KLUG, SENIOR RESEARCH FELLOW IN PHILOSOPHY, ST. BENET'S HALL, UNIVERSITY OF OXFORD, AND AUTHOR OF *BEING JEWISH AND DOING JUSTICE: BRINGING ARGUMENT TO LIFE*

"When the Israeli human-rights organization B'Tselem condemned the State of Israel for practicing 'apartheid,' an analogy that had long been seen as unacceptable in mainstream public opinion could no longer be denied, and Jews across the globe were at last confronted with a choice: Can they continue to see themselves as adherents to an ancient and prophetic tradition that sustains a commitment to peace and justice? Or will they break this bond and declare their higher allegiance to sheer power alone, even if they must continue to deny not only the rights but the very humanity of another people? In a book that is carefully documented yet burns with moral outrage, veteran French journalist Sylvain Cypel reflects on the growing divide between Israel and the Jewish diaspora in both France and the United States. Composed with the general reader in mind, this is a superb summary of the current impasse." —PETER E. GORDON, HARVARD UNIVERSITY

The State of Israel vs. the Jews

Sylvain Cypel

The State
of Israel
vs.
the Jews

TRANSLATED FROM
THE FRENCH BY

William Rodarmor

OTHER PRESS
NEW YORK

First softcover edition 2024

ISBN 978-1-63542-534-5

Originally published in French as *L'État d'Israël contre les Juifs* in 2020 by Éditions La Découverte, Paris.
Copyright © Éditions La Découverte, 2020

Translation copyright © William Rodarmor, 2021
Preface to the 2024 Edition translation copyright © William Rodarmor, 2024

Map on page 84 by Valerie Sebestyen, based on this Wikimedia Commons map: https://commons.wikimedia.org/wiki/File: Control_status_of_the_West_Bank_as_per_the_Oslo_Accords.svg

Production editor: Yvonne E. Cárdenas
Text designer: Julie Fry
This book was set in Swift and Nobel by
Alpha Design & Composition of Pittsfield, NH

10 9 8 7 6 5 4 3 2 1

Library of Congress Cataloging-in-Publication Data
Names: Cypel, Sylvain, author. | Rodarmor, William, translator.
Title: The state of Israel vs. the Jews / Sylvain Cypel ; translated from the French by William Rodarmor.
Other titles: État d'Israël contre les Juifs. English | State of Israel versus the Jews
Description: New York : Other Press, [2021] | Originally published in French as L'État d'Israël contre les Juifs in 2020 by Éditions La Découverte, Paris. | Includes bibliographical references and index.
Identifiers: LCCN 2021005598 (print) | LCCN 2021005599 (ebook) | ISBN 9781635420975 (hardcover) | ISBN 9781635420982 (ebook)
Subjects: LCSH: Jews—Politics and government—21st century. | Arab-Israeli conflict—1993- | Jews—Attitudes toward Israel. | Jews—Identity. | Israel and the diaspora. | Citizenship—Jews. | Israel—Foreign relations—21st century.
Classification: LCC DS128.2 .C9613 2021 (print) | LCC DS128.2 (ebook) | DDC 956.9405/5—dc23
LC record available at https://lccn.loc.gov/2021005598
LC ebook record available at https://lccn.loc.gov/2021005599

To

Lila, Dan, Matti, Emmanuel,

Suzanne & Rebecca

The depressing truth
is that Israel's current behavior
is not just bad for America,
though it surely is.
It is not even just bad for Israel itself,
as many Israelis silently acknowledge.
The depressing truth today
is that Israel is bad for the Jews.

— TONY JUDT
(1948–2010)

Contents

Preface to the 2024 Edition

Dahiya: "The fate of our generation"[1]

In April 1956, a twenty-one-year-old Israeli soldier named Roi Rutenberg was killed at Kibbutz Nahal Oz, one of the kibbutzim near Gaza that Hamas would attack six decades later, on October 7, 2023. The killers were "infiltrators," the term Israelis once used to describe Palestinians expelled in 1948 who snuck back across the border to see what had happened to their homes and land. General Moshe Dayan, the army chief of staff, attended Rutenberg's funeral, and began his eulogy this way:

> *Let us not cast the blame on the murderers today. Why should we declare their burning hatred for us? For eight years they have been sitting in the refugee camps in Gaza, and before their eyes we have been transforming the lands and the villages, where they and their fathers dwelt, into our estate... It is not among the Arabs in Gaza, but in our own midst that we must seek Roi's blood. How did we shut our eyes and refuse to look squarely at our fate, and see, in all its*

brutality, the destiny of our generation?...We are a generation that settles the land, and without the steel helmet and the canon's maw we will not be able to plant a tree and build a home...This is the fate of our generation.[2]

Dayan was Israel's most revered military hero. Seventy years later, one can see the abyss that separates him from General Yoav Gallant, the current defense minister. The day after the Hamas attack, Gallant declared that Israel was dealing with "human animals." So what, exactly, was Dayan saying? Basically, that we Jews are the aggressors, and they the victims. That we seized their land, and they were robbed of it—and that we need to recognize what we have done. But ever since the first settlers arrived at the end of the nineteenth century, Zionism's mantra has been "There is no other choice." And that mantra continues to generate crimes and misery.

In the 1950s, Dayan's speech was unusual, because it clashed with the dominant denial. David Ben-Gurion, the founder of the Israeli state, had ordered the crafting of a version of history that claimed Israel had "never expelled a single Arab." In 1947–49, during the Palestinians' Nakba ("catastrophe"), they were said to have "left voluntarily." This denial has long held sway in Israeli society. Today, that society increasingly approves of the original crime, validates those crimes committed in Gaza today, and expresses the undisguised wish to see the Palestinians once again expelled from the "Land of Israel."

Politics as the continuation of war

Israeli society has greatly changed in the last seventy years. Racism and the colonial mentality are now deeply entrenched.

Since 1967, generation after generation of young people has learned to practice Jewish supremacy while manning checkpoints between Israel and the Palestinian territories. In counterpoint, a small fringe of courageous Israelis has drawn a conclusion different from Moshe Dayan's view of the crimes and deprivations committed daily against the Palestinians. To break this frightful, murderous cycle, they feel, you have to stop thinking of it as inevitable. You have to instead work toward a solution where Palestinians and Israeli Jews are both born "free and equal in dignity and rights," as proclaimed in the Universal Declaration of Human Rights. We are very far from that.

On the Palestinian side, regardless of what one thinks of the method Hamas used—spreading terror—October 7, 2023 was the most spectacular armed operation ever launched against Israel by the Nakba heirs. It left Israelis feeling battered, stunned, and enraged. In addition to killing more than a thousand Israelis, Hamas militants also seized 240 hostages, the majority of them civilians. And they committed rapes.[3]

The attack changed the geopolitics of the entire region. Just three weeks earlier, Prime Minister Benjamin Netanyahu had returned from the U.N. General Assembly in New York, where he met with Joe Biden and Saudi leaders, boasting that he had scored the greatest diplomatic success in Israel's history. A defense alliance between the United States, Israel, and Saudi Arabia would soon torpedo any vague hope of a Palestinian state. The "Palestinian question" would no longer be an obstacle to a Pax Americana with the Arab world. Palestine and its people were being swept off the map. On October 7, Hamas put them front and center in the most tragic way possible. And you can't ignore the terrible cost of this attack on the Palestinians themselves. Their territory has been devastated to an extent unseen since Vladimir Putin's war on Chechnya in 1999–2000, Bashar al-Assad's on the eastern neighborhoods of Aleppo in 2012–15, or again Putin's on Mariupol, Ukraine, in 2022.

Once its astonishment had passed, Israel launched a bombing campaign of unbelievable dimensions. "In the first six days of the air campaign, Israel dropped six thousand more bombs than the U.S.-led coalition did in any single month of the war against ISIS, even at the height of the operation," reported *Foreign Affairs*.[4] The level of lethality far exceeds the Geneva Convention's Rule of Proportionality. Israel also forced the 1.4 million people living in the northern Gaza Strip to leave for the south, toward an even smaller area. It then destroyed the north's infrastructure and homes, to keep anyone from returning once the war was over. Ethnic cleansing, in short. During Israel's earlier strikes on Gaza in 2012, 2014, and 2021, the air force dropped its bombs on 110 to 200 targets a day, on average. In 2023, the tempo was 430 a day in just the first thirty-five days. The mass killing of civilians, combined with their forced displacement, doubtless constitutes a war crime.

Five months after the start of the Israeli offensive, Tedros Adhanom Ghebreyesus, the director-general of the World Health Organization, declared that Gaza "has become a death zone." On October 7, 2023, Israel lost almost 1,200 people, two thirds of them civilians, and at least 3,400 people were wounded. As of this writing, on April 7, 2024, i.e., exactly six months after the deadly Hamas attack, in addition to more than 1,140 Israeli civilian and security victims who fell that day, the 3,400 people wounded, and the 250 taken hostage, the Israelis, according to official military sources, counted 604 soldiers fallen in the following Gaza war and 3,188 wounded. For its part, on April 29, 2024, the Gaza Ministry of Health announced that the number of Palestinian deaths had reached 34,488 in Gaza (and 491 in the West Bank), more than two thirds of them civilians, and that the number of wounded stood at 77,643 in Gaza, and more than 4,800 in the West Bank. The number of dead still lying under the bombardment ruins is unknown for now. According to UN sources, women and children account for two-thirds of victims.

Following bombardment and attacks by Israeli soldiers, two thirds of the thirty-six hospitals in the Gaza Strip were no longer operating, according to the United Nations, and the rest were seriously dysfunctional, with staff working in extremely challenging conditions. But the worst seems yet to come. On February 22, the United Nations Office for the Coordination of Humanitarian Affairs reported that "most of the population is suffering from extreme hunger." It estimated that 2.2 million people, or 90 percent of the population, faced an imminent threat of famine. The day before, the agency's coordinator said that between January 21 and February 18, the number of daily entries of trucks carrying food, medicine, and other humanitarian aid, had numbered between 0 (after five attempts) and a high of 210, for an average of 100 a day. This was just 20 percent of what had entered Gaza *before* the war, when Gazans were meeting 80 percent of their food needs by producing vegetables, fruits, eggs, and chickens, none of which exist anymore.

The article's title doesn't pull any punches: "A Mass Assassination Factory."[5] On November 30, 2023, in the online Israeli journal *Local Call*, reporter Yuval Abraham described the method used by the Israeli army against Gaza in its Operation Iron Swords. Active and reserve officers, many of them members of intelligence units, told Abraham that the army's killing of civilians is deliberate. His verdict: We are seeing "a significant expansion of bombing of targets that are not distinctly military in nature" where "the number of civilians likely to be bombed is calculated and known in advance."

Artificial intelligence (AI) plays a dominant role in this. The Targets Administrative Division, the unit tasked with targeting, has hundreds of officers and soldiers. On November 2, an army spokesman boasted that an AI system elegantly named "The Gospel" "processes enormous amounts of data that 'tens of thousands of intelligence officers could not process,'" and "produces targets at a rapid rate." This is what one former officer of the unit labels "a mass assassination factory." Why call it that? Because "the emphasis is on quantity and not on quality" of human targets, he said. "The number of civilians who are certain to be killed is known in advance…Nothing happens by accident," Abraham was told. Official sources report that in the first six days of the offensive, four thousand tons of bombs were dropped on Gaza infrastructure, office buildings, and residences. Most of the strikes hit civilians, just as in 2014 and 2021, but on a far greater scale.

One military doctrine dictates this multipart destruction of goods and lives. It is called "Dahiya," after a southern neighborhood in Beirut that the Israeli air force practically leveled during the 2006 war against Hezbollah in Lebanon. Developed by General Gadi Eizenkot (chief of staff from 2015 to 2019), the doctrine stipulates that when an army is facing an "asymmetrical" enemy, as in Israel's case, it must use a disproportionate and multidirectional force targeting civilians, to make them pressure the enemy forces to quit their attacks. In a rejection of the laws of war, the doctrine makes no distinction between military and civilian targets. Besides, bombing civilians has a pedagogical virtue: they will understand that the terrorists bring them nothing but misery. "Going after the population is the only way," General Eizenkot said in 2008, speaking of Hezbollah.[6] Because Gaza is the very model of an asymmetrical war, his Dahiya doctrine has become the engine of Israeli strategy. Netanyahu made Eizenkot a member of his war cabinet.

It is worth examining the role of AI in the relentless pounding of Gaza. To what is known in military jargon as "tactical targets" (weapons and soldiers) and "underground targets" (hidden arsenals), the army has added "power targets," meaning civilians. The basic idea is that manifesting "power" is key to its strategic goal, which is restoring the army's capacity of dissuasion. "The first time the Israeli army publicly defined power targets in Gaza was at the end of Operation Protective Edge in 2014," wrote Abraham.[7] In the current conflict, the Dahiya doctrine has been applied without restraint. Gazans are being shown that no one is safe. Here is one example among hundreds: The Al-Mohandessin building was in a zone announced as having been "secured" by the Israeli army. It was bombed, and 150 civilians died.

The two sides' relationship is vividly illustrated in Albert Memmi's 1957 book *The Colonizer and the Colonized*. Blind to his own actions, the colonizer creates whatever image of the colonized he pleases, unaware that it would apply just as well to himself. So it is with Israel's famous belief that "force is the only thing Arabs understand." When Israel feels it is facing a real or potential threat, its first response is always force. The Israeli army bombarded Gaza in 2008. Then did it again in 2012, in 2014, and in 2021. After each cease-fire, it declared it had "reestablished its capacity of dissuasion." That is, until it was time to reestablish it again. But here's the problem. Back in 2008, Hamas was lobbing homemade, short-range rockets at Israel. By 2021, its fighters were firing reliable missiles as far as Tel Aviv and Jerusalem. Each time, despite Israel's "dissuasion," Hamas's military capability improved. Israel's most recent bright idea was to build an "impassible" wall that would lock Gazans in once and for all. This "innovative and technically advanced project" would finally give Israelis "a sense of security," said Defense Minister Benny Gantz in 2021.[8] We all know what happened next.

The war that Israel was been waging since October 7, 2023, can't be understood without taking into account this deep-seated Israeli attitude: Since previous efforts haven't been enough, all you can do is to strike harder than ever. Especially since Hamas's attack so shocked the world that it offered plenty of leeway for retaliation. But the question arose very early: What exactly is Israel's goal in this war? The question can't be answered, because Israeli leaders turn around Clausewitz's adage that war is the continuation of politics by other means. They think that politics is the pursuit of war itself.

From the radical colonial right to the Laborite left, many Israelis feel it is essential to adhere to two vital principles: 1) There will never be a Palestinian state; 2) The ratio of military forces to the environment must always be maintained (or increased). The rest will depend on circumstances. War-time objectives held by Israeli thinkers are never precisely fixed at the outset. They depend on how successful the war turns out to be: crushing or modest, or even failed. In other words, Israeli war aims keep shifting, like the country's own borders. Israel may be the only state in the world that has never explicitly defined its frontiers. The process is ongoing and unfinished, so political objectives depend on the result of its last war. In 1967, Israel conquered the Sinai, and Moshe Dayan declared that he would rather have the Sinai without peace with Egypt than peace without the Sinai. Egypt's president Anwar Sadat then declared war on Israel in 1973. He lost militarily, but won politically. In 1978, Israel signed a peace treaty with Egypt and gave back the Sinai. Dayan applauded. Everything is a matter of circumstance.

The Godwin point in the debate

On October 8, 2023, Israel's ultimate objectives remained fluid. But it had a new strategy on tap in the meantime, the so-called Dahiya doctrine. What happened after the war would depend on the war's outcome. If all the Gazans could be expelled to Egypt, a wide range of possibilities would open up. If only half could be booted out, that would be different. And if only very few, that would require further thought. How power was exercised would determine the political consequences. That's always been the way Israel's leaders (and its people) have thought. It isn't true of all of them, and not all of them apply this position the same way. But in an emergency, old habits click in, and the only question becomes: How do we use force? This is quite extraordinary, because the Dahiya doctrine has sometimes failed. The war on Hezbollah in Lebanon in 2006 was a military failure, for example. But the colonial tropism is so entrenched that nothing has ever modified this fundamental Israeli attitude.

A demonization of the enemy accompanies this bellicose philosophy, as it does in every war. On October 30, 2023, Israeli Ambassador to the United Nations Gilad Erdan showed up wearing the yellow star that the Nazis had imposed on the Jews. The reference was clear: Hamas is the contemporary incarnation of the Nazis, and Israel is striking Gaza to head off a second Holocaust. "Hamas are the new Nazis," Netanyahu had proclaimed earlier.[9] Soon thereafter, he would call Yahya Sinwar, the Hamas leader in Gaza, "a little Hitler."[10] Not that referring to Nazism is limited only to Israel. Among Palestinians, the Jewish state is said to be conducting a genocide. The term is arguable and argued over, especially when it's raised within a "competition among victims," as if to deny Jews sole ownership of ultimate tragedy. That said, the word is appearing more and more among international jurists. But "Nazi" accusations can't be considered equivalent on both sides. Here Israel is the strong, the oppressor, and Palestinians the weak, the oppressed, not the other way around. Finally, calling one's adversary a Nazi has long been a recurring practice in Israeli communications.

It could embody what is called the Godwin point in the debate. The Godwin rule of Nazi analogies says that as an online discussion grows longer, the probability of a comparison involving Nazis or Hitler approaches one.[11] In the course of Israel's history, Egyptian president Gamal Abdel Nasser, PLO chief Yasser Arafat, and Ayatollah Ali Khamenei have all been called a "new Hitler." Today, it's a Hamas leader. Tagging the enemy of the moment with the infamous stigma of "Nazi" is designed to dismiss them, to impose the idea that there is nothing to negotiate with them. Therefore, any armed operation is legitimate, regardless of its impact on civilians. You don't negotiate with Nazis, and you don't stay your hand when battling them. This need to turn an enemy into a Nazi led Israeli officials to start generating "fakes" and spreading them on social media the day after October 7. Not that there was any shortage of crimes committed by the Palestinians, but it was imperative to present the perpetrators as "human animals." The newspaper *Haaretz* launched an investigation. Its verdict: many war crimes committed by Hamas were definitely proven, but so were the fallacious media campaigns by Israeli leaders to promote a "bestial" image of the Palestinian assailants.[12]

The number of children killed, in particular, has been exaggerated. In the end, a single baby and five children under the age of six were killed, according to the religious organization that gathers remains and the National Insurance Institute, the union of Israeli insurance companies. So why did Netanyahu tell President Biden that Hamas terrorists "took dozens of children, tied them up, burned and killed them," when investigators had concluded "there is no proof that children were gathered and killed together"?[13] A number of imaginary crimes have been claimed. In a letter to First Lady Jill Biden, Sara Netanyahu, the prime minister's wife, claimed that a nine-month-pregnant Thai woman named Nutthawaree Munkan had been dragged to Gaza, where her baby was born. In fact, she had never been pregnant. When questioned by reporters, the prime minister's office did not respond. Investigations by Israeli journalists showed how organized falsehoods were immediately promoted. It isn't true that "forty babies had been killed, some of them with their heads cut off." No "babies were hung out on a clothesline."[14] No pregnant woman had her belly cut open so her fetus could be stabbed. None of the horrible acts that were invented by the pushers of *hasbara* (Hebrew for "explaining," and a common euphemism for propaganda) and often picked up by the media actually happened. Why further darken the crime scene, if not to "animalize" the Palestinians?

Such behavior leads some pro-Palestinian circles to claim that Hamas never committed any crimes at all. *Fake vs. fake.* This accompanies an astonishing phenomenon, namely the support Netanyahu gives many racists, including anti-Semites, a topic explored in Chapter 8. Elon Musk, the head of X, traveled to Israel in late November, in the middle of the Gaza war. He was hailed by Israeli leaders and settlers, though in the United States the billionaire is seen as a creator of "fake news" and accused of anti-Semitism by the Jewish community. "Israel's repulsive embrace of Elon Musk is a betrayal of Jews, dead and alive," wrote *Haaretz*.[15] "The Israel visit comes just weeks after Musk…directly engaged and platformed the anti-Semitic conspiracy theory cited by Robert Bowers, the assailant behind the deadliest massacre of American Jews in U.S. history."[16] Netanyahu never fails to call his enemy "Nazis," yet he endorses supremacist themes.

It's worth noting that calling an adversary a Nazi while absolving real racists of any fault is exactly the tack taken by American neoconservatives when they invented categories such as "terrorist" and "global war on terrorism," while sparing their less savory allies from such characterizations. Few people know that in 1979 Netanyahu created the Jonathan Institute, a think tank that greatly contributed to the emergence of American neoconservatism.[17] Since then, "terrorism" has become a uniform category for him, a universal "axis of evil" facing "free societies." The "terrorist" becomes the antithesis of the "freedom fighter," and constitutes "a new race of men that will send humanity back to prehistoric times." The war on terror becomes a useful catch-all. And Netanyahu himself hasn't changed. In his first public appearance after October 7, he proclaimed that "Hamas is Daesh." So terrorism is pure horror—there's nothing to understand, nothing to discuss. Osama Bin Laden, Saddam Hussein, and Ali Khamenei are all peas in a pod, and the same is true of Hamas, Hitler, and Daesh. This binary view of good fighting evil, to which four fifths of Jewish Israeli society subscribes, offers an advantage and a drawback. The (questionable) advantage is that it reduces humanity to two simple categories: terrorists, and all the rest. The drawback is that in the absence of more complex thought, this vision usually winds up collapsing.

Hamas, resistance, and failure

To understand what is happening in Gaza, you cannot overlook the part played by Hamas. Israeli-British Oxford historian Avi Shlaim answered the proponents of Hamas's "eradication" in simple terms: "Hamas is not a terrorist organization pure and simple, as Israel and its Western allies keep insisting. It is a political party with a military wing whose attacks on civilians constitute terrorist acts…It is a mass social movement, a prominent part of the fabric of Palestinian society which reflects its aspiration to freedom and independence. It is the failure of the Palestine Liberation Organization (PLO) to achieve freedom and statehood that largely explains Hamas's growing influence." If you reject this reality, Shlaim argues, you will never understand what is happening between Israelis and Palestinians, which is a conflict between a colonial state and a people who reject its domination.

Hamas is an Islamic-nationalistic party ruled by an ideology that puts the practice of Islam and armed struggle for national liberation at the heart of its doctrine. At one point, it offered Israel not peace, but a decades-long truce. Israel rejected this immediately, just as it challenged the victory that Hamas—which Israel calls "a terrorist entity"—won democratically in the 2006 Palestinian elections. But Netanyahu then proceeded to do everything he could to maintain Hamas's power over Gaza. The Israeli historian Adam Raz has amply documented this strategy of the "useful enemy." During a March 2019 gathering of his party, Netanyahu said, "Whoever opposes a Palestinian state must support delivery of funds to Gaza, because maintaining separation between the PA (Palestine Authority) in the West Bank and Hamas in Gaza will prevent the establishment of a Palestinian state."[19] His counselor, Reserve General Gershon Hacohen, drove the point home. In an interview with the Ynet news website on May 5, 2019, he said, "We need to tell the truth. Netanyahu's strategy is to prevent the option of two states, so he is turning Hamas into his closest partner. Openly, Hamas is an enemy. Covertly, it's an ally."[20]

The fact remains that the charter Hamas adopted at its creation in 1988 is anti-Semitic, wrote Shlaim. The ideology that shapes the education of children under its rule is a mix of deep ignorance of Judaism and an atavistic anti-Semitism, just as in Israel, classes in the Zionist-religious rabbinical schools spread blinkered anti-Muslim racism. Hamas's religious vision is accompanied by an equally problematical concept: making armed struggle the central engine of its anticolonial battle. The Palestinian Fatah, created by Yasser Arafat, considered the Algerian War (1954–1962) to be the perfect model. And for a long time, nationalist Palestinians' modus operandi consisted in terrorist action. When the PLO was sidelined after the failure of Israel-Palestine peace negotiations and the eruption of the Second Intifada in late 2000, Hamas stepped in and adopted that method of combat.

The revolt resulted in a political defeat up and down the line. The Israeli army easily adapted to "suicide terrorism," which consisted in sending young "martyrs" to be blown up. By 2005, the revolt was checked. In 2006, Israel sealed Gaza off from the West Bank. Mahmoud Abbas and the Palestinian Authority urged a return to negotiations, which left Hamas alone in pushing for armed struggle. A series of wars between Israel and Hamas broke out periodically in Gaza. In the West Bank, the PA totally discredited itself by submitting to Israel without obtaining the least concession. This earned Hamas a growing following among the Palestinians.

On one occasion, Hamas did organize peaceful protests. From March 30, 2018 to March 2019, young unarmed Gazans demonstrated every Friday along the "separation fence" in what was called the "March of Return." Each time, Israeli snipers would kill two, three, or more of them, and fifty-eight on the day Trump inaugurated the American embassy's move to Jerusalem. The United Nations calculated that in one year 270 demonstrators had been killed and 28,000 wounded. But the popular mobilization did no more to improve the Gazans' fate than armed struggle had. So Hamas abandoned a kind of mobilization that was alien to it in any case.

The organization has never evaluated Algerian-style confrontation, which amounted to blind terrorism. Because Hamas's failure can be explained on grounds beyond simply a worship of "armed struggle." For starters, Fatah was first created in 1959, but the national Palestinian movement, which was brutally crushed by the British Army during the Great Revolt of 1936–38, only really reappeared after the June 1967 war. In other words, at the very moment when Arab nationalism was suffering its greatest defeat, which led to its decline. The Palestinian nationalists showed up at the party just as the first guests were leaving. Finally, the model Fatah was proposing—to copy Algeria—proved a fatal mistake. The balance of power between the protagonists wasn't the same in Palestine as it had been in Algeria. Westerners didn't see Israel as a colonial country, for example, and the Algerian model wasn't universally applicable.

As Palestinian leaders, neither Fatah nor Hamas ever made use of mass demonstrations, unlike the African National Congress in South Africa, for instance. Yet the only true Palestinian victory was one that followed a large popular movement organized beyond Yasser Arafat's control. The First Intifada (1987–93) won the PLO recognition by an Israeli government that had previously dubbed it "Nazi." But when the Second Intifada erupted, Arafat's Fatah and Hamas reverted to the fundamentals: armed struggle alone. Finding itself in familiar territory, the Israeli army crushed the Palestinians. In Algeria, the massacres perpetuated by French colonial troops in May and June 1945 in Sétif, Guelma, and Kheratta (15,000 to 30,000 dead Algerians, against 102 European civilians killed) were key events in pushing the nascent National Liberation Front to embrace armed struggle. It is highly unlikely that Hamas will benefit from an identical process seventy years later.

Hamas hasn't grasped the fact that terrorism is out of date as a central weapon in national liberation. The world has changed, and in particular the bipolar world no longer exists. October 7, 2023, may have thrust the Palestinians back to the center of Middle Eastern concerns, but it has also brought them the greatest tragedy since the Nakba. And it gives Israel a chance to realize its wildest hopes: to finish and permanently expel the Palestinians from their territory, or at least to crush them—and keep them crushed.

One society dismembered, the other unmuzzled

In this war, Palestinian society in Gaza has disintegrated, and Israel has descended into a kind of madness. As columnist Gideon Levy wrote in alarm, "An unbridled and terribly cruel attack against Gaza creates hatred of Israel at levels we've never seen before, in Gaza, in the West Bank, in the Palestinian diaspora, in the Arab world, and everywhere in the world where people are seeing what the Israelis don't see and don't want to see."[21] For her part, reporter Amira Hass has struggled daily to stay in touch with her many Gazan contacts. The former Gaza *Haaretz* correspondent described the facets of a horrifying tragedy: no drinking water, no food, no electricity, mounds of garbage, fear of epidemics, hunger, crowding, buildings turned into charnel houses, fleeing on foot down roads, prodded by bayonets. "People are fighting each other for insufficient supplies of food and water while the police try to maintain a semblance of order," wrote Hass.[22] The siege of Leningrad comes to mind, along with Biafra and Mariupol.

Meanwhile, fear has gripped Jewish society since October 7. Despite Gaza being reduced to a field of ruins, the feeling of insecurity persists. Something in the average Israeli's previous perception of Gaza has been broken. Before this, the Gaza Strip seemed a long way off—forty-five miles from Tel Aviv by road. People were indifferent to it. The Palestinians were in a cage. But suddenly "one of the most powerful armies in the world turns out to be nothing but a paper tiger."[23] Resentment against the elites is growing, because the government seems so incompetent. Citizens evacuated from the communities close to Gaza couldn't find anyone to help them. Soldiers wandered around, not knowing where to go. Only the NGOs continued to function. Decades of ultra-conservative economic policies has dismantled Israel's public services. "Years of political corruption have left us with an empty shell of a state," thundered journalist Haggai Matar in his appraisal of the first month of the war.[24]

For many, that insecurity is compounded by a feeling of humiliation. How could those pathetic Arabs manage to breach an "impassable" wall? How could they confound the best army in the world? Impossible! Some people on social media went looking for Jewish traitors: "leftist officers" who must have opened the floodgates to Hamas criminals. In parallel, the urge to "finish" the Palestinians once and for all has taken ever-deeper root, swelling into a colonial hatred more brazenly displayed than ever. An overwhelming majority of Israeli Jews remain deaf and blind to the suffering and dehumanization inflicted for decades on a people that share the same territory. Since October 7, this willful blindness has reached incredible heights.

In a society where the mystical and ultra-national fringe has practically reached the height of power with the wind in its sails, narratives are flourishing that inscribe Hamas's attack in a messianic perspective. Everything that happened, it's believed, had been "written." And if you believe holy writ, every crime in response is allowed. Doesn't the Bible say that when Hebrews entered the promised land, they perpetrated a great massacre in Jericho? A taste for genocide has been stirred. It is only a taste, and hasn't been acted on yet. But it is unmistakable. Asked in an interview with Radio Kol Berama whether he was suggesting that some kind of nuclear bomb might be dropped on the enclave to kill everyone, Minister of Heritage Amihai Eliyahu, a member of the racist Jewish Power party, said, "That's one option."[25] He added that "anyone waving a Palestinian or Hamas flag shouldn't continue living on the face of the earth." The supposedly more moderate Energy Minister Yisrael Katz (Likud) merely opposed any humanitarian aid for Gazans. Retired general Giora Eiland suggested exterminating them by releasing deadly viruses, as he wrote in *Yedioth Ahronoth*, Israel's most widely read daily: "After all, severe epidemics in the southern Strip will bring victory closer and reduce fatalities among Israeli soldiers."[26]

Aside from the few who are appalled and marginalized, no one in Israel is shocked by these incredible, explicit statements. The overriding idea is a great expulsion of Palestinians, embraced without reservation by the leaders of Netanyahu's party and the entire extreme colonial right wing. Cried Likud member Ariel Kallner: "One goal, Nakba! A Nakba that will overshadow the Nakba of '48!"[27] As a guest on Channel 14 on January 2, 2024, Betzalel Smotrich explained that since the two million Gazans were all potential Jew killers, the only option was to expel them. The Europeans should take them in. As the minister of finance, Smotrich runs the "civil" administration of the Palestinian territories. In his mind, you cage Palestinians and move them around like objects. Colonial thinking at its zenith.

These pronouncements accompany a brutalization of society. Commissioner of Israel Police Kobi Shabtai threatened to promptly ship to Gaza any Palestinian citizen of Israel who showed support for the Gazans.[28] Actress Maisa Abd Elhadi, physiologist Dalal Abu Amneh, and other Palestinian artists and professionals who are citizens of Israel have received summonses simply for posting comments on social networks. At Netanya Academic College, fifty Palestinian-Israeli students had to barricade themselves against a raging mob screaming "Death to Arabs!" and "Send them to Gaza!" Author and militant feminist Samah Salaime assailed the noxious atmosphere that thugs from the extreme Israeli right wing were spreading in townships with Palestinian populations. During the 2021 war against Hamas, she got harassing phone calls from racist bullies. "You whore, we're going to rape and kill you!" She was badly frightened. "When I filed a complaint with the police," Salaime wrote, "they offered me a free tip: 'Learn to keep your mouth shut when there's a war.' This time around, I really did try to keep my mouth shut."[29]

This brutalization is increasingly turned against Jews who are critical of what Israel is doing in Gaza. They have to shut up now, too. Shlomo Karhi, the Likud minister of communications, proposed a law that would penalize anyone who undermined the nation's morale. By calling for a ceasefire, for example? It takes courage to go to the West Bank to protect Palestinians who are under constant attack by dangerous reactionaries of the colonial right, for whom the war is the perfect chance to put their expulsion plans into effect. Since October 7, some five hundred Palestinians in the West Bank were killed and fifteen of their villages emptied of their population in joint raids by Israeli soldiers and armed, kippa-wearing hooligans.

In this atmosphere, a small but growing number of Israeli Jews are pulling up stakes. They are leaving the country, or telling their children to leave. "They are liberal, educated, hard-working, secular," wrote Rogel Alpher in *Haaretz*. "These are the people for whom the massacre served as the last straw that ruptured once and for all their faith in the national project called Israel."[30] Some are fleeing the "psychopaths" running the country. Others are leaving just to have a better, less hysterical, and more peaceful life.

"Genocide" "Crime against humanity"—words and facts

I wrote Chapter 12 of this book for the American edition in 2020, and described what I thought we might expect with President Joe Biden in the White House: "To box Israel in, Biden…would have to end Israeli impunity, quit systematically vetoing any Security Council resolution unfavorable to

Israel…[and] impose on Israel a proper solution to the conflict with the Palestinians, leading to the end of the occupation of their territories. If Biden could do all this, the Israelis would find themselves in great difficulty. They would view the dismantling of their domination of the Palestinians as a terrible political defeat. But it could open the path to a more peaceful future." I then asked, "Is such an option improbable today? Certainly. Is it highly unlikely? Yes. But is it unthinkable?"

Today we know the answer to that question. Biden has clearly shown how much courage he lacks. That he would allow Israel to respond to Hamas's horrible attack was expected, but not that he would let it carry out such massive carnage in an attempt to create a new Nakba. Criticism of the president has erupted at the highest levels. In *Foreign Affairs*, Maria Fantappie and Vali Nasr wrote, "As October 7 showed, Washington's beliefs about the Middle East were completely incorrect," and it "has not updated its thinking."[31] *Politico* described "a growing loss of confidence among U.S. diplomats in President Joe Biden's approach to the Middle East crisis."[32] In early November 2023, a petition circulated within the State Department asking that the United States demand a complete cease-fire. The diplomats were worried: In Middle Eastern public opinion, America's unconditional support for Israel was making it look like "a biased and dishonest actor."[33] Polls showed that initial massive support for Israel began to erode with reports of the crimes it was committing in Gaza.

In France, President Emmanuel Macron followed in his American counterpart's footsteps. On a visit to Israel in late October 2023, he proposed that France and the United States

work together to eradicate Hamas, the way they have collaborated in Iraq and the Sahel. You can almost see a grinning
Netanyahu telling his generals about this offer: "Macron can
chatter away, so long as he lets us do what we like." The proposal vanished without a trace. In France, public debate was
initially nonexistent, partly because French public opinion
was still affected by Hamas's horrors. The Israeli bombing that
followed didn't get many people worked up, including nearly
all the media. Solidarity with Israel remained dominant while
efforts to silence voices defending the Palestinians multiplied.
In the beginning, the government allowed pro-Israel demonstrations while forbidding those supporting the Gazans.
Hasbara revived the view that Israel represents the "advance
bastion" of civilization in the face of Arab-Muslim barbarism.
In France and throughout Europe, a newly self-confident right
is riding high.

In the United States, a similar phenomenon gained traction, with the difference that the forces resisting the "clash
of civilizations" thesis reacted more strongly. To be sure,
pro-Israel lobbies were successful in delegitimizing all critical
voices. From the very start of Israel's bombing of Gaza, a campaign was launched to accuse critics of anti-Semitism. Two
words became Satan incarnate: "apartheid" and "genocide."

As I see it, the term that best describes Israel's relationship
with the Palestinians is *apartheid*, along with *colonialism*. The
right-wing slogan "From the Mediterranean to the Jordan"
certainly fits the United Nations' definition of apartheid.[34] But
the facts don't support the use of "genocide" because they fail
to meet its main criterion, which is the intention to physically
wipe out a body of people, partly or completely.

On the other hand, some of Israel's methods against the Gazans are similar to those imposed on ghettos, namely starving people and keeping them in a state of extreme insecurity. By resorting to the most drastic measures, you terrorize an entire population, with the goal of physically expelling them. That intentionality clearly supports a different crime, which is *ethnic cleansing*. And it is probably because Israel hasn't succeeded in physically expelling the Palestinians from Gaza that its destructive fury has increased.

I'm not challenging the use of the word "genocide" because I'm afraid of it. As the Israeli journalist Anshel Pfeffer wrote, Israel may not be committing genocide, "but genocidaires are present at the highest level of its government."[35] I object because this debate—is it genocide or not?—is systematically used to skip over the facts on the ground and focus on a pointless polemic over the use or misuse of certain words. It's as if the moment genocide is said to be happening, a comparison with the Holocaust becomes legitimate. And inversely, if genocide isn't completely established, then Netanyahu can laud his war, "the justice and morality of which is without peer."[36]

Using the word "genocide" actually benefits Israel in a way, because it implicitly raises the Holocaust issue. A much more indisputable term would be *crime against humanity*. Israel's actions are clearly designed to starve a population of 2.4 million human beings, for example. Starting on October 7, the minister of defense ordered "a complete siege of the Gaza Strip. There will be no electricity, no food, no fuel, everything is closed."[37] He then sent his air force on a campaign of devastating, indiscriminate bombing. What more is needed to qualify this as a crime against humanity? Who needs a pointless debate to determine whether genocide is happening? If it is, then the debate lets Netanyahu and his cronies act as if they were the offended party, while destroying the homes of an entire people. (In Israel, a new word has even appeared to describe this: "domicide.")

That said, the pro-Israel lobby doesn't worry about such subtle distinctions. It simply threatens to label someone as anti-Semitic, or puts pressure on them for allowing the use of "forbidden words." In the United States, some people have suffered the consequences. Elizabeth Magill, for example, was forced to resign as president of the University of Pennsylvania. Claudine Gay, the president of Harvard, also had to resign after a bitter and unworthy fight. Former Harvard president Larry Summers, Barack Obama's treasury secretary, called for sanctions against students who wrote a piece stating that Israeli violence had shaped every aspect of Palestinian life for the last seventy-five years, which made it "entirely responsible" for Hamas's attack.[38] Before she resigned, Gay publicly apologized and distanced herself from the students, while calling on people to respect the right to one's opinions. The most serious threats to freedom of expression came from wealthy donors who threatened to withdraw their donations to private universities if they didn't act against what they saw as "growing anti-Semitism." A few followed through. Overall, however, these pressures didn't make the critics back down. On the contrary: the mobilization of American students to denounce Israel's crimes has only increased since the start of the war in Gaza, and this mobilization has ended up having a major impact on French university students for the first time in a very long while.

On the other hand, divisions within the progressive wing of the American Jewish community appeared from the very start of the war, and they persist. A large share of the critics of Israeli policies toward the Palestinians "came back to the fold" of the majority Jewish viewpoint.[39] The split became visible on the occasion of the March for Israel for the return of the hostages and against anti-Semitism, held in Washington, DC, on November 14, 2023. The organizations that are still part of the Zionist movement continued their unstinting support of Israel long after its bombing began. This was also the case for J Street, a "pro-peace" Jewish lobby. Ditto for Jill Jacobs, the president of T'ruah, a rabbinical group for human rights. Up to then, she had strongly condemned Palestinians' treatment, but now felt "the need to affirm [her] connection with the rest of the Jewish world."[40] Others, like Jewish Voice for Peace and IfNotNow, demanded an immediate cease-fire in Gaza and the end of the military occupation of the Palestinians. The journal *Jewish Currents* ran an article titled "Building the Case of U.S. Complicity"—meaning American complicity with Israel's crimes in Gaza.

But the most vivid illustration of the crisis in the American Jewish community occurred in the limited turnout—between 100,000 and 200,000—at the March for Israel, as if its most significant evolution was disaffection for Israel. By contrast, Arab and Muslim associations had brought out between 200,000 and 300,000 marchers at the same place in Washington ten days earlier. Yet there are only half as many

Muslims in the United States as Jews, and their associations have been subjected to pressure and threats. For years, the Council on American-Islamic Relations (CAIR) held its annual meeting at a Virginia hotel outside Washington. But in 2023, the hotel withdrew from the event at the last minute, under pressure from the right-wing Zionist Organization of America, which said that "hosting CAIR was equivalent to sponsoring terrorists."[42]

It made no difference. Arab and Muslim associations have demonstrated their capacity for mobilization. That isn't good news for Joe Biden in the presidential election. The Muslim community in the United States may be very small, but it constitutes 2.5 percent of the voters in Michigan, for example. In 2016, Donald Trump won Michigan by just 0.2 percent of the vote. In 2020, Biden won it by 2.8 percent. If Biden loses half the Arab and Muslim votes in Michigan in 2024, he could lose a state that is key to his reelection. Worse, he may also be losing the youth vote. "Biden can't save America from Trump if he alienates young voters over Gaza," wrote Trita Parsi, a cofounder of the Quincy Institute for Responsible Statecraft.[43] He explained why by quoting his friend Shivshankar Menon, India's former ambassador to Israel, who says that by supporting Gaza's total destruction, "Biden has put the final nail in the coffin of the so-called rules-based international order."[44]

Biden, Macron, and the failure of the West

What will historians say about the war in Gaza fifty or a hundred years from now? That it was emblematic of an era in which Israel played a key role in legitimizing a new world order no longer founded on right, but on might? Or, to the contrary, that it symbolized the last gasp of colonialism? On December 12, 2023, the U.N. General Assembly passed by an overwhelming majority a resolution calling for an immediate cease-fire in Gaza. The United States voted against it, joined by just nine other nations, which showed how isolated it was. The same day, Biden told a gathering of Democrats that Israel was losing support by its "indiscriminate bombing" of Gazans.

The State Department was gathering evidence of this, but as a precaution refused to publish it in real time. Commented Brian Finucane, a former State Department legal advisor: "It's really disingenuous for people in the government to claim it's too hard or we can't do this in real time. It's simply a choice. They choose not to do this."[45] *Politico* noted that of the Israeli air force's 28,000 strikes on Gaza in the first two months of the war, half were "dumb bombs," that is, bombs without targets that are simply dumped on people.

Posterity will view Joe Biden and Antony Blinken as the people who allowed Israel to perpetrate one of the greatest massacres and human displacements of the early twenty-first century, on a scale that matches those carried out in Syria by Assad against his own people, and by the Saudi leader MBS in Yemen. With this difference: those crimes were committed by autocratic regimes, whereas Israel proclaims itself "the only democracy in the Middle East." In a world in which xenophobia and racism are again on the rise, along with the appeal of strongmen and muscular regimes, Biden, followed by Macron, has chosen a path that further reinforces them. They have led their countries into supporting a state, Israel, that has become the very embodiment of racist and colonial policies. They have bowed to the hackneyed "clash of civilizations" thesis now enjoying a heady revival. Biden, Macron, and the West will be the great losers in this intellectual debacle. By exonerating Netanyahu and implicitly endorsing the bombing and displacement of two million people, they and their fellows have not only lost any right to tell others how to behave, they have paved the way for their own adversaries.

Israel has long challenged the international order that arose from the Second World War. Though often scorned and far from perfect, that order has the advantage of formally promoting a world founded on the rule of law, and drawing lines not to be crossed. This is why Israel aims to change the paradigm in its war against Gaza, to modify or even cancel the Geneva Conventions and the laws of war. The world order isn't that of the Trumps, Putins, or Netanyahus. Yet Biden, Macron, and nearly all the other Western leaders have ratified those figures' notion of sovereignty by their unconditional support of Israel in the Gaza war. Who will believe in Biden's sincerity the next time he denounces fresh war crimes committed by the Russians in Ukraine? We don't know if Donald Trump or Marine Le Pen will take power tomorrow, but if it happens, we will know who carried water for them.

One last word on the responsibility of Western leaders. If any hostility to Israel's policies is an expression of anti-Semitism, then Zionism's failure is paradoxically proven by *reductio ad absurdum.* The aim of Zionism, remember, is to constitute the only option to stop anti-Semitism. But the more Israel embodies brute force, the more anti-Semitism flourishes. It exists among Palestinians, of course, just as anti-Arab and anti-Muslim racism exists among Israelis. But these would be much more effectively fought if the crimes being perpetrated by Israel stopped, instead of multiplying. Finally, Netanyahu's policy for the last twenty-five years can be summed up in a single slogan: "With me, you'll have security." But if that's the promise of contemporary Zionism, what it has achieved is catastrophic. Is there any country in the world where Jews are more threatened on a daily basis than Israel?

Today, anti-Semitism seems to be spreading at the international level. It is manifested in an atmosphere that reinforces the appeal of strongmen like Trump, Putin, and Modi, and the lure of simple, radical solutions ("A plague on minorities!"). In such an atmosphere, who really thinks that the main forms of racism currently at work in the West—anti-Arab and anti-Muslim in Europe, anti-Black and anti-Latino in North America—will spare the Jews? By cozying up to the worst racist elements, starting with those in the United States, Netanyahu and other Zionist leaders could drag Jews—all the Jews, since they claim that they alone represent them—into the abyss. What is to stop idiotic, ignorant, or evil people from seizing on Israeli crimes to fan hatred of all Jews, the way crimes by Daesh and Al Qaeda are being used to fan hatred of all Muslims?

Destroying Hamas will "take more than a few months," said Defense Minister Yoav Gallant on December 15, 2023. At the cost of how many dead Gazans? Words alone won't stop Israel from pursuing its carnage, especially as its goals still look as vague as ever. It's not impossible that at the end of a long war of the same intensity Israel will manage to completely expel the Gazans from Palestine. It will then definitely become a pariah state. If that aim isn't achieved, and Israel retains control of the Gaza Strip for an indeterminate period, as Netanyahu hopes, the self-described pro-Israel columnist Thomas Friedman fears that Gaza will eventually become for Israel what Afghanistan and Iraq have been for the United States: a trap and a terrible fiasco.[46]

Joost Hiltermann, an analyst with the International Crisis Group, described the options that might be available to Israel and the United States to find a solution to the Palestinian question. All of them strike him as unworkable, including Washington's idea of handing the keys to Gaza to the Palestinian Authority, an institution that has been totally discredited in Palestinians' eyes. "If the PA can barely govern the West Bank, how could it expect to do better in Gaza?"[47] What about America? "If the Biden administration wants to undo some of the enormous damage inflicted on U.S. credibility in its unqualified support for Israel," wrote Hiltermann, "it is clear that any solution would require far stronger U.S. pressure on Israel than has been evident to date." Netanyahu doesn't even want to discuss a two-state solution, and neither does 80 percent of the Jewish Israeli political class. In short: You broke it, you fix it. Meanwhile, the Palestinian Center for Policy and Survey Research published the results of an early poll that found that 72 percent of Palestinians supported Hamas's action, and 80 percent felt it was in response to the Israeli occupation. Not a single European country garnered as much as 10 percent approval of its attitude after October 7. The United States got just 1 percent.[48]

On December 4, 2023, reporter Amira Hass published excerpts from a November 7 letter to friends with psychology and psychiatry backgrounds from her friend Bassam Nasser, a Gaza Palestinian who holds an American master's degree in Middle Eastern history. "I kindly request that you refrain from attempting to diagnose my situation," he wrote. "I am neither post-traumatic nor entirely 'normal.' Please do not look at me with pity or sympathy...Our primary issue is our aspiration for freedom and self-determination...We refuse to live in captivity, whether in enclosed spaces or open-air prisons...We will not tolerate humiliation. We will not turn the other cheek to those who oppress us or give our coat to those who steal our shirt."[50] An animal . . .

A month later, on January 4, Defense Minister Gallant set out his "postwar plan." Neither annexation nor recolonization of Gaza, but military control by the Israeli army unlimited in time and an undefined Palestinian civilian management. Reconstruction of Gaza would be entrusted to an international force under American leadership and helped by European and Arab countries in cooperation with Israel. In other words, we destroy, you pay. We're not responsible for anything that's happening in Gaza, but will continue to control everything there: which Palestinians have the right to make decisions and which don't, entry and exit for people and products from fuel to medication, distribution of water and electricity, etc. In other words, the Palestinians will remain in their cages. That way, the security of Israel will be absolutely guaranteed.

Who could believe that, even for an instant?

The State of Israel vs. the Jews

Introduction

An unbridgeable hiatus

The year was 1990. My father was nearly eighty, and he was patiently answering my questions. He and my mother lived in Charenton then, a tiny suburb just outside Paris. It was a Sunday morning, and like every Sunday in those years, I had come over to ask my father about his life. My mother was probably in the kitchen, cooking. My wife and children would arrive in a few hours, and we would all have lunch.

My father often spoke about his family, Judaism, and his complicated relationship with religion. The son of a somewhat unorthodox Orthodox rabbi, he became an atheist but remained devoted to the Bible (things aren't always simple). He talked about why he turned his back on religious practice, but also about his youth in Poland, his love of Yiddish literature, why he didn't go to Palestine when he had the chance, and much else.

On this particular Sunday, my father was recalling life in his birthplace, Vladymyr, in what is now Ukraine. It was a typical town, buffeted by the region's constant upheavals. Its nearly forty thousand inhabitants included twenty thousand Ukrainians, fifteen thousand Jews, two or three thousand Poles, and a few others. In 1911, when my father was born, it was a part of the Czarist Empire. As an eight year old, he watched the Red Army march into the town, and remembered how this raised the Jewish population's hopes. The pogroms would finally end! But the Bolsheviks were defeated two years later, and withdrew. The town fell under the control of the nationalist Polish state, with its anti-Semitic aggressions and quotas for Jewish students.

My father left for France in 1938, when he was twenty-seven. It was a lucky move, because the town was occupied by the Soviets the next year, then in 1941 by the Germans. On September 1, 1942, Nazi *Einsatzgruppen* killed nearly the entire Jewish population, including my father's parents, his brothers, their wives and all their children, his uncles, aunts, and cousins. In 1945 Vladymyr became Soviet again, and was eventually named Volodymyr.

In the 1920s, as my father told it, young Jews like him eager to break free of the oppressive anti-Semitic atmosphere and the stifling rule of shtetl rabbis, had only three options. The one chosen most often was Bundism, a worker-oriented ideology behind Polish syndicalism during that country's industrialization. The Bund advocated a socialism in which Jewish "nationality" would enjoy broad cultural autonomy built around its language, Yiddish. The second option was Communism—Workers of the world, et cetera—and many young Jews signed on. Its path was the steepest, but it seemed the most promising. An end of exploitation for all, including Jews, and the dawn of a wonderful society whose concomitant universal brotherhood would necessarily lead to the end of anti-Semitism. The third option was Jewish nationalism, which combined two great currents. The largest by far joined ethnic nationalism and socialism; the other was ultranationalistic and chauvinistic, like most such movements in Eastern Europe. This Jewish nationalism, which melded all those tendencies, was called Zionism. Its goal was to build a Jewish state in Palestine, which was then under British colonial rule. At fifteen, my father threw away his kippah and joined socialist Zionism.

On the Sunday in 1990 when we were talking—it was soon after the fall of the Berlin Wall—my father interrupted himself in midreminiscence and said, "So you see, we won in the end." "We" meaning Zionism and the Zionists. The Bundists, he noted, had been exterminated in the Nazi genocide, and Stalin took care of the ones Hitler didn't kill, sending their leaders to the gulag or the firing squad. Of Bundism and Yiddish-based culture, practically nothing remained. Communism had failed as well, as anyone looking around Eastern Europe could see, and my father predicted there would soon be nothing left of it, either East or West. "But we Zionists are still here," he said. "Israel is a tangible reality." A strong state with a developed economy, a powerful army, and an active society. "We won," he repeated. It was one way of continuing a very old conversation with me, arguing that the choice he'd made in his youth, the one that shaped the rest of his life and his political consciousness, had been the right one.

I remember not saying anything. And sadly thinking that the story wasn't over, and that deep down, my father knew it. We had a very close relationship, but an unbridgeable hiatus called Zionism lay between us. It had been his whole life, and it was mine no longer.

Israel, I hardly knew you

My father had been the main leader of labor Zionism in France for a quarter century, and ran its Yiddish-language daily *Unzer Wort*, a socialist-Zionist paper, for twenty years until it closed in 1996. My family was living in Bordeaux when I was born in 1947, and we moved to Paris when I was nine, at which time I was enrolled in a Zionist youth labor movement. Besides French, I spoke Yiddish pretty well, but found it frowned on during my several stays in Israel, which included military service, life in a kibbutz, and university study.

I went to Israel after high school to train as a youth movement leader, but I wound up drafted into the Israeli army, serving in a paratroop brigade. When I got out, I stood six feet tall, weighed one hundred forty pounds, and was in the best shape of my life. I returned to France before turning twenty, still very much a Zionist.

But change was in the air.

In 1969 I returned to Israel, lived briefly on a kibbutz, then enrolled at Hebrew University in Jerusalem. The colonial attitudes I found there astonished me. This was only seven years after Algeria's successful war of independence, and the Israeli students talked about the Palestinians exactly the same way French settlers there used to talk about the Arabs.

Israel had seized the West Bank and Gaza, and the Golan Heights in the Six-Day War two years earlier, and these students were confidently appraising their new real estate. They were positive the Palestinians would meekly bow to Israeli power. I felt otherwise, and our conversations got heated.

"They'll never give up their land," I said.

"Sure they will. We'll give them some olives and pita bread, and it'll be fine."

"You're fools to think that," I said.

"You don't know the Arabs. They're liars and cowards, and couldn't run a state of their own. They only understand force."

My mind reeled, and my doubts grew.

I had always thought that when Israel was founded as a refuge for the persecuted Jews of the world, justice had been on the Israeli side. I knew that founding the State of Israel hadn't been a bed of roses, but you can't create a country without stepping on a few toes. But I was gradually discovering that the expulsion of the Palestinians and the seizing of their land had been deliberately brutal. And Israel was evolving into something no idealist could stomach: a racist, bullying little superpower.

As I became an increasingly active anti-Zionist, my life in Israel got harder. My wife and I were ostracized because of our beliefs, and we lost jobs. Paradoxically, I had many Israeli friends, some of whom vehemently disagreed with me. At the time, that was still possible. It isn't anymore.

When the Six-Day War ended in June 1967, hadn't my father said that Israel should give up the conquered Palestinian territory, lest it begin a fatal colonial occupation? As he and I talked, twenty-three years had passed, and Israel still occupied the Palestinian territories. But that, I didn't mention. During my time in Israel, seeing the yawning gap between the promise and the reality of Zionism had driven me away. And after frequently clashing, my father and I had quit discussing Zionism and Israel. What was the point? We had said all there was to say. I knew how far Israel had moved from what my father had dreamed of, but when he died in 2000, nothing had made him change his mind. So I just sat on the sofa in the Charenton apartment and listened. The morning was wearing on.

A country at an impasse

In 2005, I published a book about the evolution of Zionism and the Israeli and Palestinian societies that came out two years later in English as *Walled: Israeli Society at an Impasse.*[1] In 2014, my publisher suggested I write a sequel, but for a long time I resisted. The great paradox of the Israeli-Palestinian conflict is that there's something happening every day to slake the news media's unquenchable thirst for breaking news, yet at the same time nothing fundamental really changes. Israel is still occupying another people's land, and that people is vainly struggling to advance its national ambitions. And then there are the deaths on both sides (ten on one side, one on the other), the expulsions of people (100 percent on one side, zero on the other), the land seizures, the sealed wells, the security wall, the Palestinians' grinding daily shuffle between check-points and constant administrative hassles, the repeated bombings of Gaza, the desperate kids with knives and screw-drivers lashing out in the face of these assaults…This has all been said, written, seen, and commented on a thousand times. The incessant repetition is wearisome, overwhelming. Its logic is implacable. The balance of power between Israelis and Palestinians is too uneven, but at the same time, it's ineffective. Israel is too powerful to lose, but it isn't able to win. The Palestinians can't succeed, but also can't afford to lose. The mere fact of their existence makes a final Israeli victory impossible, and the Palestinians' defeat preordained.

While I can't remember what event triggered it, I gradually began to recall that Sunday morning conversation with my father more often. And it led me to realize that I was mistaken: gradually, things in Israel *were* changing. Some were very new. Laws were being passed that would have been unimaginable just a decade earlier. That was also true of some statements by Israeli leaders as well as political messages spreading through Jewish Israeli society. These were often due to an exacerbation of long-standing tensions, some from the earliest days of Zionism. The appropriation of Palestinian land by any means possible was fairly typical. But other instances were truly unprecedented, like Israel's rapprochement with the Arab–Persian Gulf monarchies.

Today, to all appearances, Israel has "won." The national Palestinian movement hasn't been this fragmented and powerless since the end of the 1930s. Israel continues to daily, systematically, and methodically occupy Palestinian territory, and does it with international diplomatic support that even Barack Obama couldn't head off. This is accompanied by a policy of dispossession and repression of the inhabitants so violent that it has settled on the land like a bleak new normal that no one talks about anymore, except when something truly unusual happens. As appalling as this new normal is, nobody can see how to end it, or who could do so. And Israel's power doesn't only stem from its formidable military domination of the Palestinians, whom it grinds down a little more every day. It is also manifested in practically every other field, whether political, diplomatic, economic, technological, scientific, academic, or artistic. Who could ever imagine, even a little while ago, that Israel would have practically normalized its relations with most of the Eastern Arab countries without first settling the Palestinian "precondition"? The situation is still in flux, but this is Israel's greatest international relations coup of recent years. That breakthrough has been accomplished, and it represents a radical change, even though the Palestinian question could conceivably erupt again tomorrow. Nor has Israel ever had such close relationships with such major emerging nations as China, India, and Brazil.

But there's more. Israel's ideological influence has never seemed so visible. It is a major player in the war on terrorism. It effectively silences its critics by threatening to label them anti-Semitic. Diplomatically, it persuaded important international figures to adopt a new definition of anti-Semitism that includes any criticism of Zionism or Israel. But at the same time, Israel's image is undergoing a noticeable, steady deterioration in public opinion in most places, including in France and the United States. Its policy toward the occupied Palestinians, especially, has left it open to an ever more frequent and damning accusation: the crime of apartheid.

In 2018, on May 14, to be exact, I decided to write a new book, this time focusing exclusively on Israeli society. On that day, the State of Israel was celebrating the seventieth anniversary of its founding. It was also celebrating another unprecedented event: the United States embassy's move to Jerusalem, with Donald Trump in attendance. Israel had long urged that the embassy be transferred from Tel Aviv, but without success, because a near-unanimous United Nations refused to recognize Jerusalem as the capital of Israel so long as a peace accord to settle the issues in the aftermath of the 1948 war hadn't been reached. But Trump didn't care about international law. And Israel celebrated its triumph in spectacular fashion.

On that same day in Gaza, while the world's eyes were on Jerusalem, Israel Defense Forces (IDF) snipers were shooting at the crowds of young people who had been demonstrating every Friday for a month and a half at the wall that Israel had erected along the Gaza Strip. The Israeli soldiers fired real bullets, killing three, five, or ten of these youths each time. But May 14 was a red-letter day. Some 58 Palestinians died and 1,350 were wounded, shot at long range by Israeli snipers whom they hadn't threatened in any way.

This raised a few eyebrows in international opinion, but drew much less interest than the American embassy's move to Jerusalem. Neither London, Paris, Berlin, Moscow, Cairo, nor Riyadh protested. As for the media, that day's news was unquestionably the transfer of the embassy. After all, people were always dying along the Gaza border, though that day's toll was unusually high. In shaking hands that day, Trump and Netanyahu were expressing their total contempt for international law. There was something truly unprecedented in the picture they made. It spoke both to how drastically Trump had intended to change the rules that had determined international relations since 1945, and to Israel's preeminent role in that strategy. Might was making right.

If force doesn't do the job, apply more force

At the heart of the connection between Israeli leaders and the conservatives around Donald Trump during his term was the idea that force is the determining element in interstate relationships, and that it shapes those relations nearly exclusively. American studies show that Jewish Israelis had supported Trump more strongly than anyone else in the world. That's no accident, because a belief in force has been at the core of Israeli society, virtually since its creation. In the Bible, Zechariah 4:6 says what can be obtained "not by might nor by power, but by my spirit." In the biblical sense, spirit refers to God, but in modern Hebrew, the phrase suggests that what you can't obtain by force you can obtain by intelligence. But popular Israeli wisdom has turned the prophet's verse into a well-known and more radical (though not especially intelligent) slogan: "If force doesn't do the job, apply more force."

That says it all: force, and nothing but force. This is a line that Israel has followed for a long time, in both successes and failures. In a kind of Pavlovian reflex, it always turns to force first, under all circumstances. In case of failure, the only conclusion to be drawn is that force failed because it wasn't sufficient. The corollary of this attitude is a deeply rooted contempt for international law. It's true that international law has revealed its shortcomings on countless occasions. But it exists, and it sets some limits on the strong's freedom to impose its will on the weak, just as respect for human rights is an intangible marker, even if its application is regularly rejected. From its earliest days, Israel has challenged the legitimacy of international law in the same way America Firsters hate the United Nations, precisely because it imposes regulation, judicial limits on the use of force. This issue came up when I interviewed Carmi Gillon, a former director of Shin Bet, Israel's domestic intelligence service, in 2004.[2] My opening question was "In the struggle against adversaries who use terrorism, is it possible to respect international humanitarian law, or is it necessary to break it?" The spy master's answer: "I'm not a specialist in international law. I can only speak to Israeli law."

International law? Sorry, not my department. This kind of thinking has been at work in the Zionist settlement of Palestine from the very beginning, and has been maintained and reinforced over the decades. For example, in the early 1960s it led the IDF to adopt "preventive war" as a basic strategic theory, even though the concept is wholly rejected by international law. That was almost forty years before Condoleezza Rice, George W. Bush's national security advisor, adopted the legitimacy of preventive war to justify the American invasion of Iraq without international sanction. In Israel, this cult of force with its decades of immunity as official policy rose to an unprecedented level when Benjamin Netanyahu returned to power as prime minister in 2009.

The man's pronouncements are worth listening to, because they summarize the entire drift of Israeli society. Whenever Netanyahu talks about peace, his favorite expression is "peace of deterrence," in other words, one imposed by the stronger party on the constrained, subdued, weaker one. "We believe in peace through strength," the Israeli prime minister said during the annual gathering of his diplomats in August 2018. "In the Middle East, and in many parts of the world, there is a simple truth—there is no place for the weak. The weak crumble, are slaughtered, and are erased from history while the strong, for good or for ill, survive. The strong are respected, and alliances are made with the strong, and in the end peace is made with the strong."[3]

That is the quintessence of the majority attitude in Israel, with or without Netanyahu. Actually, it has always been this way, including the 1948–77 period when Labor was in power. Since then, the nationalistic colonial right has ruled for thirty of the last forty-four years. Over time, this attitude has hardened into a veritable dogma that a huge majority of Jewish Israelis endorses, to the exclusion of all other ways of political thinking. Nor is this the exclusive purview of the right. In the run-up to legislative elections in April 2019, Netanyahu accused his then rival, General Benny Gantz, of being a "leftist" and a "weakling." What was Gantz's response? To boast of having killed 1,364 terrorists during the bombings of Gaza he had ordered when he was army chief of staff. (International observers say those bombings killed 2,200 people, including more than 1,500 civilians.) Gantz's campaign staffers put photographs of bombed neighborhoods up on Facebook, claiming 6,231 Hamas targets destroyed, and boasting that "parts of Gaza were sent back to the Stone Age."[4] Gantz and his people know that to win, you can't afford to be labeled weak when dealing with the Arabs.

This typically colonial mentality of domination has led IDF strategists to adopt the so-called Dahiya doctrine, which makes war crimes committed against civilian populations part of Israel's official strategy in its fight against terrorism. First formulated in 2008 by General Gadi Eizenkot (chief of staff, 2015–19), the theory holds that in asymmetric wars, when the enemy controls terrain that is hostile to you or is supported by the local population, massive destruction of the enemy's infrastructure and civilians' houses by disproportionate force is essential to achieve your ends. The doctrine is named for the Beirut neighborhood where the Lebanese Hezbollah's headquarters was located during the 2006 Israeli intervention. Israel reduced Dahiya to a heap of ashes.[5] So Israel has adopted the same strategy that Vladimir Putin used against the Chechens, and Bashar al-Assad against his own people, but with one crucial difference. While Putin and Assad applied the strategy much more aggressively than Israel ever has, they never admitted it publicly, to preserve the appearance of a respect for the laws of war. Israel, on the other hand, made it part of its official strategic thinking, as it had much earlier with preventive war.

Israel's trumpeting its forceful public rejection of the norms of international law—in the name of refusing racial, ethnic, or religious dilution of their country—has attracted the new ethnocentric leaders emerging around the world. Where some believe in an open, transborder world, most support walled tribalism, an ethnic or national circling of the wagons. In this, Israel today looks like the end product of a coherent, deliberate affirmation of specialness against the tenets of a universalism that it perceives as weakness itself. The extreme right-wing international leaders are dubbed "illiberal," but they mainly embody authoritarian xenophobia, with strong popular support. These include India's Modi,

Brazil's Bolsonaro, Italy's Salvini, Hungary's Orban, and the rulers of the Philippines, Poland, and Austria—without forgetting Donald Trump, of course. In recent years they all made the pilgrimage to Jerusalem, forging relationships of proximity and common interest with Israel, the little state that leads the way in so many fields, and has so much to teach them.

Israel fascinates the new ethnocentric leaders

These leaders are fascinated by Israel's ability to deny basic rights to an entire people—the Palestinians—for decades without seeming to suffer any political consequences. Also fascinating is Israel's congenital nativism, its bald assumption of its right as a dominant ethnicity to impose its laws on minorities, and to claim rights for itself that it denies them. These leaders admire Israel's wholesale rejection of international law. In March 2019 Trump abruptly endorsed Israel's annexation of the Syrian Golan Heights, which it had formalized in 1981 by an Israeli law never recognized by the United Nations. "There is a very important principle in international life," Netanyahu told journalists afterward. "When you start wars of aggression and you lose territory, do not come and claim it afterwards." On the plane bringing him home from Washington, D.C., he revisited this diplomatic innovation: "Everyone says you can't hold an occupied territory, but this [American decision] proves you can. If occupied in a defensive war, then it's ours."[6] Since the wars waged by Israel since its founding are by definition all "defensive"—even when Israel attacks, which it always does so as not to be annihilated—this casts a new light on the potential consequences of future occupation by force on foreign territory. It's worth remembering that the conquest of the Golan Heights on day four of the Six-Day War in June 1967 took place when Israel had already destroyed the Syrian air force in the first hour of the first day, and the Syrians hadn't fired a single shot at Israeli troops.

Another thing that fascinates these leaders is the striking impunity Israel enjoys. Likewise Israel's trick in labeling anyone opposed to its wishes as a terrorist. When Mahmoud Abbas, the Palestinian president, announced in 2014 that he intended to ask the United Nations General Assembly to endorse the State of Palestine's Declaration of Independence, Avigdor Lieberman, a minister in various governments from 2001, called this "diplomatic terrorism."[7] More generally, Israel appeals to rulers as the leader in policies in areas as varied as the fight against terrorism, the closing of borders, and the expulsion of undesirable foreigners.

Finally, right-wing leaders are fascinated by the political mindset reigning in Israeli society. While the massive support the Israelis once gave Trump was unique in the world, what he stood for isn't a political novelty. When George W. Bush launched the invasion of Iraq in 2003, Israelis were the people who most strongly supported the American decision. But for a long time, Bush had hoped to preserve the forms and enjoy an international consensus before acting. Trump, on the other hand, never sought consensus. He operated to break norms, and that especially appeals to Israelis, who seem to say, "Welcome to the club."

When Trump was still in office, *Haaretz* Washington correspondent Chemi Shalev summed up Trump's appeal this way: "It is his indifference to refugees, cruelty to immigrants, war against the rule of law, hatred for foreigners, never-ending lies, abusive invective, nod to racists, and disdain for women that make Israelis, for obvious reasons, feel right at home with Donald Trump. The abrasive, impatient, shoot-from-the-hip novice who speaks the favorite Israeli lingua franca called *dugri*—roughly translated as trash talk—is one of us, an honorary member of the Israeli tribe, the macho man of our dreams, and whoever doesn't like it can lump it."[8]

Lieberman, the former defense minister, was talking *dugri* when he said, "There are no innocents in Gaza"[9] to justify the army's bombing civilians.

In this oppressive atmosphere, some parts of Jewish society are still fighting to preserve rational thinking, a sense of humanity, and the notion of universal rights. Its members feel consternation and at times disgust at where their country is going. These Israelis—few in number but admirable in their determination—are fighting for Palestinians' rights in the same way white activists fought segregation in the American South in the 1950s and '60s and supported the fight against apartheid in South Africa in the 1970s and '80s.

Many of these Israelis say they are doing battle in the name of Jewish values, basing their activities more on morality than on politics. You will find many messianic religious Jews in Israel's ultranationalist and openly racist circles, but many Israeli anti-occupation NGO leaders are either religious Jews or were raised in religious settings. Whether religious or not, they despair at seeing Israel so radically abandon a worldview that characterized Judaism in the modern era, one primarily rooted in a progressive conception of humanity and society. They are revolted by the conditions imposed on the Palestinians, but also alarmed at what fifty years of occupation will do to future Israeli Jews, dominated as they are by a triumph of racist tribalism, groupthink, the rejection of immigrants, and contempt for any universalist vision of the world.

I finished writing the original French text of this book in November 2019. The American version was finished fourteen months later. In that interval, the political map of the United States changed profoundly. With regard to the Middle East, Donald Trump's electoral defeat has opened the possibility of ending the veritable "axis of evil" he created with Benjamin Netanyahu and Saudi Crown Prince Mohammed bin Salman. The Israeli political scene, on the other hand, is unchanged. With or without Netanyahu, Israel remains a country where polls show that 77 percent of the population (the Jewish population, that is) supported Trump, and only 22 percent supported Joe Biden. A country where, beyond the debate over the utility of attacking Iran militarily, a state of mind prevails that is vigorously hostile to its Arab environment and now even more so to Iran, which Israel sees as a grave existential threat.

In the diplomatic arena, the new American president has made it clear that he feels it absolutely imperative for the United States to return to the 2015 accord limiting Iran's military nuclear capability, a deal signed by Iran and all the great powers, and from which Trump unilaterally withdrew. For Biden, only a return to the terms of that deal will prevent nuclear proliferation in the entire region. Without such an accord, Iran will eventually build its bomb, and that will drive states such as Saudi Arabia, Turkey, and Egypt to acquire nuclear weapons as well. As Biden recently put it, "the last goddamn thing we need in that part of the world is a buildup of nuclear capability."[10]

But if Biden plans to revive the nuclear deal with Tehran—and would like to extend it to other, non-nuclear weapons—he will inevitably clash with Israel, which opposes any negotiations with Tehran. Israelis overwhelmingly favor using strongarm methods in dealing with Iran.

How far is Biden prepared to go? Would he risk taking measures to compel Israel to yield? If so, what would be the repercussions on the conflict between Israel and the Palestinians? On the American side, will there be a revival of interest in the Palestinian issue? Or would Washington use abandoning the Palestinians as a bargaining chip to get Israel to tacitly acquiesce in progress on an accord between the U.S. and Iran?

We are now talking prospectively, and history has shown time and again how rarely predictions correspond to reality. Nonetheless, I feel it is necessary to devote a short chapter at the end of the book to the Middle East after Donald Trump. I want to explore what has changed since his leaving office, and which of the fundamental issues in the Israeli-Palestinian conflict remain the same despite the change in the White House.

We are living through a period when the international situation looks increasingly chaotic. A period where anti-Semitism is on the rise, and we see an Israeli prime minister—Benjamin Netanyahu—cozying up to admitted anti-Semites, while at the same time accusing anyone critical of Zionism of being anti-Semitic. A period where some see anti-racism as a new totalitarian threat to liberties, where being openly racist is increasingly accepted from the United States to Myanmar, from the Arab world to the European democracies, with each brand of racism feeding the next, in a vicious cycle. A period in which globalization is inevitably leading to more race mixing, a phenomenon that some whites think they can deter by barricading themselves behind walls, barbed wire, and absurd, not to say obscene, immigration policies. This is happening as any number of countries slide from what was once called the Third World into harsh and xenophobic nationalism— incarnated by India's prime minister, Narendra Modi, one of Israel's most important new friends.

The confusion generated by these phenomena is manifested in the frightening evolution of Israel and its society. This has consequences for the Jewish diaspora, and in particular for its two largest components, in the United States and France. It is essential to try to know and understand this evolution before weighing the consequences it entails for Jews living outside Israel.

In one way, Israeli society affords the observer an unusual advantage. It's a paradoxical society: extremely dynamic, not very democratic, but very liberal. Israel has been at war since its founding, and has a highly developed and respected culture of secrecy. At the same time, it enjoys astonishing freedom of speech. Go beyond the press releases, the clichés, and the travel posters, and it isn't very hard to discern the essence of the country's evolution. Almost everything in Israel is said, written, or broadcast, often very crudely, so it's fairly easy to find out what is happening. Which is why the chapters in this book devoted to that society are based on sources, mass-market publications, and interviews that are almost exclusively Israeli.

1

Imposing Fear, Teaching Contempt

The reality of the military occupation

Sometimes you have to call things the way they are. Especially when you're talking about things so endlessly repeated without any prospect of change that your sense of urgency gets dulled. We're talking about Palestine here. A Palestine that is just a stone's throw from suffering Syria, two stones' throw from devastated Yemen, a spectacular horror show that makes the Israeli occupation seem like a dull headache by comparison. And yet...

It's true that the occupation has never reached the levels of terror inflicted on those countries, but three factors make it particularly oppressive: its initial basis (expelling people from their land by force); its long duration (seventy-plus years since that expulsion, fifty years of military occupation over most of those people), and finally, its modalities (the slow but steady confiscation of land, the seizure of resources, the occupying authorities' deliberate policy of making Palestinians' daily lives unbearable in hopes of eventually making them leave). This constellation of elements has shaped a sociopolitical landscape to which the world has grown accustomed, whether out of passivity or ignorance, or because there is misfortune everywhere, and we can't solve all the world's problems. But this is a landscape to which the Palestinians—like victims everywhere—can't ever grow accustomed.

The most moral army in the world?

The purpose of this initial chapter is to make clear that we're dealing with a military occupation in which one group of people is daily subjected to the whims of soldiers from the other side. To head off possible skepticism, consider this: anyone who wants to find out what is happening to the Palestinians can just read the newspapers. What follows is a list of news items published in the Israeli press over a six-month period. The stories are mostly but not exclusively from *Haaretz*, the only media outlet that regularly reports on the IDF's actions:

"Israeli border policewoman arrested on suspicion of shooting Palestinian for fun." Subhead: "Judge says suspect shot the man, who was seriously wounded, 'as a dubious form of entertainment.'" (October 15, 2018)

"Israeli army denied soldiers threw gas canister into a Hebron school. Then a video surfaced." Subhead: "After the video surfaced, the IDF altered its response," saying that the soldiers did throw grenades, because the students threw stones at them. (December 6, 2018)

"Israel said a Palestinian was killed in clashes. A video shows he was shot in the back." Subhead: "While the army says Mohammad Khossam Khabali was shot during violent clashes, video shows him walking with friends on the main street." (December 9, 2018)

"Deterrence? Israel demolishes Palestinian assailant's home—for the third time." (December 16, 2018)

"The disabled Palestinian slowly walked away. Then Israeli troops shot him in the back of the head." Security cameras showed they were 80 meters away. (December 17, 2018)

"After shooting a Palestinian teen, Israeli troops dragged him around—and chased an ambulance away." Subhead: "The Palestinian from the Jalazun refugee camp died after soldiers kept him from receiving medical care." (December 20, 2018)

"Palestinians recall settlers dressed in white firing at them, as soldiers stood by." (January 28, 2019)

"[Five Israeli Soldiers] beat a detained Palestinian and made his son watch." (January 31, 2019)

"Without saying a word, Israeli troops beat up a blind man in his bed." Subhead: "Israeli soldiers invaded the home of a Palestinian family at night, and battered a man in the face in front of his wife and children. He is 47, blind and on dialysis, and his toes have been amputated because of diabetes." The soldiers only stopped beating the man when they realized that he couldn't be the suspect they were after. No legal action was taken against them. (February 28, 2019)

"Israel forces Palestinian to raze his and his daughter's homes with his own hands." Subhead: "In East Jerusalem, the Israeli authorities require residents to demolish their 'illegally built' homes by themselves or to pay the city exorbitant sums for doing it." (March 7, 2019)

"How the Israeli army shot dead a Palestinian paramedic in a refugee camp." Subhead: "Sajed Mizher, a volunteer paramedic…walked over to a man wounded by a gunshot [and] was shot himself." (April 5, 2019)

Let's take stock of the situation. We are no longer in a period of major confrontations. The Second Intifada ended more than fifteen years ago in a stinging Palestinian defeat. So we are now talking about events that are happening during the "normal" occupation. And make no mistake; those news items aren't the only ones that happened during that six-month period. On the contrary, there might be as many as ten virtually identical ones every week, which the military authorities don't deny. Each month, some number of additional cases fail to reach the awareness of the media or humanitarian associations, which can't be everywhere. An example: Muhammad al-Khatib al-Rimawi, 24, beaten to death in his bed by soldiers who broke into his house in the middle of the night on September 18, 2018. These are everyday events experienced by people powerless to stop them.

In fact, those acts mark a shift in the Israeli army's operational modes following their victory in the Second Intifada. Since the conquest of the Palestinian territories, criminal acts by Israelis have been legion. But they have been presented as exceptional, shortcomings by what innumerable Israeli generals and politicians have called "the most moral army in the world." The first uprising by the occupied Palestinians in 1987–93 ended with a political victory. Israel was forced to recognize the Palestine Liberation Organization (PLO), which no previous Israeli government had done. Which is why, when the Second Intifada started in late September 2000, the Israeli army unleashed means of repression out of any proportion with those used during the previous insurrection. In the very first days, a month before the first Palestinian bombing took place, an Israeli helicopter gunship fired missiles at a "terrorist target" in Ramallah that turned out to be a Fatah youth center.

That October, at the very start of the Second Intifada, a Palestinian mob at a police station lynched two Israeli soldiers who had gotten lost in Ramallah. In retaliation, ABC News reported, "Israeli rockets hit the police station where the killings of the Israeli soldiers took place and the official Palestinian TV station, which had been broadcasting extensive video of the violent clashes of the past two days. The police station was reduced to rubble, and flames were pouring from a second building."[1] Israeli gunships later fired rockets at five targets in Ramallah and Gaza City, including the Fatah youth center. I was in Ramallah at the time, and saw the burned building the next day.

During the First Intifada, no Israeli tanks entered a Palestinian city. This time around, tanks immediately poured in and shot up the cities. Nor did the end of the Second Intifada in 2005 bring an end to those aggressions. Quite the contrary. The Israelis' victory led them to feel more than ever that "if force doesn't do the job, apply more force." Instead of new negotiations, the end of violence by the Palestinians led to much greater tightening of the screws on them and an escalation of violence by the Israelis, launched with total impunity.

According to an extensive study, Israel incarcerates an average of eight hundred to a thousand Palestinian minors, nearly all of them boys, every year. "Some are under the age of fifteen; some are even preteens," wrote Netta Ahituv in

Haaretz.[2] They are jailed for an average of three and a half months. When an IDF spokesman was asked why the arrests were always made at night, the answer came with jaw-dropping cynicism: "So as not to upset the normal course of civilian life." The boys are taken away in handcuffs and blindfolded. Their parents are often not informed where they are being held. The study went on to reveal that these adolescents were made to sign predrafted confessions (in Hebrew, a language they usually can't read). Some were told "If you don't confess, we'll take away your father's permit to work in Israel. Because of you, he'll be out of work and your whole family will go hungry." Or: "I'll bring your mother here and kill her before your eyes." Whether the boys sign or not, they are hauled before a military court, where they are unfailingly convicted. That's generally the first place that their parents see them again. According to the NGO Military Court Watch, 97 percent of the children arrested are from villages near settlements, because the military assumes that it's mainly minors throwing the stones. The Military Court Watch advisor Gerard Horton says these operations have two purposes: to frighten the whole village and to make examples. "Each generation must feel the strong arm of the IDF."[3] The sharp escalation in physical and psychic violence against the Palestinians has had an important impact on the attitude of IDF soldiers, and even more so on their officers. In the vast majority of cases, they quickly cover up once-scandalous practices that have now become commonplace.

Her name was Nour Iqab Enfeat. The sixteen-year-old West Bank Palestinian girl was approaching a checkpoint. She may have been told to stop, but no order can be heard in the video of the scene. She doesn't appear to be holding anything. Suddenly we see her running away, with two Israeli soldiers in pursuit. Then shots are heard. Nour falls to the ground. Their backs to the camera, the soldiers surround and start cursing her. A civilian is with them, wearing sandals; probably a settler. The huddled girl moans. We hear the soldiers screaming: "Croak, you whore's daughter." "Die, suffer, you *kahba*" (a Moroccan Arabic word for prostitute). Writes journalist Gideon Levy: "If the soldiers at that checkpoint are not prosecuted and punished, one thing will be made clear: Barbarism is the true moral code prevailing in the IDF."[4]

Three years later, I asked the IDF public information office if an investigation had been opened, in light of the images of the girl's killing. On April 21, 2020, it answered that since the Palestinian girl "assaulted an IDF soldier with a knife and stabbed him in the hand and abdomen...It was decided that no steps will be taken in relation to those involved in the incident."

For this kind of barbarism to become established, it must have enjoyed explicit—or more often implicit—approval from the highest levels of the military hierarchy on down. A lieutenant stationed at Hebron testified that his battalion commander gave a "long leave" (from Thursday to Sunday) to any soldier who killed a terrorist or kneecapped one, which means shooting at a person's knee, crippling them for life.[5] Such occurrences have become so common, and happen with such impunity, that B'Tselem, an organization whose Israeli and Palestinian volunteers closely follow human rights violations in the Occupied Territories, made an unprecedented decision in 2016: It stopped sharing with IDF military courts the evidence it had gathered about abuses by soldiers. After twenty-five years of experience, the NGO concluded it was pointless, since the incriminating evidence practically never led to investigations, much less convictions. "It made us accomplices in a farce that consists in pretending that the verifications are actually conducted by the army," says B'Tselem director Hagai El-Ad ruefully.[6] In the month of March 2019, Israeli soldiers killed seventeen Palestinian civilians without any investigation being launched. It was a month like any other, like those that have occurred for years and years.

Daniel Kronberg is the executive editor of the *Israel Journal of Mathematics* at Hebrew University of Jerusalem. He is also a longtime member of Ta'ayush—it means "coexistence" in local Arabic—a Judeo-Arab association that helps Palestinians in the Occupied Territories resist the devastation that settlers wreak on their land. Kronberg himself helps villagers south of Hebron. In the field, he says he has noticed a big difference between older reservists and younger soldiers. To the latter, "Palestinians are completely dehumanized, and Jews who support them are traitors." Kronberg showed me his arm, which is marked by a huge brown scar from when settlers savagely beat him with an iron bar. This has happened to him several times, but he no longer bothers filing a complaint. "The last time, instead of taking a statement, the police arrested me," he said. "When the police and the IDF are in cahoots with thugs, what's the point of filing a complaint? The settlers' abuses are so numerous that in most cases nobody bothers to complain, neither the Palestinians, nor the Israelis who help them. It's useless. It took me a while to understand that what's happening is no accident; it's a system. To varying degrees, an entire society is on a dreadful slippery slope in dehumanizing the Palestinians."[7]

A very coherent incoherence

At the military level, this system isn't supported only by abuses. In dealing with the Palestinians, the IDF implements a policy it calls "making your presence felt," says Yehuda Shaul, the executive director of Breaking the Silence (BtS), an organization founded in 2004 by army reservists that publishes soldiers' accounts of crimes committed by their fellow troopers and by settlers.[8]

I met Shaul in January 2019 at his organization's headquarters in a Tel Aviv suburb, after showing my credentials at a heavily reinforced steel door. At thirty-nine, Shaul is a big man, over six feet tall and almost as wide. He's friendly and warm, with flashes of sardonic humor, but you can feel his inner fire. Shaul founded Breaking the Silence in March 2004 with two other former soldiers, and became its first executive director. When we met, he had only recently shed the kippah he had worn from birth. His father is American; Shaul was born in Jerusalem to an Orthodox Jewish family and raised in a religious settlement. It was his military service, during the months he spent in Hebron as an infantry sergeant, that changed him, forcing him to reevaluate his life and beliefs. Today, he reflects an uncompromising rejection of the Palestinian occupation.

"Making your presence felt," Shaul explains, is designed to give the Palestinians "the feeling that no matter what happens, whether it's rainy, windy, or sunny, they're all under permanent control."⁹ The system has two advantages: it controls the Palestinians, and it gradually gets the young Israeli recruits accustomed to behaving badly. As an example, Shaul cites *maatzar demeh*, meaning "fake arrests."

"You go to a house chosen at random, having first checked that it doesn't include anyone on a list of suspects. You get everybody together. You search the place. Sometimes you tear it apart. After half an hour, you leave. You don't arrest anyone. You don't tell them anything. This rouses the whole neighborhood. Nobody knows why you came." Why do that sort of thing? Only the soldiers know that these are fake arrests. The first time, recruits may ask what the point of the operation was. They're told "It's to train you." When it happens again, they understand that this is also a kind of intimidation, a way of "making your presence felt." In addition, says Shaul, "it breeds suspicion in the village." Why was the operation at night? Why wasn't anybody arrested? In Hebrew, it's called *hatalat eima*, "imposing fear."

These regular nighttime security checks are also a way of gradually shaping the troops. The first time they do it, says Shaul, "the soldiers feel uncomfortable breaking into a Palestinian house to frighten people. The second time too. But when it becomes a regular thing, it takes an unusually independent personality to keep one's sense of dignity." Turning away from your fellow troopers and going against the current is the hardest thing to do, especially in the military, where following orders is the rule. "It takes a while to get the recruits used to behaving at their worst," says Shaul. "In the beginning, shooting at a twelve-year-old isn't the easiest thing for a sniper to do. Same thing for a soldier who enters a house to tear it apart. You're terrifying an entire family, and the first time you do it, it's hard. If you have to take a piss, you step outside. By the twentieth time, you're used to it, and you just piss on the people's carpet. The dimension of habituation is essential. No one comes through unscathed." Not getting "used to it" takes a person of unusual strength of character, like Shaul himself. Once a soldier is habituated, he'll participate in real searches, real arrests. And will beat blind diabetics in their beds at night during operations whose only goal is to keep the Palestinians in a state of submission and anxiety. "Generations of Palestinian children have grown up with this fear, with the traumas and scars it leaves," says Shaul sadly. And generations of young Israelis have become habituated to the role the IDF has given them. "In this system, unpredictability, the unexpected, and seeming incoherence are completely planned," he adds.

An article in *Haaretz*[10] recounting the experience of a foreign student at Hebrew University of Jerusalem illustrates what Shaul means. The student had spent the night with friends in Bethlehem in the West Bank, about six miles from Jerusalem. The next morning he showed up at Checkpoint 300, which anyone who wants to go in or out of the city has to transit. It was early, barely six in the morning, and the four gates were closed. But many Palestinians were already lined up to pass. Many had arrived at three or four a.m. to be sure to get through in time to go to work. At one point, a green light lit up over one of the gates. The crowd surged in that direction, a few people got through, and then the light went out for no apparent reason. A few moments later, this happened again. A light went on, but at a different gate. More shoving and pushing. Then the light went out. Baffled, the student began to feel anxious; he would be late to school. The Palestinians were worried about missing a day's work. As the line grew longer, a young soldier showed up shouting "*Wahad, wahad,*" Arabic for "One at a time." She seemed amused. The puzzled student soon understood why. Each time, the light would go on at one gate before going off, then on again at a different gate. You never knew which of the four gates would open, how long it would stay open, or when the next one would open. Would it be three minutes? Or twenty? It was all a cruel game.

When the student finally got through, the checkpoint soldier in her fortified bunker merely glanced at his papers, completely impassive. As if everything was normal. "I realize that what I had gone through that morning happens to the Palestinians every day," he said. And it's been going on for years. Why should getting through a checkpoint have to be so deliberately cruel and complicated? he wondered. Why should people have to undergo a long series of useless, ugly, and depressing abuses? Everything was arbitrary, indifferent, hard-hearted—just plain mean. What did that have to do with Israel's security? It struck the student as incomprehensible and incoherent. "I know my story is nothing dramatic," he said. "It's not bloody or anything. It's just a little story, but maybe it symbolizes what is happening here."

In fact, the anecdote reflects ordinary daily life in the Occupied Territories. But the student's conclusion is wrong. The "long series of useless, ugly, and depressing abuses" is neither incoherent nor useless from the point of view of the occupation system, any more than the IDF soldiers' indifference or meanness is. It is all part of what Shaul calls "planned apparent incoherence." The checkpoint soldiers' attitude had been considered, tested, and evaluated. The whole point is to make people's lives unbearable through repeated daily constraints and the incoherence they convey. The young recruits that the IDF assigns to the moral cesspools called checkpoints, where they learn not to fight but to exercise police control over a defenseless civilian population, gradually learn to behave with that same indifference until meanness—mental cruelty, really—becomes the approved norm.

For Palestinians, the meaninglessness of the waiting they have to endure is part of a deliberate policy aimed at making them feel sick of life. For generations of young Jews who put on the uniform, this systematic cruelty serves as a school where teaching contempt toward the population they have to control, along with implicit colonial racism and the dehumanization of the Palestinians, becomes the only way to preserve one's self-respect. Because if a Palestinian were seen as a human being, a person equal in rights and dignity, the behavior of soldiers who break into houses night after night just to frighten their inhabitants, or the ones who enjoy humiliating Palestinian workers just trying to earn their daily bread, would feel unacceptable.

This deliberate cruelty, which is part of a very coherent incoherence, has been studied by many psychologists, in particular by Martin Seligman at the University of Pennsylvania. The founder of "positive psychology," Seligman spent years researching what he called "learned helplessness." Experiments he conducted determined that when endlessly confronted with a situation whose logic escaped them, and which they could neither control nor escape, animals and humans alike sank into a kind of depressed lethargy due to the accumulation of anxiety and despair.

Seligman is a former president of the American Psychological Association, which, unlike the American Psychiatric Association, agreed to cooperate with the CIA in supervising the torture of prisoners in Guantánamo and the black sites the agency created in a number of countries in the fight against Al Qaeda. (In 2014 and 2015, various articles accused Seligman of cooperating with American intelligence, which he denied. The polemics failed to reach any definite conclusions, and eventually died down.) But it does seem probable that various intelligence services have studied Seligman's theories on learned helplessness. To judge by the IDF's nighttime raids, fake arrests, and checkpoint humiliations, it's likely the practitioners of "the imposition of fear" had heard about them.

Amira Hass, the *Haaretz* correspondent in the West Bank and Gaza, reported the story of a Palestinian Gazan woman who was trying to bring her father, who had cancer, to an Israeli hospital to see a doctor. Each time, she made an appointment with the Israeli specialist several months ahead of time, to justify the two exit requests she made to the authorities. Each time, Shin Bet's authorization failed to arrive in time. Each time, she repeated her desperate request. "Why add abuse to the pain of illness?" asked Hass. "The answer is well known. Abuse is part of the control."[11] And that's the way it is in the Palestinian territories—every day.

The flourishing of a Jewish Ku Klux Klan

The Israeli army isn't managing the West Bank occupation alone. It is supported by the Jewish settlers there (though in

THE STATE OF ISRAEL VS. THE JEWS

fact soldiers are more often the ones supporting the settlers). The extremists among the settlers, many of them religious-Zionists, are the most organized activists. They combine an exalted, messianic view of the Land of Israel, which the Lord gave to the Jews alone, with an astonishing indifference to the lives of the inhabitants whose land they are appropriating. It's estimated that these settlers represent a little more than a quarter of the Israeli population living in Palestinian territory. According to government figures, there were about 427,000 settlers in the West Bank at the end of 2017, not including a little more than 220,000 Israeli Jews who settled in the East Jerusalem neighborhoods conquered by Israel in 1967. In 1993—the date of the Oslo Accord that led to mutual recognition by Israel and the PLO—there were only 116,300 settlers in the West Bank, excluding Jerusalem. This means that three times more settlers arrived in the twenty-four years since Oslo than in the first twenty-six years since the Israeli conquest in 1967. The figures for Jerusalem are even more impressive.

Most of these settlers have been encouraged by both right and left Israeli governments, which have given them preferential treatment that includes no-interest loans, low rent, and no property taxes. They differ from the ideological settlers, who enjoy the same advantages but arrive bearing messianic ideas and weapons to "conquer the land." Over time, those settlers have acquired an unbridled arrogance born of continued impunity. As with the IDF abuses, newspaper reports bear this out. Here is a two-week tally in 2019 from the pages of *Haaretz*:

"Masked Jewish settlers filmed attacking Palestinian family; no arrests were made." (April 14)

"Two settlers shot and killed a Palestinian who threw stones at cars, and then the army deleted videotaped evidence." (April 19)

"Israel lets settlers spend Passover at evacuated outpost but forbids entry to Palestinian landowners." (April 28)

There aren't as many of these items as there were reports of IDF crimes, but the number of incidents is steadily increasing. In particular, depredations of Palestinian farmland have never been so widespread. According to the Palestinian Ma'an News Agency, settlers in the West Bank destroy a thousand olive trees every month. In October 2018, 90 olive trees were chopped down on land near the village of Al-Mughayyir, 70 destroyed and 60 damaged at Turmus Ayya, 40 cut at Bruqin, 30 at Tal, 18 at Deir Nidham, and 22 uprooted at Far'ata, in addition to attacks on Palestinian farmers in their fields at Deir al-Hatab and Burin. And the list goes on. The authorities always take the same position: to avoid friction between settlers and Palestinian farmers, the Israeli army prevents the Palestinians from getting to their fields. Which leaves the settlers free to do whatever they like. Later, when the Palestinians go to the Israeli police, their complaint is noted—or not. "The villagers' complaints have never resulted in criminal charges or convictions that might deter others," writes Amira Hass.[12]

The Israeli NGO Yesh Din (Volunteers for Human Rights) has studied six villages in a ten-square-mile area of the West Bank (about 0.4 percent of the territory). Between 2008 and 2018, it reported 275 attacks by settlers, or more than two a month. Of the 152 complaints filed by Palestinian farmers, only five led to charges. No verdicts were handed down. Michael Sfard, an Israeli lawyer with Yesh Din, asked the police why investigations never turned anything up. "Lack of public interest," he was told. In other words, why bother investigating if nobody gives a damn?

Between January 1 and May 20, 2019, the U.N. Office for the Coordination of Humanitarian Affairs tallied eighty-nine incidents of violence by settlers, and forty-five Palestinian victims. Crimes involving great bodily harm are also on the rise. In late July 2015, four settlers set fire to Saad Dawabsheh's house in the village of Duma. He, his wife, and their 18-month-old child were burned alive. Eight months later, other settlers torched the house of the victim's cousin, who was the main witness to the crime. (On May 19, 2020, the *New York Times* reported that a settler named Amiram Ben-Uliel was convicted of murder for firebombing the Dawabsheh family home.)

"We are witnessing the flourishing of a Jewish Ku Klux Klan movement," says Yesh Din lawyer Sfard. "The whole thing is allowed by Attorney General Avichai Mendelblit, who condones taking land from Musa to give it to Moshe." (Moses is "Musa" in Arabic, "Moshe" in Hebrew). The only difference? In the United States the KKK is white; in Israel, it's Jewish.

Sfard cites one week in which settlers launched attacks in five villages, burning cars in the streets and painting death threats on walls. "No Jewish rioter has been arrested," he says. "Routine." In another week, Yesh Din counted twenty-five West Bank attacks in twenty-four hours. Injured civilians were hospitalized, vehicles destroyed, and shots fired into houses. And trees were ripped up, of course. This is a highly symbolic gesture that settlers regularly make as a way of saying that "Arab" trees have no business growing in Jewish soil. Says Sfard of this new KKK: "Like its American counterpart, the Jewish version also drinks from the polluted springs of religious fanaticism and separatism." And, as was long the case in the American South, the highest judicial authorities turn a blind eye.[13]

One gruesome murder highlights the growing acceptance of the "Jewish Ku Klux Klan" by Israeli political elites and the general public over the last fifty years. In January 2019, five young students from a yeshiva (Talmudic school) in the West Bank settlement of Rehelim stoned to death Aisha al-Rabi, a forty-seven-year-old mother of seven. Nor was the killing the first committed by settlers. Such acts started soon after the Gush Emunim movement[14] began building the first "illegal" settlements in the 1970s, and they haven't stopped. The attacks are carried out by small groups of fanatics, usually urged on by their religious leaders' frightening rhetoric. Two of them are sadly well known. The first is the 1994 massacre carried out at the Tomb of the Patriarchs by Baruch Goldstein, a Brooklyn-born Israeli settler. This was followed in 1995 by the assassination of the Israeli prime minister Yitzhak Rabin by Yigal Amir, a religious-nationalist fanatic.

In the 1980s an important terrorist organization emerged from Gush Emunim settler circles. Dubbed the "Jewish Underground" by the media, it carried out a series of attacks, including one aimed at three mayors of large Palestinian townships. (The mayor of Ramallah lost one of his legs; the mayor of Nablus lost both.) The terrorists were caught in 1984, as they were planning to plant bombs on Palestinian buses. These weren't marginal actors, either. The group included rabbis, military officers, and university professors. Twenty-five of them were tried and given sentences of up to life in prison. None

spent more than six and a half years behind bars, and several became settlement leaders after their release.

For fifty years, these actions have enjoyed the tacit support of leaders of the religious-Zionist movement. Followers regularly visit the grave of Goldstein, the Tomb of the Patriarchs assassin. Each time a murder is committed by one of these fanatics, the rabbis of the movement distance themselves slightly from the act while showing great compassion for, not to say connivance with, the killers. We shouldn't be surprised by any of this, because the whole messianic-national vision is founded on an ambiguity.

On the one hand, you have the religious-Zionist settler movement, whose rabbinical schools teach their flocks that the interests of Judaism as they understand them—that every square inch of the Land of Israel is sanctified—are above the laws of the state. They usually add that the Palestinians are at best strangers on the land where they were born, and at worst, subhuman.[15] So it's with a clear conscience that the settlers of this movement build their illegal outposts and commit crimes against Palestinian civilians. Blessed are any means that advance the will of God. On the other hand, what is the government doing? It condemns "blunders" when they are too flagrant, but protects the proponents of those ideas while providing the settlements, including so-called illegal ones, with all the means of subsistence, including water mains, telephone cables, gas and electricity, etc. And the state views their inhabitants as new pioneers and a source of national pride.

Why should anyone be surprised that over time an entire society gets used to hypocrisy that eventually becomes the norm? Who can be surprised that the most extreme settlers

should feel increasingly justified in committing their crimes? An article titled "I was a Settler. I Know how Settlers Become Killers"[16] described how the yeshiva boys who killed Aisha al-Rabi were trained. It was written by Shabtay Bendet, a former settler who eventually saw the light. Bendet lived in the Rehelim settlement from 1996 to 2009. Several of his children were born there. He knows its rabbis and their speeches. How could the settlement's religious leaders greet the murder of this Palestinian woman in a way that "ranged from shameful silence, to apologetics, even to an outright defense," he asks. Because "years of education in which a hyper-nationalistic religious ideology and vision finally led them to abandon any sense of human dignity."

Shmuel Eliyahu, the rabbi of Safed and one of Israel's most influential religious leaders, defended Aisha al-Rabi's killers in his weekly biblical commentary following her death. He even promised them glory, quoting Ecclesiastes 4:14: "For out of prison he cometh to reign." In other words, don't worry about being jailed for your crime, because you'll soon be in power.

This evolution, says Bendet, is no accident. It stems from the authorities' deliberate desire to protect the settler movement. For a long time, attacks by settlers on Palestinian civilians and their property were condemned in Zionist circles, even those on the right. "But today there are no such voices," he writes. Too many unpunished crimes, plus force of habit; people wind up shutting their eyes. "Years of trampling morality and law have clumped local residents into one collective bloc, along with all settlers and the right wing generally. This collective won't even condemn despicable acts of terror, and

even devalues the significance of human life, for anyone who isn't Jewish."[17]

Israel, the leader in the war on terrorism

All the constraints that Israel imposes on the Palestinians are carried out under the ideological banner of the "war on terrorism." This system of control ultimately reduces them to a simple identity: collectively, they are a "terrorist people." Every violent Palestinian act—not just an attack—is called terrorism, even if it's a boy throwing a stone or a girl slapping a soldier. Even passive resistance or unarmed demonstrations are now considered terrorism.

In its public statements and its effort to undergird its diplomatic successes, the State of Israel forcefully promotes its savoir faire in the fight against terrorism—and I have to admit it succeeds. Let's just take the case of France. Following the July 4, 2016, Islamist attack that killed eighty-six and injured two hundred in Nice, there were hosannas praising the Israeli model of fighting terrorism. The day after the attack, the French radio network RTL ran a long interview with Israel's ambassador to France. *L'Express* ran this headline: "Why Israel is a model in the war on terrorism."[18] France's former defense minister Hervé Morin spoke of "'Israelizing' our security." On July 22, the Israeli embassy in Paris put out a pamphlet titled "The Israeli example in the face of the terrorist threat." The embassy was pleased to see the French media finally becoming aware of the terrorist problem and Israeli expertise. Since then, each time a new criminal act of this kind is committed in France—and there have been several, of lesser magnitude— the media heat up with talk about "Israeli expertise" in the fight against terrorism.

Let's summarize this so-called expertise. Though terror activity has waxed and waned, the Israeli model has been consistently dealing with what it first called Arab and then Palestinian terrorism since the 1920s, practically without a break, to the point where no Israeli so-called expert would risk proposing a method to defeat terrorism today. At best, the aim is to control it as much as possible. The first lesson the Israeli model teaches is that terrorism, a sui generis category, is like malaria: a recurring illness whose outbreaks can be managed, but never totally cured.

In this model, terrorism is a uniform entity, everywhere and under all circumstances. The Islamic State, Palestinian Hamas and Fatah, Al Qaeda, Shiite Hezbollah, etc., all belong to the same category of terrorism. As the former French prime minister Valls says, there's no point in trying to understand the differences between them, because "to explain is to excuse." The fight against terrorism is a technical problem, a logistical issue and nothing else. Choose the right method, provide adequate means, and you will succeed in reducing terrorism—not permanently, but to a great degree. Israeli "experts" practically never raise the question of the legitimacy of means used in this war, of course. Abu Ghraib? Never heard of it. The barred manure pits in which Vladimir Putin's army tortured Chechen "terrorists"? Never heard of them either. Since 1948, Israel's Emergency Defense Regulations have turned the country into a kind of Guantánamo on the Mediterranean, where thousands of people have been imprisoned indefinitely, without charges or trial. It's all perfect.

The big value supposedly added by Israeli savoir faire hinges on the society threatened by terrorism to consent to the methods used to defeat it. Success in the fight against terrorism increases to the extent that the population facing it is prepared to quit defending human rights and just focus on the technical factors that lead to success. The *L'Express* article cited above says that "the Israeli antiterrorist policy rests on a strategy that is both defensive (security zones, barriers, military checkpoints) and offensive (infiltration, preventive arrests, targeted assassinations)." Moreover, the Israeli public's "sensitization and adaptability are major assets," according to an Israeli "expert," who boasted of his people's "culture of responsibility." That culture of responsibility comes down to Jewish Israeli society's acquiescence in despicable behavior. Fifty years of occupation have trapped all but a very few Israeli Jews in a way of thinking in which dehumanizing the adversary is the norm. When successive classes of young conscripts become accustomed to treating a civilian population badly, with what *New York Review of Books* contributor David Shulman calls "systemic cruelty inflicted over generations on innocent populations," accompanied by "the continuous theft—literally hour by hour—of Palestinian land,"[19] it leaves a more or less inalterable mark on the parties' attitudes and how they see each other. The real content of Israeli society's culture of responsibility is just that: getting accustomed to systemic cruelty.

So how has Israeli society changed, in the half century since the initial occupation of Palestinian territory? It's clear that major resources were brought to the oppression of Palestinians and the pillaging of their resources from the very beginning, and that it was largely supported by public opinion. But it's also worth realizing that over time, "quantity has transformed into quality," as Hegel says. The acquiescence with measures inflicted on the Palestinians has expanded to a degree we couldn't have imagined fifty or even twenty years ago. In an article with as much fury as despair, Amira Hass writes that in systematically shooting young, unarmed Gazans—empty-handed terrorists, so to speak—"Israel is conducting a mass psychological experiment in Gaza." But not on the Gazans. The guinea pigs are actually the Israelis. How far will their society go in its acquiescence? she asks. "The experiment is about compliance and cruelty; it's an experiment in adapting to increasing cruelty." And the results, she concludes, are much more successful than even psychologist Stanley Milgram's notorious "shock" experiment.[20]

Conducted at Yale in the early 1960s, Milgram's experiment was designed to test how obedient people would be when confronted by demands made by a superior authority that they judged to be legitimate. The subjects were asked to press a button that sent an electric shock to a person each time that person gave the wrong answer to a question. The subjects couldn't see the victims, but could hear their reactions to stronger and stronger shocks. The unseen people weren't actually being shocked; they were actors who pretended to be in more and more pain. When the subjects were reluctant to keep raising the level of the shocks, the experimenter urged them on, with prompts ranging from "Please continue" to "You have no choice but to continue." A great number of the subjects obeyed orders right to the end. Milgram concluded that conformity and obedience largely outweighed their sense of morality. In spite of the mock screams by the supposed victims, most of the subjects went so far as to inflict a shock which, if real, would have been lethal.

In Gaza, the Israeli army is experimenting to see how far the Jewish population of Israel will go in accepting the worst, writes Hass. She lists the increasingly painful measures being inflicted on Gazans without objection from Israeli society—except for the usual activists working at human rights NGOs, who are dismayed by how cruelly the Palestinians are treated. Israel refuses to connect Gaza to the national water network, for example. This leaves more than two million people dependent on the same coastal aquifer that supplied water to just eighty thousand in 1947. There is no water treatment, because Israel won't let in enough diesel to power the generators. The soil is incredibly polluted, electricity is available only a few hours a day, and sick people are forbidden to leave the territory to seek treatment elsewhere. And now unarmed demonstrators are being shot at every week. The intensity of this "cruel madness" keeps growing, Hass writes. "And we continue pressing the button."

It's conceivable that the things that outrage Amira Hass are the very ones that attract people to the Israeli method of fighting terrorism, whether their names are Trump, Bolsonaro, Modi, Orban, or Valls. On one hand, you find a level of disdain for human rights when they involve an undesirable minority—immigrant, religious, ethnic, or national—and the public's total support for deliberately ignoring the rights of other people. On the other hand, you find the astonishing impunity at the international level enjoyed for decades by Israeli leaders in conducting their war on terrorism. As we will see, that impunity is the biggest reason for the massive shift of Israeli public opinion in favor of radical colonialism. Why stop pressing the button if you've never suffered the least consequence?

2

Pissing in the Pool from the Diving Board

How Israel has changed in fifty years

In the spring of 2017, the Israeli director Anat Even released a documentary about Jaffa's Manshiya neighborhood called *Disappearances*.[1] In one scene, a municipal urban planner is telling a group of students about the history of a place. He talks about the Jews, many of them of Moroccan origin, who settled there in the 1950s and were evicted from their homes between 1960 and 1970 to make way for a commercial complex. The teacher accompanying the students asks the urban planner why he doesn't also mention that the same neighborhood was previously inhabited by Palestinians who were forcefully driven out in 1948. The planner answers that he doesn't see why he should talk about that. "Because those are historical facts," says the teacher. "Fuck history!" says the planner, laughing. History is written by the winners, he adds. The anecdote can serve as a metaphor for the most important change that Jewish-Israeli society has undergone in a half century of occupation.

The end of denial

The urban planner didn't bother denying the reality of what happened in 1948 in Jaffa, a Palestinian city where 95 percent of its inhabitants had been driven out or fled during a Jewish military offensive a few weeks before the creation of the State of Israel. Quite the contrary; he admitted it, and to hell with history. His attitude is emblematic, and it's the opposite of the one that has long been promoted in public discourse. When Israel was founded, denying the expulsion of Palestinians lay hidden in the heart of the Zionist position. David Ben-Gurion repeatedly claimed that Israel didn't drive out a single Arab. In the national Israeli epic, to which the whole society subscribes and which generations of children learn in school, "the Palestinians all left voluntarily." While many people suspected that the story glossed things over and that a few stains may have smudged the country's birth certificate, the essence of the argument was defended. By denying the expulsion of 85 percent of the Palestinians living on territory that would ultimately belong to Israel, the state preserved its positive self-image.

Behind the denial of the expulsion of the Arabs from Palestine lies the awareness that this act didn't conform to the ethics Zionism wanted to display. The subject of a "transfer" of the Palestinian population from the future Jewish state was long debated at the Twentieth Zionist Congress in Zurich in 1937, eleven years before the country's founding. Those debates, long kept secret, came to light only in the 1990s. So when the ethnic cleansing happened between 1947 and 1950, Zionist leaders felt it was so dishonorable that they denied it—while accusing the victims of being the cause of their own misfortune. What has gradually disappeared in Israel is the secret shame underlying this denial, accompanied by a growing legitimization of the transfer idea. "Fuck history!" What the Jaffa urban planner expressed has become widespread in Israel, far beyond just ultranationalist circles. People now feel that not only was expelling the Palestinians a legitimate thing to do at the time, but that the mistake was not to have pushed them *all* out. Driving the Arabs out, being sole master of Israel's territory, living only with one's own kind, were all devoutly to be wished. But people also knew it was morally indefensible. Hence, its denial. And that is the barrier that has gradually crumbled over fifty years of occupation: the sense of having committed an unforgivable crime at another people's expense.

Even if that initial denial lives on in Israel, the past expulsion of the Palestinians has become more accepted for one simple reason: the idea of expelling the Palestinians living under Israeli authority today is now more desirable, and increasingly seen as legitimate. For a large share of public opinion, it is *the* solution. Over the last two decades, Israelis have been regularly polled on their opinion about a "transfer"—the politically correct version of the word "expulsion." Being in favor of transfer means wanting to get rid of the Arab population. What would people in France, the United States, or elsewhere say if a pollster asked people how they felt about getting rid of all Arabs, or Muslims, Blacks, Jews, homosexuals, or hunchbacks? In Israel, very few people now find asking the question improper. It has become possible because in fifty years of occupying another people, Israeli Jews' mindset has progressively shifted to a point where a colonial outlook and the dehumanization of the adversary have become totally dominant.

This didn't happen all at once, but the process was relatively quick. In the 1980s and '90s, a significant number of Israeli scholars called "New Historians" began to explore the real conditions under which the State of Israel was born. And the more progress they made in their research, the more it confirmed the Palestinian version of history. The Arabs' "voluntary departure" was an invention.

A few eminent historians, like Shabtai Teveth and Anita Shapira, did their best to shore up the Zionist national epic. Others tried to explain the mass Palestinian exodus as the price that civilians always pay, as happens in many modern wars. But that overlooks the fact that the Palestinian expulsions began more than a year before the war for independence began. The Oslo Accord, signed in 1993, brought the New Historians some brief notoriety, but the failure of peace talks and the second Palestinian insurrection that began in 2000 swept the debate about Israel's origins under the rug. Who has time to worry about the past when terrorism is threatening a country's very existence?

Today, few people bother focusing on what happened to the Palestinians in the creation of Israel. Still, new pieces of information occasionally emerge, all supporting the Palestinian argument. On May 27, 2019, *Haaretz* published an article about the declassification of archives describing the destruction of Palestinian homes whose inhabitants had been driven out between 1947 and 1950: "Israel made sure Arabs couldn't return to their villages," it found, "chiefly by razing structures and planting dense forests" in their place.[2]

But who cares about those old stories? People in all sorts of circles, both secular and religious, are now weighing a new idea: that the big mistake in 1948 was not to have conquered the entire territory of Mandatory Palestine and driven all the Palestinians out. It would have made things so much simpler. No more Arabs, no more "Palestinian problem." This mindset has become widespread today. That's very different from the denial that Israel's founders maintained, and a major shift in people's thinking. It represents a legitimization of crime, and freedom from guilt.

The meaning of the Azaria affair

"Guilt and shame have disappeared" in Israel, says B'Tselem director Hagai El-Ad.[3] Not only is responsibility for a crime being acknowledged, it is boasted about without any political or moral cost. One notorious incident provides an exemplary illustration of this: the case of a soldier, Elor Azaria.

On March 27, 2016, a knife-wielding sixteen-year-old Palestinian boy named Abdel Fattah al-Sharif was shot by an Israeli patrol. This happened during a brief period when young Palestinians were attacking soldiers and settlers with knives or screwdrivers. They were almost always shot before they could act, which is what happened here. With the wounded attacker lying on the ground in a pool of blood, Azaria walked over and shot him in the head, killing him. He wasn't the first soldier to act that way, but this time a Palestinian was filming the scene, and the images are appalling. The army was forced to arrest the soldier.

Right-wingers immediately mobilized to defend the legitimate act by a "hero" who eliminated a "terrorist." Netanyahu visited the soldier's family, government ministers got involved. All felt that Azaria's court-martial was uncalled-for. He was sentenced to eighteen months in prison, which the IDF soon reduced to fourteen; he was let out after eight. This matched the sentence previously given to a young Palestinian girl named Ahed Tamimi for slapping an Israeli officer who burst into her home. A few days earlier, the IDF had shot her fifteen-year-old cousin in the head at point-blank range. On one side, eight months for a killing; on the other, eight months for a slap. That's the kind of justice you might expect in South Africa under apartheid, Mississippi in the 1920s, Kenya under the British, or Algeria when it was part of France. On Azaria's release, he was greeted with a huge banner reading "Welcome Home, Hero Azaria." In an interview three months later he said, "I did the right thing, as I saw it." He expressed no remorse, and added that "I would act in exactly the same way…because that is how one has to act."[4] A young man just out of his teens, Azaria was convinced he did only what was expected of him.

His case "symbolizes what is now happening all the time in the Occupied Territories," says "silence breaker" Yehuda Shaul. "Azaria isn't a rotten apple. The whole barrel is rotten."[5] Palestinians are shot dead every week far from any cameras, and the soldiers are never prosecuted. Even when there is no dispute over the facts, it is rare for the IDF to refer the cases to its tribunals. But on March 12, 2019, a military court finally accepted a case it couldn't evade. A video was circulating of five Israeli soldiers brutally beating a pair of handcuffed and blindfolded Palestinians, a forty-seven-year-old man and his young son, battering them with their weapons while an officer silently watched. The soldiers were members of the Netzah Yehuda (Judah's Eternity) battalion, which is made up exclusively of religious ultranationalists. They suspected the Palestinians of having information about the killing of two of their comrades in arms one month earlier. (In fact, they had no connection with the event.)

The video is deeply shocking. "The nausea and disgust are overwhelming, and then comes the anger and shame," wrote journalist Gideon Levy. "All of it takes place very quickly...The sounds of blows to the head, blow after blow, the father and son moaning, the sounds of the helpless, the giggles of the abusers. The soldier taking the pictures so he would have something to show his buddies."[6]

This crime is even worse than Elor Azaria's, if evil can be measured on a scale. Azaria reflexively killed a teenager he saw as subhuman. These soldiers sadistically enjoyed inflicting pain on two helpless human beings. But in both cases, government officials and eminent rabbis rushed to their defense. When the host of a televised debate was bold enough to say "The occupation is turning our soldiers into animals," Netanyahu immediately tweeted: "Proud of our soldiers!"

The convicted troops were given laughably short sentences. And ten days later, several of their comrades in the unit committed the same crime again. Confronting a group of Palestinian shepherds, they savagely beat a father and his son as their family watched in horror, then dragged the two off for interrogation, further hitting them about the face and body.

It is no accident that the young soldiers of the Judah's Eternity unit are religious ultranationalists. In the course of fifty years, fanaticism has played an ever-larger role in the units that are most engaged in repressing the Palestinians. This is embodied by the *yeshivot hesder*, Talmudic schools that offer a mixed educational and military curriculum, and play an outsize role in the dramatic change of the IDF officer corps. Yesterday's second lieutenants are today's generals, and more and more of them are ultranationalist fanatics.

In October 2018, Yair Nehorai, a lawyer with Rabbis for Human Rights, asked the Supreme Court to curtail the activities of the Bnei David military academy in the West Bank settlement of Eli. The mission of the academy, which receives many public subsidies, is to form the future elite of the Israeli army. Founded in 1988, several of its graduates have ascended to the higher echelons. One of them is General Ofer Winter, military secretary to the Defense Ministry in 2018. He caused something of a scandal during the Israeli offensive in Gaza in 2009, when he published an order to his troops that described the operation as the execution of "divine will." In front of his soldiers, Winter had prayed: "God, Lord of Israel, make our mission successful, as we are about to do battle for your people, against an enemy that curses your name."[7]

The Bnei David academy receives millions of dollars in financing from the ministries of Education and Defense, and also from private sources. Its name, which means Children of David, reflects the belief that the Messiah will be born in the lineage of King David, and the education it dispenses is related to the coming of the Redeemer. The IDF's chief rabbi is connected to that academy.

In his complaint to the Supreme Court, Nehorai noted that the academy walls are adorned with phrases like this one from Rabbi Eitan Cooperman: "The IDF is the tool through which

God's might acts in the world." Likewise, from Rabbi Joseph Kalner, a line that should have drawn a formal IDF reprimand: "All secular Jews are traitors and the state can do anything to sanction them, including putting a bullet through their heads."[8] This is an unchecked invitation to crime amid a total lack of culpability.

Modern Hebrew is a colorful language, and it includes the expression "To piss in a swimming pool from the diving board." I'll explain what that means. We've all peed in a swimming pool at least once in our lives, right? But to do it from a diving board, with everybody watching, is less common. "These days, Israel is pissing in the pool in front of the whole world," says B'Tselem director Hagai El-Ad. "The result is the same, but the impact is different."[9] Why are Israelis openly flaunting what they always used to hide? Why would they now admit that they expelled the Palestinians in the past? Why make a hero of a soldier who so egregiously violated the code of military conduct? What need do they have to openly advocate for the partial or total annexation of the West Bank, given that they've been continuously dispossessing the Palestinians with impunity for fifty years? "You would think that from their point of view it would be an error," says El-Ad. "But what if it were actually a strategy?"

The B'Tselem director thinks that many Israeli leaders have decided they can now get much more than before, and at minimal political cost. The cautious might say, "Be careful!" But the forceful, who have become by far the most numerous, answer, "The time is right. Why should we keep from pissing in the pool when we can do it with complete impunity?" And up to now, events have proven them right, says El-Ad. Under

Donald Trump the U.S. handed Jerusalem to Israel for its capital without much international backlash, and its so-called peace plan met all of Netanyahu's demands. Trump also backed out of the nuclear deal with Iran, which was a huge victory for Netanyahu. In November 2019, Washington said it no longer considered Israeli settlements in occupied territory to be illegal. And Europe went along, out of cowardice or impotence. So why should Israel refrain from promoting its interests?

El-Ad's view is probably right. It's certainly the logic that most Israelis and their leaders follow. You piss from the diving board, and then you raise it a little higher each time. Who's going to stop you? But that way of thinking has a price, and one that could prove fatal in the long run. Later on, we will see that Israel's supporters overseas, and especially within American Judaism, find this behavior increasingly unacceptable, and even dangerous. And the danger is stalking the Israelis themselves. Driven by a feeling of impunity, and buoyed by the sense of being a regional superpower, an entire society is starting to think it can act any way it pleases, and never pay a price. In particular, this impunity pushes the society's penchant for colonizing to extremes.

In July 2018, Israel decided to expel the members of the Bedouin Jahalin tribe from their West Bank village of Khan al-Ahmar. "Unlike the expulsions of 1948–49, this time the expulsion is taking place openly," writes Amira Hass,[10] "and it is being videotaped and documented on the WhatsApp accounts of dozens of journalists. International diplomats stationed in East Jerusalem and Ramallah know every detail of the saga of the Bedouin village. [They] also know that Khan al-Ahmar isn't alone. Other villages earmarked for expulsion include Susya, Zanuta, villages in the Yatta area and the Jordan Valley, and dozens of other Bedouin communities in the West Bank that Israel's Civil Administration plans to relocate to new, poverty-stricken townships, where the Bedouins' way of life will be destroyed."" ("Civil Administration" is the name of the Israeli military administration that deals with civilians in the West Bank.)

European countries have been helping these communities, so what must they think as they watch Israel forbid new construction and cut off water and electricity, with the sole aim of making the Bedouins leave "voluntarily"? What does it matter? How many divisions does Europe have?

Impunity and the coarsening of society

As you might imagine, this generalized sense of impunity has had an impact on Israeli society. Sociological studies and frequent media commentary have shown that being blunt and generally crude are typical Israeli personality traits. The word to describe this attitude is chutzpah. Having it means to shamelessly display nerve, gall, and boorishness. It's usually defined in a classic joke: the lawyer for a man who killed his mother and father asks the court for mercy, on the grounds that his client is now an orphan.

This trait is being displayed with vigor, at a rising level of violence, both verbal and physical. TV series and social media are devoted to it. The images are all over the Internet, and they reveal the anger, violence, and impunity that increasingly characterize an entire society. In little scenes filmed on the street or in stores, the most frequently heard manifesto is "I'll do whatever I like. So fuck you, and fuck the rest of the world!"

In April 2016, the ex–Shin Bet director Carmi Gillon drew a direct line between the occupation's corrupting effect on society and the rise of today's "Ugly Israeli," who combines rudeness with vulgarity.

When I met Gillon in 2004, he was the mayor of Mevasseret Zion, a town near Jerusalem. He had previously been Israel's ambassador to Denmark, and most notably director of the Shin Bet from 1994 to 1996. When Prime Minister Yitzhak Rabin was assassinated by a religious fanatic in 1995, Gillon felt responsible for failing to protect him. He resigned some time later. An affable man from a large South African Zionist family (his brother was a well-known judge), he was one of six former domestic intelligence chiefs interviewed in *The Gatekeepers*, Dror Moreh's fascinating 2012 documentary. Today he is openly opposed to Netanyahu's policies.

"The occupation is characterized by violence and aggression, and it's responsible for the phenomenon of the 'Ugly Israeli,'" says Gillon. "The occupation corrupts, and this shows up in violence in nightclubs, and behavior by the Ugly Israeli in the latest video clips. There is a very violent atmosphere here. The occupation is destroying us."[12]

On that score, an infamous video shot on an airplane ricocheted round the Internet in 2015. In it, a Hebrew-speaking woman passenger vehemently demands that a flight attendant immediately bring her the chocolate she ordered. When he doesn't act quickly enough, she screams, "I paid for this flight! I want my chocolate!" Another passenger promptly backs her up. Calling the poor flight attendant "a piece of garbage," he shouts, "Sell her the chocolate! What is she, an Arab?"[13] As if high-flying chutzpah weren't enough, a dash of racism had to complete the scene.

David Shulman, a former professor at Hebrew University of Jerusalem, writes that the Palestinian occupation has dragged Israel in "a seemingly inexorable process of moral corruption and decline." Before 1967, he says, "there was widespread fear and even hatred of Arabs...but it was nothing like the rampant racism one now hears every day on the radio and TV. Shame, sincere or not, had not yet disappeared from public life."[14]

The writer Shai Stern specializes in playing the insult comic. In a long YouTube video, you can watch him strolling around the Old City of Jerusalem on July 14, 2014, chatting in Hebrew with a series of Palestinian shopkeepers. To the first one, Stern says, "We just want peace and quiet. Couldn't you change Hamas? Pick somebody else to represent you?" The shopkeeper: "What about you, why don't you change Israel?" "No, 'cause we're a country. You'd never know how to make a real country. I really don't like the fact that you keep staying here. I want you to leave." Further on, he asks a young man, "Wouldn't you really rather be a refugee? We really know how to pamper people in refugee camps. It would be great for you. Everything would be taken care of, and subsidized." In a shoe store, he asks to buy a pair of "Arab shoes." The seller says that his shoes aren't either Arab or Jewish. "Sure they are," says Stern, "The Arab shoes aren't as good." To the seller: "What's your name?" Seller: "Ahmed." Stern: "Why in world do you have an Arab name? It's not good for you to have a name like that in our country."[15] The rest of the clip is more of the same, somewhere between slapstick and colonial contempt. And Stern's delighted audience eats it up.

These racist tropes wouldn't be that significant if they weren't enjoyed by so many in Israel, and shrugged off by many others. They are part of the evolution of an entire society. In February 2019, a group of parents in the Karnei Shomron settlement managed to have all the school's Palestinian cleaning women fired. Explaining their demand to the school principal, one parent wrote: "The lives of our children come first. We are racists, and we love the Jewish race."[16]

For their documentary *War Matador*, Macabit Abramson and Avner Faingulernt in 2009 filmed families who came to picnic on the hills overlooking Gaza and watch the bombing of the city by the Israeli air force during Operation Cast Lead.[17] They cheer the spectacle of Palestinian buildings being destroyed. "What a marvel, those bombs! Our air force is wonderful." People are eating and drinking, enjoying the show, not unlike those white crowds in Mississippi and Georgia who after church on Sunday came out to watch Negros accused of touching a white woman or stealing apples being hanged. Why should they feel ashamed, when the legitimization of racism comes down to them from the very top?

In October 2015, an asylum-seeker from Eritrea named Haftom Zarhum was assaulted and killed by four men in the town of Be'er Sheva. The men later explained that they had "mistaken him for an Arab terrorist." (An attack had just taken place near the city's main bus station.) The trial of one of the accused, David Moyal, took place in July 2018. He had been free on bail, and for his participation in the murder was sentenced to do one hundred days of community service and pay 2,000 shekels (about 550 dollars) in reparation to the victim's family. In other words, not a day in prison and a few hundred dollars' fine for doing vigilante justice, mistakenly killing a person with dark skin. Eyatar Damiri, one of the other attackers, had also pleaded guilty, and was sentenced to four months in jail. The last two attackers, Yaakov Shamba and Ronen Cohen, pleaded not guilty and were acquitted in another trial in 2020. Pathology examinations revealed that the victim had been hit by eight bullets. The judge ruled that those bullets (fired by persons unknown) had more likely killed the victim than the blows struck by the attackers, which he recognized had occurred. He justified his decision by saying that "the series of terrorist attacks created an atmosphere of fear and panic among the public."[18]

This is where a society is going, whose institutions, including its high officials, are sinking into racism.

In this area, Miri Regev takes the cake. A Likud Knesset member, she had not yet been named culture minister when she participated in a session of the Interior Affairs Committee on July 17, 2014. As it reviewed a report by the police commissioner, Yohanan Danino, Regev asked him to explain why, when his forces intervened on the Temple Mount, the police had stopped only the Jewish demonstrators, and not the Muslims. (By common consent the Temple Mount, which Muslims call the Dome of the Rock, is managed by a Jordanian organization, a waqf, and Jews have access to it only within very narrow limits.)

Jamal Zahalka, the chairman of the small Arab party Balad, responded to Regev that the Dome of the Rock is located in occupied Palestinian territory, and that the Israeli police had no business entering it. He added that Commissioner Danino's hands were covered in blood. Regev wheeled on Zahalka, demanded an immediate apology, then told the ushers to remove him from the hall. A verbal battle erupted in which Regev repeatedly insulted the Arab member of the Knesset (MK). Two visibly embarrassed ushers walked over, grabbed Zahalka under the armpits, and tried to escort him away. "Get that garbage out of here," screamed Regev. "Haters of Israel here in the Knesset! Trojan horses, traitors, and terrorists!"[19]

During this entire exchange, neither the Knesset speaker nor any committee member asked Regev to stop her insults. Finally, the ushers were able to get Zahalka out of the room. What matters in this whole sorry episode is the general master-slave relationship it illustrates. And this is far from a unique case. It's just how barefaced racism operates within the halls of Israel's so-called democracy.

So why should we surprised when, before the elections of 2019, Netanyahu and his party should strike a deal with the Jewish Force list, which included two Kahanist candidates? Historically called the Kach Party,[20] the group owes its name to the American rabbi Meir Kahane, a Jewish supremacist and violent hypernationalist who founded the Jewish Defense League. (Yigal Amir, Yitzhak Rabin's assassin, sprang from its ranks.)

The Kahanist party was excluded from participating in the 1994 election, officially because of racism. But in 2019 it ran candidates under the banner of a party called Jewish Force without any problem. Piotr Smolar, Le Monde's Israel correspondent, explained the deeper significance of the movement's rehabilitation this way: "The lines have shifted, the moral norms erased. Electoral speeches stigmatizing the Arab minority are now a dime a dozen. The whitewashing of Jewish Force is neither a break in Mr. Netanyahu's political trajectory nor that of the evolution of the Israeli right. It is the conclusion of their long ethnocentric drift."[21]

A whiff of fascism

As the April 2019 elections approached, Ayelet Shaked, a leading figure in the colonial movement, aired an unusual TV spot.[22] Against a black background, she gives a sensual toss to the dark hair framing her face. Next to her, you can see a perfume bottle with the label *Fascism*. Zoom in. "Fascism is a judiciary revolution," she says in Hebrew. "Activists are curbed. Judges are appointed by the government." Shaked, who was justice minister at the time, was promoting a "revolution" she hoped would lead to a less permissive judiciary, a Supreme Court subservient to the government, and leaders able to enact laws without the approval of a court she despised. Zoom back. Slogans on the wall: "The two-state solution isn't working. Governance. Separation of authorities. Restraining the Supreme Court." The spot ends when Shaked picks up the perfume bottle, spritzes herself, and says, "Smells like democracy to me."

At first, you would think it was parody, but it wasn't. That really was Netanyahu's minister of justice from 2015 to 2019, promoting an Israeli-style democracy with a delicious whiff of fascism. Shaked would later claim her message was misunderstood.

The fact is, Shaked's proposals aren't that unusual in today's Israel. The government, the Knesset, and political leaders' entourages are full of characters whose ethnocentrism would make people like Steve Bannon and David Duke turn green with envy. In Israel, they move in the highest circles of the land.

One of the most famous was the billionaire Sheldon Adelson, who died on January 11, 2021. He held no official position, but his influence was unparalleled. Adelson owned a string of casino hotels in Las Vegas, but made his fortune in Macao, the Chinese gambling paradise. Once one of the richest men in America, he fell to seventeenth on the *Forbes 400 List* in October 2019. (Damn those rich techno bros!)

A generous donor to Netanyahu's and Trump's political campaigns, Adelson also supported Ariel University in the Occupied Territories and the most extremist West Bank settlements. He lavishly supported AIPAC, the pro-Israeli lobby in Washington, and helped underwrite Birthright Israel, which is famous for having organized free trips to Israel for 750,000 young Jews between the ages of 18 and 26 from sixty-eight countries. American evangelicals such as John Hagee, who heads Christians United for Israel, also benefited from the billionaire's largesse. In 2007 Adelson bought the popular free daily *Israel Hayom* and put it at Netanyahu's disposal.

At a Washington conference in 2014, Adelson was asked about the risk of Israel's formally abandoning democracy if it continued controlling the Palestinian territories and its people. "I don't think the Bible says anything about democracy," he replied. "God didn't talk about Israel remaining as a democratic state…Israel isn't going to be a democratic state—so what?"[23]

Adelson was as blunt as a kick in the shins, and with his wealth, who among all the recipients of his manna would criticize him? When he made that statement in 2014, he didn't know that three years later Israel would prove him right, making ethnic segregation a part of its Basic Laws.

And then there is Miri Regev, the one who screamed at a Palestinian MK, "Get that garbage out of here!" She was culture minister from 2015 to 2020, which many people thought was a bad joke. She embodies the ignorance, vulgarity, and raw strength that once made Donald Trump so appealing to Israelis. Like Trump, Regev has a limited vocabulary, a loud voice, and unmitigated gall. She was born in one of those "development towns" in the semidesert south where Israeli leaders stuck the poorest Jews from the Arab and Middle Eastern countries in the 1950s and '60s. She spent her career in the IDF, becoming its spokesperson from 2005 to 2008. She then joined Likud, becoming an MK in 2009. Regev is very *dugri*—a classic Hebrew trash-talker. Her main targets are "the Arabs" and "the Muslims," whom she sees as backward barbarians, and collectively as criminals and anti-Semites. She also trains her guns on Israeli leftists, whom she calls "beautiful souls" for not being Zionist enough, or for treacherously supporting a fifth column—Palestinians who are Israeli citizens, whom she would happily strip of their nationality.

Speaking from the Knesset podium, Regev once addressed the Zionist left this way: "I'm told it's good to start a speech with a quotation. It looks cultivated. So I'm going to give you one." She then screamed, in English, "Cut the bullshit! Cut the bullshit!"[24] At every turn, Regev displays her contempt for intellectuals, "those fine talkers," in a crude, populist-fascist vein. Like Trump, she calls her opponents liars and purveyors of fake news. In the Knesset, to the Arab member Haneen Zoabi: "I'm going to say this in Arabic so you understand: get the hell to Gaza, you traitor." But Regev isn't disgusted only by Arabs; Israeli artists are also among her usual suspects. That's ironic, since she was supposed to promote them when she was culture minister. In order to muzzle those disgraceful defenders of Palestinians, she pushed for a law demanding "loyalty to the state in the arts" from writers and artists. To the artists who jeered her, Regev claims it wasn't censorship, but healthy public discourse.

I also have to mention Avigdor Lieberman, a ferocious defender of secular interests who has been a minister several times. He would like to see "disloyal" Arab citizens "decapitated," and in 1998 suggested bombing the Aswan Dam to punish Egypt for supporting the PLO.

A natural politician, Lieberman has climbed every rung of the Israeli political ladder, starting at the very bottom. He was born in Moldova when it was a Soviet Socialist Republic (and still speaks Hebrew with a strong accent), coming to Israel when he was twenty. He worked odd jobs—he was a nightclub bouncer for a while—before joining the Herut (Freedom) Party, a forerunner of Likud. A clever, determined political operator said to have connections among Russian oligarchs, he has served in many ministries. He also became close to Netanyahu, serving as his chief of staff in 1996–97. But Lieberman was extremely ambitious, and moved on to found the secular-nationalist Yisrael Beiteinu (Israel Our Home) Party in 1999, initially attracting immigrants from the former Soviet Union. Lieberman's party is small, but it can play a kingmaker role when the larger parties are deadlocked.

I interviewed Lieberman for *Le Monde* in 2002 about his plan to resolve the conflict with the Palestinians by "balkanizing" them in many unconnected enclaves. After the interview, he asked if I was Jewish. When I said yes, he said, "Don't you see what's happening in France? Don't you understand that Muslims are taking over, and soon there won't be any place for you?"

We should also consider Eli Yichai, a member of Shas—a religious Sephardic Orthodox party—and a former interior minister. During an Israeli military operation in 2012, he urged the IDF "to send Gaza back to the Middle Ages...destroying all the infrastructures, including roads and water."[25] On another occasion, Yichai spoke from his heart: "I sound like a racist, a benighted man or a xenophobe, but I'm motivated by love for my country."[26]

Those sentiments were echoed in 2012 by Ariel Sharon's son Gilad Sharon, who wrote, "We need to flatten entire neighborhoods in Gaza. Flatten all of Gaza. The Americans didn't stop with Hiroshima—the Japanese weren't surrendering fast enough, so they hit Nagasaki, too...There should be no electricity in Gaza, no gasoline or moving vehicles, nothing."[27]

And then there's Oren Hazan, who seems unable to speak of Palestinians, "that nonexistent people," without insults. After making his fortune in Bulgaria in casinos and "no-tell" hotels, he became a Likud MK. Hazan enjoys performing in videos he shoots. In one, he can be seen saving a young Jewish girl in danger of being "soiled" by an Arab man. He is joined in the video by Ben-Zion Gopstein, a rabbi with Youth of the Hills, a group of messianic Jews who clash with Palestinians. The video is a sketch, of course, but it reeks of racism, and the dialogue wouldn't be out of place at a KKK rally.

I could mention dozens of other leaders in the hyperethnocentric state that Israel has become. But I've saved the case of Bezalel Smotrich for last, because he is distinctly more organized. At forty-one, Smotrich is a rising star of the extreme right. He grew up the Beit El settlement and lives with his wife and their six children near Kedumin, another messianic outpost. He has made any number of racist and antidemocratic statements. Declaring himself a "proud homophobe," he organized an anti–Gay Pride "beast parade" in 2006 that portrayed homosexuals as goats and donkeys given to "deviant acts."[28]

Smotrich's ambition is to head a unified colonial religious right that would gather all the scattered supernationalist and messianic factions. And unlike most of Israel's foul-mouthed political figures, he is articulate, which lends apparent coherence to his rants. Among other things, he has proposed separating Jewish and Arab mothers in hospital maternity wards. He also wants the death penalty imposed on "Arab criminals," and has volunteered to serve as executioner. (The death penalty is outlawed in Israel except for the crime of genocide.) Even when settlers firebombed a home in the Palestinian village of Duma,[29] Smotrich argued the term "terrorist" could never be applied to Jews in Israel, since any Jew confronting an Arab is by definition acting in legitimate self-defense. It's no surprise that Smotrich favors the immediate annexation of the West Bank.

Asked in 2016 what he would do to young Palestinians

throwing stones at settlers or soldiers, Smotrich said, "If we show an iron hand, there won't be children who throw stones. Anyone who throws stones will not be here." So what he would do with them? "I will shoot them, or jail them, or expel them."[30]

The worst of it is that Smotrich isn't spewing his racist venom in isolation. He has been the deputy leader of the Knesset, and his arguments are considered completely legitimate in Israeli political and intellectual circles—as are those of the other people mentioned above. In Israel, leading figures express them freely, and instead of dismay, they draw popular acclaim.

3

But What's Your Blood?

The nation-state of the Jewish people

In the Knesset debate before the vote on the nation-state of the Jewish people bill, something happened that didn't get much notice at the time, but sums up the entire law. The members belonging to what Israelis call the "Arab List"—formally the Joint List, it comprises groups that defend Palestinian rights, including Jews—suggested an alternative text, one that promoted "the principle of equal citizenship for each citizen," whether Jewish, Arab, or other. It was the exact opposite of the law under consideration, which explicitly gave full citizenship only to Jews. What do you suppose happened? The alternative proposal wasn't rejected; it simply wasn't put to a vote. Opponents argued that its language violated Knesset rules, which forbid any statement denying "the existence of the State of Israel as the state of the Jewish people."

That's a remarkable tautology. Since the Knesset is the product of a democratic vote, its rules are the expression of democracy. So if the Knesset decrees antidemocratic norms, any vague impulse to preserve democracy must necessarily conflict with the democracy embodied by the parliament. But let's not quibble. The message the Knesset was sending was simple: Arabs have no say in the matter. Israel as the state of all its citizens? Forget about it. The country was already behaving like an ethnocracy even before the vote. Netanyahu described in no uncertain terms what adopting the law meant: "Israel is not a state of all its citizens…It is the nation-state of the Jewish people—and it alone."[1]

The first law of this sort was proposed in 2011. Seven years later, it was a done deal. On July 19, 2018, the Knesset adopted the law, officially writing into law segregation between the Jewish ethnic majority and everyone else, namely Palestinian Arabs, who make up 95 percent of the non-Jewish citizens of Israel. Until then, international opinion had focused on the "apartheid" that Israel was imposing on people in the Occupied Territories. But now even Palestinians who are citizens of Israel—they are fully 20 percent of the population—are excluded from full citizenship. In the Knesset, the majority rejoiced. It had pissed in the swimming pool from the diving board on a subject of the greatest importance, and nothing happened.

"Bad for Israel and the Jewish people"

Overall, just what does this law imply? The country's 1948 Declaration of Independence says that State of Israel "will uphold the full social and political equality of all its citizens without distinction of race, creed, or sex." By contrast, the new law decrees that "the right of self-determination" is unique to Jews alone, and therefore denied to all non-Jews. To make things crystal clear, the very word "equality" of citizens was dropped from the law. Finally, whereas the Declaration of Independence says that "Israel will promote the development of the country for the benefit of all its inhabitants," the new law recognizes only "the development of Jewish settlement as a national value and...[will] encourage and promote its establishment and consolidation."

The original text of the proposed law contained an even more radical segregationist passage. Paragraph 7-b, which was still part of the draft law when it passed on first reading in May 2018, reads as follows: "The State can authorize a community composed of people having the same faith and nationality to maintain the exclusive character of that community." In other words, a Jewish municipality would have the perfect right to forbid an Arab from living there. The paragraph was deleted at the very last moment, for fear that the Supreme Court would strike down the whole law. In a well-known case, the court had ruled in 2000 that it was against the law to refuse to rent or sell an apartment to anyone on ethnic, religious, or other grounds.[2]

The entire law passed with a small majority, 62 to 55, and the welcome deletion of paragraph 7-b didn't change anything of its overall spirit. Ayelet Shaked, the justice minister at the time, clearly defined that spirit when she declared before the final vote: "Israel is a Jewish state. It isn't a state of all its nations. That is, equal rights to all citizens but not equal national rights...There are places where the character of the State of Israel as a Jewish state must be maintained, and this sometimes comes at the expense of equality."[3]

To make sense of that gibberish, it helps to understand that since its founding, Israel has made a distinction between *nationality* and *citizenship*. A Jew was Jewish by nationality, and Israeli by citizenship. A Palestinian could be Arab, Druze, or something else by nationality, and be a citizen of Israel. (Until the 1990s, nationality appeared on the I.D. cards Israel issued to its citizens.) In this view, nationality is considered the equivalent of *ethnic* identity, and citizenship is the equivalent of *juridical* identity. By implication, "the Jewish state" is a state that belongs to its nationals, those born of the right ethnic group or nationality (Jews), but not to its citizens as a whole.

The vision that this law embodies goes back a long way. It was rooted in original Zionism and heavily influenced by ethnic national movements in Eastern Europe. Naturally, it occurs in the "Jewish" nature of the first juridical texts relating to the State of Israel, which de facto assumed the predominance of Jews over other citizens. But it conflicted with the universalist aspirations that are also written in the state's Basic Laws. This ambivalence allowed Israel to present itself as democratic or even progressive, while still practicing discrimination. It has done so for more than seventy years, and its leaders have made good use of that ambiguity. But that is exactly what a majority of the Likud, along with its far-right allies, wanted to get away from. On another occasion, before the vote, Justice Minister Shaked carefully dotted the i's and crossed the t's: "There is a place to maintain a Jewish majority even at the price of violation of rights" of non-Jewish citizens, she said. To make sure no one mistook what she meant, she added: "Zionism should not—and I'm saying here that it will not—continue to bow its head to a system of individual rights interpreted in a universalist manner."[4]

Those pushing to establish the nation-state of the Jewish people are aiming squarely at the principle of universal and inalienable individual rights.

The nation-state bill is "bad for Israel and the Jewish people."[5] Who do you suppose could have said that? Ayman Odeh, the head of the Arab List? Or maybe leftists like writer David Grossman or the late historian Zeev Sternhell? In fact, it was Reuven Rivlin, the president of Israel and a Likud Party founder. Many voices were raised to protest passage of the law, and not only from what remains of the Israeli left. The harshest probably belonged to Amos Schocken, the owner of *Haaretz* and a man of few words, who addressed the big Tel Aviv demonstration against the law. Speakers spoke of "shame," and a "stain" on the face of Israel. Writing in *Haaretz,* the journalist Gideon Levy pretended to rejoice. Finally, he said, a law "that tells the truth" and will "put an end to the farce of Israel being 'Jewish and democratic.'" Sounding bitterly amused, he said, "All those years of hypocrisy were pleasant. It was nice to say that apartheid was only in South Africa...To say that Hebron is not apartheid, the Jordan Valley is not apartheid, and that the occupation really isn't part of the regime...It was nice to claim that since Israeli Arabs can vote, we are an egalitarian democracy...It was comfortable to ignore that the land owned by the Jewish National Fund, which includes most of the state's lands, were for Jews only...Now Israel is for Jews only, on the books...Israel's new friends will be proud of this law."[6]

Levy is right on two points. The practices he names have long existed in Israel, and the new law will indeed please ethnocentric movements and their supporters. Israel has once again shown itself to be a pioneer in the modern age. But Levy is wrong about the fundamentals. The passage of the nation-state bill isn't some routine confirmation of ongoing behavior. It enshrines the triumph of ethnocentricity. The text of Israel's initial Basic Laws has long served as a fig leaf hiding the reality. Non-Jews in Israel were in fact tolerated residents who had no rights except being able to vote every four years. But inscribing that reality in a juridical, constitutional codex is far from ordinary.

The same is true of the passage of the nation-state bill. Zionism has always contained the idea of an ethnic state, and the new law doesn't change much of what existed before its passage. But it marks the end of an era. Until now, the law allowed people to challenge discrimination, even if the challenges didn't have much effect. But henceforth, Israel is officially a segregationist country. Until now, the Jewish state's ethnic nature had to be balanced by the appearances of a formal democracy. It was part of the shadow side of Zionist ideology, and had to be hidden, to protect Israel's positive self-image. The nation-state bill proclaims that this no longer needs to be hushed up. The essentially ethnic character of the state is acknowledged. Sheldon Adelson succeeded: Israel is no longer officially a democracy. "So what?"

"It was axiomatic that there was an intimate link between Judaism and universal human rights," writes David Schulman.[7] From the Enlightenment to the days after World War II, that link was forged and passed on by people, very many of them Jews. Within a variety of political settings, they tried to promote social justice, human dignity, and the values embodied in the idea of progress. That is the link that the nation-state bill has definitely broken.

In his 2016 book *East West Street,* Philippe Sands describes how Hersch Lauterpacht and Raphael Lemkin, two Jewish jurists from the same town of Lemberg (Lviv today) in western Ukraine, originated the contemporary concepts of genocide and crimes against humanity.[8] Lauterpacht even helped draft Israel's Declaration of Independence. Without fear of contradiction, one can say that the passage of the nation-state law would have left him slack-jawed with indignation.

The triumph of ethnocracy

The following incident happened less than a month after passage of the nation-state bill, and became known only because of excellent reporting by *Haaretz.*[9] On August 11, 2018, Nadim Sarrouh was preparing to cross the border from Jordan into Israel with his wife, Venus Ayoub, and her Palestinian family. Sarrouh has a doctorate in computer science; Ayoub has a degree in architecture from Technion in Haifa. The couple and the family were headed for their home in northern Israel, after a visit to Jordan.

An Israeli border policewoman first asked Sarrouh if his wife was pregnant. When he said no, she said, "Okay, then she'll be fine, waiting in the heat." This was the Arava desert; it was 113 degrees that day. Inside, Sarrouh was interrogated by the policewoman and a female Shin Bet agent. Where was he from? What did he do? What was his father's name? Born in Haifa in 1940, Sarrouth's father had been expelled to Lebanon in 1948. In 1968, he went to study and eventually settled in Germany, which is where Nadim was born, in 1984. Traveling with his German passport, Nadim returned to Israel, and reconnected with his Palestinian family.

"But where are you really from?" asked the Shin Bet agent. Sarrouh: "From Germany. I'm a German citizen." The agent: "Yes, but what's your blood? German or Palestinian?" Sarrouh: "I don't know about that, but if my blood is anything, it's probably also Polish." (His mother was Polish, though born in Germany.)

A long interrogation followed, in which, among other things, the agent asked Sarrouh what he thought about the situation in Gaza. Exasperated, he said he didn't think they were allowed to ask him that sort of question. "We can actually do anything we like," she replied angrily. "This isn't Germany! We aren't letting refugees in just like that, like your Merkel is doing." She pointed to the flag flying outside and said, "You see that? You're in Israel. It isn't your country. And if you don't like it, you can take your passport and go back to Jordan."

A second Shin Bet interrogator soon joined them, repeatedly saying, "Don't lie if you want to see your wife again." The agent said something to Sarrouh in Arabic, and when he said he didn't understand, she shouted at him for being an Arab who didn't speak the language of his blood. When she asked him about Jerusalem, the issue of his "blood" came up again. The Shin Bet agent refused to believe that he felt no special connection with Jerusalem, that someone with his blood must have feelings for the Holy City. When she asked him, "When did you last throw a stone at an Israeli?" Sarrouh couldn't help it; he burst out laughing. Shortly afterward, he got his passport back and was reunited with his family.

Asked for comment, the Shin Bet denied that its agents had acted improperly, and accused Sarrouh of having been "aggressive." But the scene remains extraordinarily revealing. First because it shows the ignorance of the security service interrogators, and the way they view their environment: Palestinians, Arabs, Islamic State, Iran...they're all terrorists. Second, because it is symptomatic of the ideology behind that attitude. The casual racism in leaving a woman out in the hot sun just because she's an Arab. And especially this: you might be born in Germany, but your blood isn't, and that criterion outweighs anything else. You are born Palestinian, and Palestinian you remain. In Israel, nationality—your ethnicity, your birth tribe, your blood—forever stamps your real essential identity, as opposed to citizenship.

What is there to say? To Jews, any ideology that prizes the preeminence of blood should bring back terrible memories. Yet young Israelis have been educated along these lines for generations. Especially because Likud and its allies have been almost continuously in power for more than forty years, the current generation is notoriously prone to the "teaching of contempt." In the 2015 legislative elections, Benjamin Netanyahu claimed that "hordes of Arabs" "brought by the Left" were heading for the polls, and called on people to mobilize to keep them from preventing his reelection. Those hordes were made up of citizens of Israel, needless to say, just not from the right ethnic group. Because they were Arabs, their blood didn't have the same value.

Israeli society's growing stress on ethnicity is showing up in news stories like this one: "Israeli hospitals admit to segregating Jewish and Arab women in maternity wards."[10] Representatives of the health and retirement system didn't deny separating the women, and in fact they doubled down, claiming it was necessary to make the mothers comfortable, and "not create an artificial melting pot." In a statement, Hadassah Hospital in Jerusalem said: "Given the differences between various populations, women often ask to be in a room with other women from their own community."[11] Three Arab women sued the hospital, saying they had not asked to be put in rooms separate from the Jewish mothers.

Nowhere is the creeping spread of this unbridled ethnocentricity more apparent than in housing. In mid-June 2018—at the very moment that the nation-state bill was being debated—hundreds of Jews demonstrated in the Galilee city of Afula, demanding that the sale of an apartment in their neighborhood to an Arab family be canceled.[12] The Afula march was led by Mayor Avi Elkabetz and Deputy Mayor Shlomo Malihi. "The residents of Afula don't want a mixed city but rather a Jewish city, and it's their right," said Elkabetz. "This is not racism."[13] In the same city, forty-three Arab Israelis had submitted successful bids for housing in a new neighborhood. The court ruled that the grants violated regulations, and nullified the sale.

In itself, that was nothing new, says Raghad Jaraisy of the Association for Civil Rights in Israel. "There's always been racism against Arabs in this country," she says. "What's different is that it's out there now…What was once whispered about behind closed doors, people are no longer ashamed to say out in the open."[14]

We've seen this phenomenon before, of course. In 2010, Shmuel Eliyahu, the chief rabbi of the city of Safed, published a rabbinical edict calling on the Jews of the city not to rent apartments to Arabs. But, says Tzachi Mezuman, the director of the Racism Crisis Center, "that involved a private person who was known for his racist opinions. The Afula case involved elected officials."

Two months before the Afula demonstration, Sivan Yechieli, the mayor of Kfar Vradim, suspended the sale of building lots when he realized that several Arabs had bought them. His justification: "to preserve the secular Jewish Zionist character" of his town. He had earlier polled his constituents; more than 50 percent said they wanted to live in a town without Arabs. Events like this are now happening constantly. When Arab residents of Nazareth Illit petitioned to have a new school built in their neighborhood, the mayor said that as long as he was mayor, "no such school would be built, because it would harm the 'Jewish character' of the city."[15]

This kind of attitude has long been common, but it's now being expressed without any moral restraint. Polls show that a majority of Israelis would prefer to live in places without Arabs. According to Professor Joseph Jabareen of Haifa Technion, more than nine hundred of the country's townships would reject Arab families. What's next? Would such places refuse to let an Arab enter a Jewish store, the way Arabs are now denied entry to Jewish neighborhoods? On the very day that the people of Afula were demonstrating, a Bedouin family went to the municipal swimming pool in a small town in the south of the country. They were turned away. Why would they even bother?[16] In early June, the former Housing and Construction minister Yoav Galant said, "The south is under attack not just from Gaza; the illegal and hostile construction in the Bedouin [community] in the Negev and in the area near Be'er Sheva in recent years is out of control."[17]

With a long list of examples in hand, the Coalition against Racism in Israel in May 2018 described the spread of racist language among Israeli politicians and rabbis in recent years. "When political leaders and rabbis, who are supposed to be role models, express such thoughts, they give legitimacy to others to act and speak in a certain way."[18] Anti-Arab racism has always been widespread in Israel, ranging from the casual racism of colonial superiority to something more virulent. But today, it has taken on a deeper dimension.

"Vital space" for the Jewish people

A nation-state needs more than a basic law enshrining its ethnicity; it also needs a suitable territory. In 2002, to get the colonial right wing's political vision, I spoke with Effi Eitam, a retired general who once led the National Religious Party. Eitam doesn't look like a lunatic. But when he quit the army, found God, and became the head of the most extreme right-wing political party in Israel, a lot of people thought he'd lost his marbles. A lanky man with close-cropped gray hair, he limped slightly as he led me out to his patio to explain why Israel should own every inch of land between the Jordan River and the Mediterranean. And he's not alone in thinking that way.

"The western part of Eretz Yisrael"—the biblical Land of Israel—"from the Mediterranean to the Jordan; that's the Jewish people's vital space,"[19] he said. Eitam, who apparently skipped his history classes in school, didn't seem to know that "vital space" was at the heart of the Nazi lebensraum concept. Otherwise he might have suggested another formulation. But the fact remains that the idea came to him spontaneously. And in that space, only Jews would be allowed to rule. People who talk about "human rights" and "peace" were "psychopaths," he added.

Eitam didn't last long, either in the government or at the head of his party. But his ideas have taken root, and nowhere more deeply than in promoting the annexation of Palestinian territory. This idea enjoys much more popular support than it did two decades ago, and has spread far beyond the religious-nationalist camp.

Three weeks before the legislative elections in April 2019, *Haaretz* published the results of a poll about annexation.[20]

Of the respondents, 42 percent said they favored a partial or total annexation of the Palestinian Territories in the West Bank, in particular Area C,[21] which is by far the biggest in area, but which also has by far the smallest Palestinian population. On the other hand, 28 percent of those polled were hostile to annexations, and 30 percent had no opinion. If you exclude those with no opinion, 60 percent favor annexations. If you further deduct the 20 percent who were Arab respondents (we can safely assume they oppose annexation), some 72 percent of Israeli Jews in one way or another favor annexing all or part of the Occupied Territories. Three-fifths of the proannexation group wouldn't allow Palestinian inhabitants of the West Bank any civil rights at all.

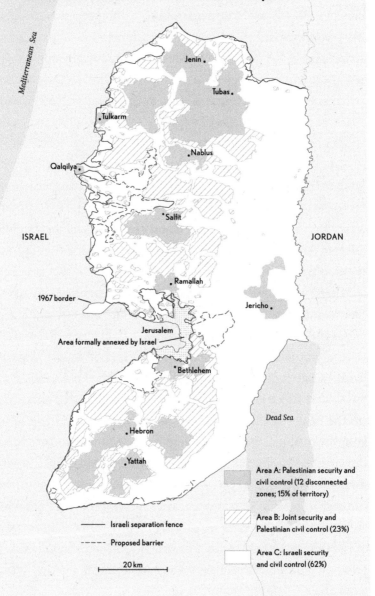

The Palestinian West Bank Under Israeli Occupation

Mediterranean Sea

Jenin

Tubas

Tulkarm

Nablus

Qalqilya

Salfit

ISRAEL

JORDAN

Ramallah

Jericho

1967 border

Jerusalem
Area formally annexed by Israel

Bethlehem

Dead Sea

Hebron

Yattah

Area A: Palestinian security and
civil control (12 disconnected
zones; 15% of territory)

Area B: Joint security and
Palestinian civil control (23%)

——— Israeli separation fence

----- Proposed barrier

Area C: Israeli security
and civil control (62%)

20 km

If that isn't an outlook that has embraced the most rabid colonialism, what is?

In February 2019, a movement named Nahala circulated a petition titled "I, the undersigned..." that read:

> I hereby commit to be loyal to the land of Israel, not to cede one inch of our inheritance from our forefathers. I hereby commit to act to realize the settlement plan for the settlement of 2 million Jews in Judea and Samaria...as well as to encourage and lead the redemption of all the lands throughout Judea and Samaria. I commit to act to cancel the declaration of two states for two peoples and replace it with the stately declaration: The land of Israel: One country for one people.[22]

The petition was signed by the ministers of justice, education, transportation, tourism, environment, Jerusalem affairs, public security, culture, communications, social equality, and others, as well as many deputies from the extreme right, the Likud, and the religious parties. And this kind of commitment isn't just wishful thinking. Annexations are being actively considered in study groups, daylong conferences, seminaries, *yeshivot*, and elsewhere.

In August 2018, *Haaretz* asked a number of nationalist ideologues how they envisioned West Bank annexations. The answers are edifying, and give some insight into current Israeli thinking about what fate might have in store for the Palestinians.[23]

Naftali Bennett, then head of Jewish Home, the national-religious party, suggested immediately annexing Zone C and offering Israeli citizenship to some 75,000 Palestinians, provided they signed a declaration of loyalty to the State of Israel. The 2.8 million other West Bank Palestinians would be scattered among some thirty bits of territorial confetti and given autonomous status. Security would remain in Israel hands, and no Palestinian refugee would be allowed to settle in these mini-Bantustans. The situation would be frozen for an indefinite period. Said Bennett: "It's less than a state, but it seems to me to be as good as it gets." In a second phase, all of the West Bank would become Israel's. If Jordan agreed, the Palestinians could become Jordanian citizens.

Ze'ev Elkin, the Likud minister of Jerusalem affairs, proposed a "gradual annexation," starting with big blocks of settlements. The international community would harrumph a little, but would accept it in the end, as it had already accepted everything else. Elkin would then proceed by the "salami method," annexing one slice of territory after another, not all at once. But an obstacle would remain. On one hand, "granting citizenship and equal rights to Palestinians is a dangerous solution," he said. On the other, it's impossible to officially annex territory without granting some rights. The minister wasn't sure what solution he would choose.

Martin Sherman, the founder and CEO of the Israel Institute for Strategic Studies, said he would want to annex everything, both the West Bank and Gaza, as fast as possible. For one simple reason: to empty them of their Palestinian population. How? War. While waiting for that delightful event, "a series of incentives is needed so they'll leave," he said. Sherman could think of positive incentives (money, for those who would accept it), and negative ones: "Declare the Palestinians an enemy and start to gradually reduce the provision of services and goods to them." Isn't that a bit radical? No, because Israel isn't morally obligated to support the presence of an enemy. But Sherman said that the only real option is a general "transfer," a term used since the 1930s to mean the expulsion of Arabs. "Let them go to Indonesia or India, for example. Transfer isn't a dirty word."

Columnist Caroline Glick (*The Jerusalem Post*, *Breitbart News*) also pushed for the immediate annexation of the entire West Bank. The Palestinians "wouldn't want to become Israelis," she said, so why worry about them? By their own choice, they would remain without citizenship under an Israeli government. On the other hand, they would have to be given a status of "residents." Annexing Gaza would be out of the question, however. Who would want to run that madhouse? asked Glick. "Gaza is an independent state."

Finally, Mordechai Kedar, an expert at the Begin-Sadat Center for Strategic Studies, came up with a totally original solution. He argued that the notion of "Arab peoples" is an invention of colonialism. Arabs actually have no identity beyond that of the "great families" to which they belong, he said. As a tribal people, they have no sense of nationhood. So the Palestinians could be split up into any number of entities, one in Gaza and a scattering of little "emirates" around the cities (Hebron, Jericho, Nablus, Ramallah, etc.) Those emirates would have no sovereignty, of course (the Arabs wouldn't complain since they don't understand the term, said Kedar), and would be completely controlled by Israel. The rural zones, comprising 80 percent of the West Bank territory and 10 percent of its population, would be annexed, and their inhabitants offered Israeli citizenship.

Such are colonialist thinkers in Israel: eager to see their wishes come true, and totally devoid of scruples. Nobody knows what will become of these rants, but the people spouting them are serious; they want them put into practice. Left unspoken is their dream of some unforeseeable opportunity to rid themselves of the original inhabitants once and for all. A full-scale war, or some kind of chaos that would finally give Israel the chance to finish the job left half done in 1948. This would achieve the common dream: one state for one people in its "vital space," extending throughout Mandatory Palestine, now rid of the last Palestinian. Bezalel Smotrich, the religious settler ideologue we met in Chapter 2, makes no secret of the need to prepare for D-Day, when the great expulsion can be launched. Addressing Ayman Odeh, the Arab leader of the United List in the Knesset, on Twitter, he wrote that "We [Jews] have just been the most hospitable people in the world since the days of Abraham and so you [Palestinians] are still here. At least for now."[24]

In the meantime, there's work to be done. In Gaza, it's limited to periodically bombing that tiny strip of land while keeping Hamas in power, which is useful in stalling any real diplomatic progress. The West Bank, where most of the Palestinians live, requires a different approach. Right now, Israel's main strategy has two parts.

The first is to perpetuate and enlarge the settlements, while making life increasingly miserable for the Palestinians. Legalizing the so-called illegal settlements has long been done on the sly, but on February 6, 2017, the Knesset tried to do so on a massive scale. It passed a "regularization" law that legalized the existence of all settlements imposed on Palestinian land that were built "in good faith." "It was a land grab, pure and simple," said Hagai El-Ad, the director of B'Tselem.[25] Israel clothed the land seizure in legality, and why shouldn't it? Up to now, says El-Ad, "it's been one hundred percent settlements and zero percent consequences" at the international level. The regularization law was the tip of an iceberg of a slew of other laws passed in recent years, all designed to tighten Israel's colonial grip a little more each day.

Israel's Supreme Court struck down the regularization law as unconstitutional almost four years after it was passed. In her ruling, Chief Justice Esther Hayut said that the law "seeks to retroactively legalize illegal acts perpetrated by a specific population in the region while harming the rights of another." "It creates discrimination between Israeli and Palestinian residents regarding the regulation of illegal construction in the area."[26] Netanyahu immediately denounced the court's "interference in striking down an important law for the settlements and their future." He promised that the coming annexation of Palestinian lands "will solve most of the regulation problems."[27]

The second part of the strategy consists of emptying the countryside and pushing the Palestinians into areas around cities. These are often crowded, impoverished exurbs in Areas A and B, officially run partly or wholly by the Palestinian Authority. (In Area C, there are already more settlers than Palestinian residents.) To accomplish this, the Palestinians are made to abandon their villages by cutting their livelihood (by denying them access to their fields, for example) but also by "the imposition of fear," as we saw earlier.

Here's an example. The town of Yatta, six miles south of Hebron, had a few thousand inhabitants in 1980. By 2007, it had 48,000. Today, it has 70,000. Every day, more land is being confiscated to become a "military zone," a "public space," or included in a "natural park." "As soon as a settlement is created, the entire surrounding area is emptied of its inhabitants," says mathematician Daniel Kronberg.[28] Meanwhile, the Palestinians are systematically denied building permits. Some of the other ways to make them leave are truly perverse. For example, thousands of families, maybe tens of thousands, have been refused "family reunification." So if a Palestinian wants to marry someone who lives outside the West Bank, they can't have that person join them. The only way to live with them is to leave. It's very effective.

This policy reinforces the balkanization of Palestinians that Avigdor Lieberman urged back in 2004. By herding Palestinians into cities and their exurbs—which settlement opponents call "rampant ethnic cleaning"—Israel is preparing to annex most or all of Area C. During Trump's term in office, it enjoyed the unconditional support of the White House. With a Biden administration in Washington, all bets are off.

4

This Country Belongs to the White Man

An emerging idea: racial purity

The date was July 3, 2012. Over the previous few months, a series of violent attacks had been launched against certain refugees, most of them from Sudan and in particular from Darfur, with its terribly repressive regime, and Eritrea, where the authorities' death squads had unleashed a reign of terror. In Israel, voices were increasingly being raised against the presence of undocumented aliens, which they called "infiltrators." The choice of name is no accident. In the 1950s, "infiltrators" is what Palestinians expelled between 1947 and 1950 were called when they tried to come back to see what had happened to their village and their possessions. "Infiltrator" was the equivalent of "terrorist."

On that day in 2012, the Netanyahu government's interior minister, Eli Yishai of Shas (ultra-Orthodox Sephardic), gave an interview to the newspaper *Maariv*. "Most of those people coming here are Muslims who think the country doesn't belong to us, the white man," he said. "I will continue the struggle until the end of my term, with no compromises." He said he would use "all the tools to expel the foreigners, until not one infiltrator remains."[1]

A plague on Black "infiltrators"

Yishai's statements are interesting for several reasons. First, because they were made in a supposedly democratic country by an interior minister who had earlier sided with the racist rioters against the victims. Second, because they reveal his ignorance: Eritreans (about 72 percent of the undocumented Africans in Israel) are more usually Christian than Muslim, and like the Sudanese (20 percent), include many animists. Finally, and especially, because the undocumented aliens the minister hoped to expel were Black. This involved 40,000 people among the 180,000 to 200,000 immigrants then in Israel, most of them Asian or Eastern European, and most of whom were also undocumented.[2] Undocumented immigrants from countries other than Black Africa often work in construction or as farm labor, and are regularly underpaid and denied social rights in Israel, where associations defending them protest their mistreatment. But unlike Africans, they have never faced calls for their mass expulsion.

We are witnessing a phenomenon unprecedented in Israel. Up to now, anti-Black racism has been virtually nonexistent. And Israel's putting itself under a banner defending "the white man" is foreign to Zionism's ideology and history. Defense of the West? Sure, but of the white man? You would search in vain for such a reference in Zionism's foundational texts and the historic debates in Israel. So this is something new. Is it anecdotal or significant? It's true that the Black Israelites who began to arrive from New York in the 1970s had trouble integrating. They were mainly settled in "developing" cities— meaning poor and distant—in the Negev desert. The Ethiopian Jews, who were once known as Falashas and who were recognized as Jewish by the Israeli rabbinate in 1974, came in two great waves between 1984 in 1994, and today number more than 100,000. Though Jews, they continue to be harshly discriminated against at times, especially in housing, and remain confined to particular neighborhoods with high unemployment rates. Some mayors refuse to enroll the migrants' children in schools. But a few Ethiopian Jews have found spectacular success, especially in sports and show business, and several have become members of the Knesset. So their integration has been problematic, but nowhere near as hard as that of refugees from East Africa, who soon became the target of radical hostility.

The first such refugees began to arrive in the second half of the 2000s. The flow accelerated in 2011 and 2012. They very quickly congregated in three southern Tel Aviv neighborhoods: Shapira, Hatikva, and Neve Sha'anan. At first, the government took steps it hoped would discourage them. A special immigration police was created to manage them and keep them from coming. In 2010, the government launched a project to build a wall along the border with Egypt to keep them out. In addition, when these immigrants find work, their employers are supposed to deduct 20 percent of their wages and give it to the government, to provide the funds necessary for future expulsions. As for requests for asylum, of 15,205 applications made to the Interior Ministry between 2013 and 2018, only eleven—about 0.07 percent—were granted. By comparison, in the European Union at the same time, requests for asylum were granted to 57 percent of Sudanese, and 92 percent of Eritreans.

The first actions against the immigrants' presence soon began. Settlers in Hebron vented their hostility on the ones in their neighborhoods. Racial attacks multiplied. Municipalities like Kiryat Shalom passed laws that stipulated that no private apartment, and not even a room, could be rented to one. Eliat's city hall rejected Black children in its schools. In Tel Aviv, separate kindergartens were created for them. Writing in the *Washington Post*, journalist Gershom Gorenberg described meeting Emanuel Yamani, an Eritrean refugee to whom an Israeli policeman had once said: "Soon we'll deport all of you. You can go sit under a tree, open your mouth, and wait for a banana to fall into it, like monkeys." When Yamani answered that he was a human being, the amused policeman said, "Haven't you looked at yourself? Don't you see you look like a monkey?" Gorenberg asked the Interior and Immigration ministries for their reaction, but got no response.[3] Everyday racism was spreading, winked at by public authorities.

Netanyahu noticed the shift in the wind. "If we don't stop the problem," he said in 2012, "60,000 infiltrators are liable to become 600,000 and cause the negation of the State of Israel as a Jewish and democratic state."[4] This led to a series of similar statements, each more alarming than the rest. In May 2012, several violent attacks were made against places where Africans gathered, including a clinic for refugee children, which was torched. Miri Regev, the future culture minister, agitated to have the immigrants deported. Lashing out at the "leftists" (several Labor members had taken up the African refugees' cause), she declared that Sudanese infiltrators were "a cancer in the nation's body."[5] When they responded with outrage, Regev apologized for the comparison…to the cancer sufferers! From then on, xenophobic and racist talk exploded, both in the media and on the street.

Likud member Danny Danon said, "We must expel the infiltrators from Israel. We should not be afraid to say the words 'expulsion now.'"[6] Danon would go on to become minister of science and technology, then Israel's ambassador to the United Nations. Member Yulia Shamalov-Berkovich said that lawyers assisting asylum seekers should be interned with them in the detention camps.

In December 2013, the government began a policy of "voluntary departures" for these immigrants, in exchange for a small payoff. NGOs supporting them protested, pointing to the history of the Wandering Jew and to Hillel the Elder's edict: "That which is hateful to you, do not do to your fellow. That is the whole Torah." But Netanyahu, riding a wave of popular support, persisted. Immigrants were interned in camps in the Negev and deprived of their papers.

Saimon Fisaha, an Eritrean who had lived and worked in Israel for six years, wound up in the Holot camp. There, he was offered $3,500 and a one-way ticket to Rwanda. He was assured that when he arrived, he could ask for asylum and find work. Three days later, he was on a plane with ten fellow refugees. Writing in the *New Republic*, Brian Goldstone described what happened next.[7] On arrival in Kigali, Fisaha had to hand over his identity papers. When he asked how to begin the asylum request process, the agent said it couldn't be done and refused to return Fisaha's papers unless he paid him $500 and left the country. Fisaha and the others had fallen into the world of human trafficking. He would wind up traveling to the Mediterranean through Sudan and Libya, experiencing "beatings and imprisonment, theft and extortion, extreme hunger and dehydration, [and] the threat of deportation back to Eritrea"—in other words, possible death. Held captive in Libya under dreadful conditions, he witnessed the enslavement of men and women, rape, and torture. Fisaha finally reached Europe on a leaky boat carrying three hundred people like him.

On January 3, 2018, Netanyahu launched a major new policy he claimed would "resolve" the problem of African asylum seekers. "The government approved a plan today that will give every infiltrator two options: a plane ticket out or jail."[8] Refugees would be offered $3,500 in cash, plus repayment of the money deducted from their pay if they had been working (20 to 40 percent of their wages). Refusal would be punished by incarceration in the high-security Saharonim detention center in the desert (with no exemption for the five thousand children born in Israel to African couples). Israel claimed to have signed agreements with Uganda and Rwanda to welcome the deportees, but the two countries denied such an agreement existed. Accounts of the fate experienced by refugees flown to Rwanda began to spread, and they sounded like what Fisaha had experienced. Amnesty International published a damning report that said that those who arrived hadn't been offered refugee status, residency visas, or jobs.

Soon 750 asylum seekers at the Holot camp began a hunger strike. In late February 2018, 20,000 people demonstrated in Neve Sha'anan in support of the refugees. But polls showed that two-thirds of the Israeli public still supported their mass expulsion. And hatred for the Black immigrants joined hatred for the "beautiful souls" who supported them: intellectuals, artists, and NGO militants. It was similar to the way some Trump supporters hate the people who support Blacks and immigrants in the United States.

In March 2018, hundreds of additional refugees were interned in the Negev. On April 2, Netanyahu announced a dramatic reversal: Israel had reached the "best possible agreement" with the United Nations High Commissioner for Refugees, he said. The U.N. agency would take charge of settling half of the refugees in countries like Germany and Canada; the other half would receive residency permits in Israel. A huge outcry against the government erupted. Naftali Bennett, the minister of education and the head of the religious extreme right, blasted an agreement he said offered "paradise for infiltrators." Three hours later, Netanyahu said he would "reexamine" the accord. Back to square one.

At the height of the Mediterranean refugee crisis, the Pew Research Center published the result of a poll taken in eighteen of the thirty-six member countries of the Organization for Economic Cooperation and Development (OECD). The question asked was, "Would you take refugees from countries where people are fleeing violence and war?" Israel emerged as the country most hostile to welcoming refugees, with 57 percent of respondents saying no. Hungary was the second most hostile, with 54 percent. (In thirteen of the eighteen countries, majorities said yes.) The admonition in Exodus 22:21 — "You must not exploit or oppress the foreigner, for you yourselves were foreigners in the land of Egypt"—seems the one least embraced in the nation-state of the Jewish people.

Links with white supremacists

While hundreds of voices in the media and even universities decry the "threat to our identity" posed by these Black "infiltrators," the Israeli companies that bring in contract workers from places like the Philippines and Thailand are quietly going about their business. For example, in 2018 the government launched a program to recruit 6,000 foreign workers for construction work, to join the 16,500 already on site.[9] According to Kav LaOved, an Israeli worker protection organization, each of those Filipinos or Thais must commit to pay their agent $10,000, to be deducted from their monthly salary. (Said salary is set beforehand with the employer, and is generally below the Israeli minimum wage.) Worth noting: the immigrant gets a work permit, but will automatically lose it if the employer lets them go. Moreover, the employer usually holds the immigrants' papers, making it impossible for them to escape their dependent status. This is all perfectly legal.

So what explains the hysteria that gripped Israel over the Black Africans—a group of foreigners making up just 0.5 percent of the country's population? "They had dark skin," said Michael Sfard. "I can't think of any other explanation."[10] Israel has welcomed foreign workers for decades, most of them from Eastern Europe and Asia, without generating this kind of hostility. What woman in Tel Aviv's elegant suburbs doesn't have a Filipina housekeeper to do the cooking and cleaning? Rejection of the Africans was strictly because of their color. As noted above, this is a new phenomenon, and probably springs from the growing closeness between Israel's extreme right wing and American evangelicals and white supremacists, who in turn share strong mutual connections.

Many Israelis liked that Donald Trump chose advisors from evangelical, right-wing, nationalist, or supremacist circles. (Former vice president Mike Pence and ex–Secretary of State Mike Pompeo are both Christian evangelicals. John Bolton, later Trump's tell-all nemesis, is an ultranationalist hawk.) Israelis also liked Steve Bannon, the alt-right ideologue, and Breitbart News, of course. Others who passed through the Trump White House include Stephen Miller, Julia Hahn, and Sebastian Gorka. Miller is a fervent Zionist and a xenophobe with a reflexive hatred of immigrants.[11]

Closeness to those thinkers, whose common denominator was the defense of white supremacy, had characterized the Israeli colonial right for the last two decades. The reverse was equally true.

That's the case of Ann Coulter, a fanatical anti-immigrant media star with a big audience, who ceaselessly praises Israel's migration policy. Likewise Richard B. Spencer, a major white supremacist who says he is surprised he isn't sufficiently appreciated in the Jewish state. "You could say that I'm a white Zionist in the sense that I care about my people. I want us to have a secure homeland that is for us and ourselves, just like you want a secure homeland in Israel."[12] Such thinking finds fertile soil in Israel, where the right and most of the public freely embrace racist positions.

Some aspects of this drift may seem laughable. After France won the World Cup in 2018, a number of Israeli commentators joked that "a premier African team" had actually won the trophy. But the consequences of this proximity with American white supremacy can sometimes take a frightening turn.

In late April 2019, Rabbi Giora Redler, who is on the faculty of Bnai David rabbinical military school in the Eli settlement, was recorded saying that Hitler was "correct in his ideology" and "is one hundred percent correct, except for the fact that he's on the wrong side."[13] Read that breathtaking statement again, and you realize it's exactly what he meant, that Hitler went after the Jews instead of getting rid of the real demons, namely the Arabs or Muslims. Rabbi Eliezer Kashtiel, the head of the yeshiva, went on Israel's Channel 13 to say "We believe in racism," and Arabs "have a genetic problem, they don't know how to manage their country, they don't know how to do anything."

When white supremacist theories spread unchecked in a society, why should such statements surprise us? Why should we be surprised when members of a U.S. congressional delegation are treated differently depending on their color? That's what happened to Donna Edwards, the first African American to represent Maryland in Congress, when she traveled to Gaza with two other Democratic representatives in 2009.[14] On their return to Israel, officials separated Edwards from her group and detained her for an hour and a half. Later, when due at the Foreign Affairs Ministry, Edwards was once again taken aside, separated from her colleagues, and interrogated for nearly two hours: Who was she visiting, and why had she gone to Gaza? Separating the Black congresswoman from her white colleagues, and doing it in broad daylight, is yet another sign of the extent to which racism is seeping into everyday Israeli affairs, even at the highest levels—and the authorities' sense of total impunity about it.

Nor should we overlook the role played by American Jews in the spread of this racism. Visit Hebron, a place where racist oppression of Palestinians is at its worst, and you'll find that the most rabid settlers, the ones who choose to live next to the Tomb of the Patriarchs, include many from the United States. Sara Yael Hirschhorn is a visiting professor at Northwestern University. In her 2017 book *City on a Hilltop*,[15] she notes that many American Jews who emigrate to Israel are also religious extremists. Repelled by American diversity and integration with Blacks, they prefer Israel's separateness. One woman was reported as referring to her Arab neighbors as "worse than the niggers."

The search for the "Jewish gene"

Behind the embrace of white supremacy—which in Israel is limited to the most aggressive settler circles—lies a phenomenon that is growing much more rapidly: the notion of preserving racial purity. The idea is linked to a deep desire for separateness, conceived as a veritable life ideal. On November 9, 2016, Netanyahu announced "a multiyear plan to surround Israel with security barriers." Aware that this idea would strongly appeal to public opinion, he explained: "At the end, in the State of Israel, as I see it, there will be a fence that spans it all…I'll be told, 'This is what you want, to protect the villa?' The answer is yes. Will we surround all of the State of Israel with fences and barriers? The answer is yes. In the area that we live in, we must defend ourselves against the wild beasts."[16]

The metaphor of Israel as a "villa in the jungle," the only civilized state surrounded by wild animals, had been used before, by Ehud Barak, the Labor prime minister at the time, after the failure of the Camp David peace negotiations in summer 2000.

The impulse to shut one's self away, to withdraw from others, which can lead to racism, is sometimes motivated by more than just a need for security. It is usually of a religious inspiration, and often from the interplay between messianic and nationalistic beliefs. In Judaism as it is practiced in Israel, a very traditional rabbinate has power over all aspects of family life (birth, marriage, divorce, death). Civil marriage is not legally recognized, and mixed marriages, that is, unions between Jews and non-Jews, are not recognized. This denial, which was originally of a theological order, is today often reinforced by more or less overt expressions of racism.

In 2014, when the news broke that Yair Netanyahu, the prime minister's son, was having a relationship with a Norwegian student named Sandra Leikanger, the revelation sparked outrage among the proponents of Jewish purity. "Any Jew who wants to maintain his roots wants to see his son marry a Jewish girl," ultra-orthodox Shas MK Nissim Ze'ev told the *Jerusalem Post.* "As the prime minister of Israel and the Jewish people, [Netanyahu] must display national responsibility via the values he presents inside his own household."[17] The relationship even caused a stir within Likud. Many noted that if the prime minister's son had children with this Norwegian woman, God forbid, they wouldn't be Jewish. (This, of course, is because Jewishness is passed down through the mother, at least according to the many people who sadly still believe that biologico-cultural nonsense.) It would be a betrayal of the race, the ultimate tragedy. But what would people say if Norway's Christian authorities said they were offended by their prime minister's son dating a Jewish girl? That they were racists, right?

Obviously, things get really sticky when a Jewish man or woman wants to marry an Arab. In Israel, "Arabness" sharply heightens the sense of race betrayal. In 2018, when the Israeli actor and singer Tsahi Halevi announced that after four years of their living together, he was going to celebrate his fictional "marriage" (fictional, because it is against the law) with the journalist and television anchor Lucy Aharish, a Muslim Palestinian Israeli, the outcry was deafening. Aryeh Deri, the interior minister at the time, felt he should warn them. The marriage "was not the right thing to do," he said on Army Radio. "Your children will have a problem in Israel because of their status." He then suggested that the lady convert to Judaism. Likud member Oren Hazan brought up the state's nonrecognition of marriages between members of different communities. "Lucy, it's not personal, but you should know Tsahi is my brother and the Jewish people are my people, stop the assimilation!" he tweeted, before accusing Halevi of having been "Islamicized." Others also spoke out against the marriage, including the secular MK Yair Lapid and the religious minister Naftali Bennett. (The couple married in a private ceremony on October 10, 2018.)

Salman Masalha, a Palestinian Knesset member, disgustedly slammed the racism inherent in those comments. He reminded the defenders of Jewish purity that Muslim countries totally ban women from marrying non-Muslims. And while in theory a Muslim man is allowed to marry outside the faith, it's essentially prohibited in practice. "People like Deri, Lapid, and Bennett are no different from their opposite numbers in Muslim countries," Masalha said.[18]

The preservation of Jewish purity isn't without consequences. In today's Israel, the most astonishing manifestation of this ideology is the emergence of a school of scientific thought that hopes to make "Jewish genetics" the be-all and end-all justification of Zionism. It would support the Jews' historic right to return to their ancestral lands, and the unique character of that Jewish nation—unique, that is, in the sense of exceptional, or chosen. In January 2014, an academic conference was held at Tel Aviv on the topic "Jews and Race: Genetics, History, and Culture." Debate among the assembled academics was heated, with some backing the concept of a Jewish "race," and others radically hostile to it. The very titles of the seminars were enough to make some people deeply uncomfortable: "Do races have a history?" "Jewish race or Jewish races?" "Can genetics determine who is Jewish?" and so forth. It makes you wonder.

Americans have a lot of influence in Israeli academia, and when they use the word "race," it has a double meaning. Without questioning the unity of the human race, it also serves to designate human groups, especially in terms of skin color, but not necessarily in a racist way. That said, many of the conference speakers used the expression "Jewish racial identity," which raised others' hackles. Poised at the confluence of biology, demography, and geography, population genetics researchers are the tip of the spear of this vogue. And their networks in Israel are increasingly active. Israel and the

United States now have academic institutions committed to the search for the "Jewish gene"—a genetic identity particular only to Jews—that they hope to uncover.

The American researcher Henry Ostrer, for example, runs a genetics laboratory at Yeshiva University's Montefiore Medical Center in New York. He caused a sensation in 2012 when he published *Legacy: A Genetic History of the Jewish People,* in which he speaks of a "genetic basis of Jewishness."[19] The titles of the book's six chapters are explicit: "Looking Jewish," "Founders," "Genealogies," "Tribes," "Characteristics," and finally, "Identity." Ostrer's thesis drew criticism in the pages of *The New York Review of Books* from famed Harvard geneticist Richard Lewontin, who rejected it out of hand.[20] Nonetheless, Ostrer has many followers in certain Israeli academic circles, including the Ramban teaching hospital in Haifa.

When I was reporting on this issue in 2014, the Israeli geneticist Gil Atzmon said, "It's been convincingly proven that Jewishness can be identified through genetic analysis, which lends credence to the notion of a Jewish people"—as if history alone weren't enough to show that. He cautiously rejected the idea of "a distinctive Jewish gene," but added, "this doesn't mean that science won't find it, as research progresses."[21] On the other hand, said Atzmon, "genes allow us to increasingly clearly reconstruct the continued history of a Jewish people through its genes and a phenotype" (a collection of common characteristics). But could this population have remained genetically homogenous over twenty-five centuries? He recognized that large conversions to Judaism had taken place, especially between the first and fourth centuries around the Mediterranean, and also more recently. "But they have not been significant enough to stop the trend." So Jews, because of persecution and their tendency to close ranks to protect themselves, would have preserved their genetic identity.

Needless to say, such theories have caused consternation among geneticists and especially historians. Whether ultranationalist or progressive, nearly all historians question these interpretations. Israeli researcher Eva Jablonka, the coauthor of *Evolution in Four Dimensions*[22] and a recognized expert on the use of genetics in social sciences, totally rejects its use by researchers looking for a Jewish gene. "They're nationalists pursuing a hidden agenda," she said, to claim that a three-thousand-year-old people could have remained unchanged, and is therefore unique.[23] That's absurd, said Jablonka. But it's an absurdity to which more and more people in Israel subscribe, especially among messianic ultranationalists. The Israeli rabbinate has started to turn to genetics to test the Jewishness of people they feel are "doubtful." That's a mistake, according to the late policy analyst Noah Slepkov. "In pushing people to take DNA tests, the Israeli rabbinate has fallen into the trap of 19th century racial science."[24]

These alarming trends—claims about Hitler being "one hundred percent correct," the phrases "Jewish genetics" and "Jewish race"—are still marginal in Israel, but their spread should be taken seriously. When Israel seized the Wailing Wall in 1967, Shlomo Goren was the head of the military rabbinate. In a moment of messianic fervor, he suggested blowing up the Dome of the Rock, a holy Muslim site, and building the Third Temple in its place. Israeli political leaders saw him for what he was: a dangerous lunatic. Defense minister Moshe Dayan is said to have wondered, "Who needs a Jewish Vatican?"

Five decades later, the people pushing to rebuild the Temple are no longer marginal types to be mocked. They include Knesset members, well-financed organizations, and influential pundits. The government has asked the Ir David Foundation, one of those organizations, to conduct archaeological digs near the Temple Mount. It would be a mistake to underestimate the influence of the extreme right, whether secular or messianic, in Israel's evolution. Its ideas are steadily spreading, and the right wing is the primary source of radical and racist thinking. It is already reaching for the major levers of power, without grasping them—yet. If the extreme right ever comes to power in Israel, the entire Middle East could be dragged into a dizzying round of terrifying conflagrations.

5

Locate. Track. Manipulate.

Cybersurveillance, Israel's new politico-commercial weapon

Israel likes to present itself as "the startup nation," and with good reason. No other country, not even the United States or China, can boast of a high-technology sector that accounts for 10 percent of its GDP and nearly half its exports. No other nation this small has such an advanced research and development sector (more than 4 percent of GDP) on the high-tech cutting edge, whether in medical robots, military drones, shipping, agricultural equipment, laser technology, and of course, computer software. In no other country is the army and military-industrial complex so deeply involved in promoting the growth and success of high-tech businesses. This is especially true in cybersecurity, an area about which little information is available, but which is of intense interest to the government, especially its defense ministry and intelligence services.

The tradition of weapons sales

"Israel has a long history of arming dark regimes, from Latin America through the Balkans and Africa, to Asia,"[1] reports *Haaretz*. Probably the most scandalous instance was the support given to South Africa's apartheid regime. And that dubious business continues today. India is led by the autocratic Hindu nationalist Narendra Modi, a rabid Islamophobe whose supporters include the racist Rashtriya Swayamsevak Sangh militias, which also attack Christians. In 2017 India was the main purchaser of Israeli weapons (air defense systems, ground-to-air missiles, radars). The Indian air force sends its pilots to Israel for training, and used the Israeli company Rafael's Spice-2000 "smart bombs" against Pakistan in the Kashmir conflict in the winter of 2019.

Israel has drawn especially sharp criticism for supplying missiles and naval corvettes to Myanmar, despite sanctions against that country for its crimes against the Rohingya Muslim minority in 2016–17. When the Burmese military commander Min Aung Hliang came to Israel to negotiate the purchase of matériel, he naturally paid the requisite visit to Yad Vashem, the Holocaust memorial in Jerusalem. The United Nations has since accused him of crimes against humanity.

In Israel, much of the weapons business happens in the shadows. The Defense Ministry can act in complete secrecy, with support from nearly all the political class and the tacit acquiescence of a patriotic public, for whom anything concerning "security" is rightly kept away from prying eyes, including their own. In no other democracy, even among Western countries, is defense secrecy protected as tightly as in Israel. Which is probably yet another reason why Israel so fascinates the emerging authoritarian democracies.

In July 2018, forty human rights activists asked the Supreme Court to order the Defense Ministry to stop shipping weapons to Ukraine, because some were going to neo-Nazi militias like the Azov Regiment, which is part of the Ukrainian armed forces. Its founder, Andriy Biletsky, had earlier revived a group called Patriot of Ukraine whose mission was "to lead the final march of the white race towards its survival…against subhumans who are led by the Semite race."[2] Israel's Elbit Systems sold them communication systems.

Israel isn't in the same league as such arms exporters as the United States, Russia, France, and Germany. But given its size, it is by far the country whose economy is most dependent on those sales. Israel has only 3.1 percent of worldwide 2014–18 sales,[3] yet is the eighth biggest exporter, while ranked only thirty-second in GDP and ninety-eighth in population. Relative to its GDP, Israel sells proportionately four times more weapons than the United States. And in this arena, it's well known that Israeli companies are subject to fewer legal constraints and public control than the big arms merchants. To repeat, Israel's selling weapons to the cruelest and most corrupt regimes on the planet is nothing new, and no different from what other nations do, including France and the United States. In this sense, nothing has changed since the days when Israel under a Labor government shipped weapons to South Africa. It also furnished weapons and advisors to the Somoza regime in Nicaragua, as it did for a while to Uganda under the bloodthirsty Idi Amin.

But there is a striking difference between the relations that Israel maintained with fascist or military dictatorships in what used to be called the Third World, and the ones it cultivates today. Historically, Tel Aviv was discreet about those relations, which were born of the realpolitik that nations pursue to protect their interests. Furnishing fissile material or nuclear expertise to South Africa under apartheid or training bodyguards for African and South American potentates came under that heading, and brought diplomatic and financial benefits. At times, the connections turned sour. Israeli agents helped bring Idi Amin to power in Uganda, only to have him turn on his mentor a few years later. That aspect of the arms trade hasn't changed. But it now comes with connections that are political in nature. Autocratic, ethnocentric, and religiously driven regimes of the kind ruling India, Brazil, and Hungary are now seeking political closeness with Israel, which returns the favor. In their eyes, Israel embodies an odd Platonic ideal: an omnipotent state eluding the norms of international law, with its citizens' overwhelming support.

The latest in cybersurveillance

In the first few decades of occupying the West Bank and Gaza after 1967, Israel could only draw on old-fashioned colonial ways of imposing its law. But over the last two decades, the occupation has allowed it to refine and export its skills in an antiterrorist specialty: the surveillance of targeted groups and populations.

There is a direct connection between the cordoning off of Palestinian cities, neighborhoods, villages, and refugee camps that Israel has been carrying out for more than half a century in the West Bank (and in an extreme form in Gaza) and the commercialization of "security methods" that it teaches the security forces of countries that want to manage big public events—or crush popular uprisings. Even the Trump administration once turned to Israel for help in securing its famous wall along the Mexican border. The Israeli company Magna BSP, which sells the surveillance systems ringing the Gaza Strip, signed a very lucrative contract with the United States to share its knowledge and experience.

That experience was highlighted in *The Lab*, a 2013 documentary directed by Yotam Feldman. Drawing on high-level interviews, the film shows in striking detail how the Israeli army turned the Gaza Strip into a laboratory in which to test new products: drones; missiles; all kinds of bombs, including those forbidden in civilian areas by the laws of war; and targeted assassination techniques. These operations have allowed companies in the Israeli defense industry—especially Raphael, Israel Aerospace Industries, and Elbit—to find new customers and significantly increase their annual revenue.

Israel's Operation Protective Edge against Gaza in summer 2014, an air attack followed by a ground intervention, had the biggest payoff of all. For the first time, the IDF was able to deploy the Hermes 900 drone, which can carry a payload up to 660 pounds, in an urban setting under difficult weather conditions. It could also evaluate Hatsav tank rounds, which penetrate concrete before exploding in a closed space, super-smart MPR-500 bombs, small new information-gathering vehicles, and more.

Over the years of the Palestinian occupation, Israel has also refined its war-on-terrorism techniques, where controlling people is the key to success. This is the domain in which Israel appears as a pioneer. What fascinates the leaders who sing its praises is the combination of control techniques and the willingness of Jewish Israeli society to accept and submit to limits on public freedoms.

There's a long list of illegitimate methods designed less to reduce terrorism than to dismember Palestinian society, in the hope of forcing it into submission. They range from collective punishment (in particular the razing of houses, which is regularly visited on the families of alleged terrorists after an armed attack on Israeli soldiers, settlers, or civilians) to administrative detentions. Authorized under the Emergency Defense Regulations, detention orders allow the jailing of anyone for up to six months without giving a reason, renewable indefinitely. Both methods were used by the British until 1948, and were adopted for the Israeli repression arsenal with the creation of the State of Israel.

In the half century of occupation of the West Bank and Gaza, the Palestinian population has grown from one million in 1967 to nearly five million today.[4] Of these, some eight hundred thousand have been arrested at least once in their lives. On December 11, 2012, the Salam Fayyad government estimated that about a hundred thousand Palestinians have been administratively imprisoned for periods ranging from a month to several years in what is essentially a Guantánamo that dare not speak its name. The record is held by Hamas member Hatem Qafisha, who spent eleven years and seven months in prison in six different administrative internments between 1996 and 2013 without ever being formally charged with a crime.

Torture is rarely cited among Israel's repressive tactics today, but not because it doesn't exist. It is still used, but even the Public Committee Against Torture in Israel admits that a once-routine practice is now less so. That's because the methods available to Israeli security forces have greatly changed in two decades, especially the sophisticated use of cybersurveillance.

It's mainly in the cybercontrol of people that Israel has earned a universal recognition in less than twenty years, winning significant financial, political, and diplomatic success. According to Yuval Noah Harari, an Israeli historian whose bestsellers have won him renown, the occupied West Bank gives Israel a tremendous "laboratory in the creation of a numerical dictatorship." Asks Harari: "How can you effectively control 2.5 million people[5] by using artificial intelligence, big data, drones, and cameras? Israel is the leader in surveillance. It tests its methods, then exports them to the world…In the West Bank you can't make a phone call, get together with friends, or go from Hebron to Ramallah without being targeted and filmed."[6]

All kinds of regimes have made use of those skills. In late 2018, *Haaretz* published an in-depth investigation that listed some of the countries that have bought Israeli surveillance and control equipment and training.[7] Private Israeli companies have sold information-gathering systems to more than a hundred countries, including Indonesia, the Philippines, Thailand, Malaysia, Bangladesh, Vietnam, Angola, Mozambique, Zambia, Botswana, Swaziland, Ethiopia, South Sudan, Nigeria, Uganda, Mexico, Ecuador, El Salvador, Panama, Trinidad and Tobago, Nicaragua, the Dominican Republic, Honduras,

Peru, Colombia, Azerbaijan, Uzbekistan, Kazakhstan, Saudi Arabia, the United Arab Emirates, and Bahrain.

The Defense Ministry, whose imprimatur is required in this trade, has never published the full list. In addition, dozens of countries have turned to Israeli training programs—which now include a large cybersurveillance component—to train their intelligence, police, and military services. In the United States, the Georgia International Law Enforcement Exchange (GILEE), a professional training program created in 1992, has close ties with Israeli security circles. A joint project with Georgia State University and a variety of international, federal, and state agencies, GILEE has sent the Israelis some 24,000 law enforcement and public safety agents for training in a quarter century.

When Netanyahu attended the inauguration of the right-wing Brazilian president Jair Bolsonaro in January 2019, he used the opportunity to offer an exchange: if Brazil moved its embassy from Tel Aviv to Jerusalem, Israel would offer cyber-surveillance matériel and training to Brazilian personnel. When Modi, the Indian prime minister, visited Israel in July 2017, he placed orders for similar matérial. The Philippines' president Rodrigo Duterte, who is a kind of Trumpian tropical satrap, did the same a year earlier. It's likely that many of the leaders of the new authoritarian democracies in Eastern Europe and elsewhere with which Netanyahu has forged links have also benefited from Israeli know-how in hunting down their opponents.

So who are the leading Israeli companies? The most prominent is the NSO Group. Founded in 2010, it gets its name from its creators' first names: Niv Carmi, Shalev Hulio, and Omri Lavie. Unlike many cybersecurity companies, NSO is not involved in data protection. Instead it offers so-called offensive cybertools. The most notorious is called Pegasus, which in 2016 *Forbes* described as "the world's most invasive mobile spy kit."[8] Pegasus had the capacity for virtually unlimited surveillance of mobile phones. It can pinpoint their location, listen in, record nearby conversations, photograph everything in their surroundings, read and write messages and email, download applications, and access applications already on the phone as well as photographs, videos, calendars, and contact lists. And it does all this in total secrecy. As NSO's Lavie once boasted, "We are a ghost…We leave no traces."[9] One of Pegasus's victims was nearly Ahmed Mansoor, a human rights activist in the United Arab Emirates. In August 2016 he received a suspicious text on his iPhone promising information about torture in his country. Partly because he'd been hacked before, he was suspicious, so he sent the text to researchers. They forwarded info about it to Apple, which fixed the exploit the software uses to spy on users. Soon after, for publishing critical information about torture on social media, Mansoor was sentenced to ten years in prison.

NSO was one of the major beneficiaries of the new relationships forged between 2018 and 2020 with the Gulf monarchies. In Israel it may be the company that financially profited most, signing commercial agreements with Saudi Arabia, Oman, Bahrain, and several of the emirates of the United Arab Emirates, one of which has a worth $250 million. NSO doesn't do business with Qatar because Israel prohibits it.[10]

Among the other most active companies are Elbit Systems, a supplier of the Nigerian National Intelligence Agency, among others, and Verint Systems, whose promotional slogan was "Locate. Track. Manipulate." Verint once installed a secret data-collecting system in Peru, but had to shut it down when the then prime minister, Ana Jara Velásquez, was caught using it to spy on voters, journalists, and businesspeople. Verint has also sold an enormous amount of surveillance and social-media tracking software to Bahrain, a small emirate in the Persian Gulf where a Sunni elite rules the largely majority Shiite population. Repression of dissidents in Bahrain is ferocious. Nabeel Rajab, its best-known human rights defender, was sentenced to five years in prison in February 2018.

We could also mention Cellebrite, Check Point, Singular, Gilat, Leadspace, and other companies. In all, some seven hundred Israeli startups are involved in cybersurveillance. The *Haaretz* investigation revealed that to avoid attracting attention and overcome reluctance to deal with Israel, company executives often set up subsidiaries in other countries. These include Cyprus and Bulgaria, which have the advantage of offering clients an EU label. "In most cases, when you want to sell in the European Union, and very definitely in the Gulf, you will need a non-Israeli front,"[11] says Guy Mizrahi of the Rayzone Group. This was confirmed by Avi Rosen of GM IoT Security, who was once vice president of Cyota, the information security company founded by the ex-minister Naftali Bennett: "When you sell in the Gulf, with a license of course, they prefer to see a Bulgarian."[12]

Some of these companies have since been acquired by others. That's the case of NSO, for example, whose legal and national status keeps changing. It was bought by the American private equity firm Francisco Partners, incorporated in Luxembourg, and then had its headquarters transferred to such tax havens as first the Virgin Islands and then the Cayman Islands. But during all this time, NSO, its directors, and employees never left Herzliya, a town ten miles north of Tel Aviv.

These companies were all founded by a small number of people, about 2,300 all told, 80 percent of whom are alumni of the same IDF signal intelligence unit, Unit 8200. Founded in 1954, the unit was merged with military intelligence, then reorganized in the early 2000s to pursue cybersurveillance of Palestinians. Getting into the unit is a hot ticket among young conscripts, because it offers successful candidates more than first-class training. Graduates of what Israelis call the Eight Two Hundreds are assured a comfortable future in a field that in the last decade has become the most lucrative in Israel. The tech companies enjoy fiscal advantages given to exporters, and pay virtually no taxes. Salaries are high, and chief executives can earn fortunes within just a few years. With so much money to be made, it's no surprise that Israeli cyberexecutives often choose to overlook the nefarious purposes to which their systems can be put.

The conclusion of the *Haaretz* investigation, which was drawn from fifteen sources in about a hundred countries: "Israeli equipment has been used to locate and detain human rights activists, persecute members of the LGBT community, silence citizens critical of their governments, and even fabricate cases of blasphemy against Islam in Muslim countries that don't maintain formal relations with Israel...Israeli firms continued to sell espionage products, even when it was revealed publicly that the equipment was used for malicious purposes."[13]

Operating under the radar

In mid-June 2018, the then public security and strategic affairs minister, Gilad Erdan, opened an international conference in Tel Aviv on the role of megadata in the war on terror. "With the experience we have now, we can help other countries deal with this kind of terrorism,"[14] he told the conferees, who had come from around the globe. By terrorism, Erdan was mainly referring to propagators of nefarious ideas, and especially BDS, the international Boycott, Divestment and Sanctions movement,[15] to which he devoted part of his speech. While boasting about Israel's capacities in using big data, Erdan stressed that algorithms alone were nothing without the experts, psychologists, and lawyers needed to effectively exploit social media and track targeted organizations and individuals. Erdan assured his audience that Israel's human and technological assets were incomparable.

Chief among Israel's advantages in cybercontrol is its ability to lie low. Take Candiru, for example. Before Amitai Ziv revealed the company's activities in *Haaretz* in 2019,[16] few non-zoologists could even explain the firm's name. (The candiru is a parasitic Amazonian catfish rumored to invade a swimmer's urethra.) The company was founded by 8200 alumnus Isaac Zack,[17] and recruited most of its 120 employees from that specialized unit. Candiru's specialty is offensive cyber: spyware tools that let users break into targeted computers and mobile devices without first having to activate an application. Where NSO specializes in offensive phone hacking, Candiru does the same to computers and servers. And it is big business: sales of offensive spyware earn Israeli companies an amount estimated by various sources at between $1 billion and $3.4 billion a year.

Exposing the secrecy surrounding these operations is the task taken on by an Israeli lawyer I met named Eitay Mack. A smiling, pudgy thirtysomething in a kippah, Mack works out of a cramped office in an unremarkable office building in downtown Jerusalem. But appearances are misleading. Mack is the man who keeps Israeli cybersurveillance executives awake at night. For one thing, he challenges the notion that Israel dominates this technological sector. "The United States, Russia, France, and others all have similar capabilities," he says. "What gives Israel an edge is that it operates under the radar." The country has two big advantages over its competitors, says Mack. Its ongoing military operations and control of the Palestinian population provide Israel with an invaluable testing ground. But more than that, Israel has no constraints. It is happy to sell its material to the highest bidders—rogue states, trench-coat spooks, shadowy clans—and rarely checks to see if their hands are clean.[18] It can do this—and here's the key to its success—because the Defense Ministry and cybersurveillance companies are free to act with practically no controls. Those freewheeling habits, born of the early days of arms sales, are now deeply ingrained in the ministry's operations, says Mack.

Unlike most of the other international actors in this field, Israeli officials and security companies enjoy extensive protection not only thanks to the state's security apparatus, but above all to its legal system. "You have debates in the U.S.

Congress over the sale of arms and matériel to dictators and military juntas," Mack says. "There's nothing like that here." In the most sensitive cases, he says, a final decision can be taken by the prime minister alone, with no debate within the government. The same culture of secrecy applies to economic matters. When *Haaretz* investigative reporters asked the Economy Ministry for figures, it got this answer from the Central Bureau of Statistics: "It is not possible to provide information about security companies, as we are unable to distinguish between security exports and civilian exports."[19]

And there is a final catch-22. When the cybersurveillance companies are criticized, they argue that their operations are controlled by the Defense Ministry, even though they are private companies. But try to sue the ministry, and it will assert the right to keep matters secret, says Mack, "and the judges always agree." Here's an example. Mack went to court to make Israel stop selling cybersurveillance to South Sudan, whose regime was accused of crimes against humanity. The court handed down a decision, but he can't talk about it. That's because before any hearings were held, the Defense Ministry demanded that all issues raised and any ultimate verdict be kept secret. "And the judges, as usual, agreed," he said with a sad smile.

Mack also ran into a court's refusal to publish a verdict and the grounds for its decision in a case involving the sale of cybersurveillance to the regime in Cameroon. He got a similar result when he petitioned the Supreme Court, asking that it make Israel respect United Nations sanctions against Myanmar. When the defense minister opined that "the Supreme

Court has no authority to rule in military affairs," the court refused Mack's petition.

Here again, Israel has a significant advantage over its competitors. Civil liberties organizations are active, but they operate pretty much on their own, because the state enjoys an unusual degree of impunity in any matter involving security. In other democracies, where challenging authority is seen as legitimate, Israeli officials often try to avoid having to account for themselves. This is especially true in matters involving the use of force, and produces dubious claims of national security. By contrast, the Israeli public invariably supports such claims the moment certain key words are spoken: "terrorism," "Arab," and "Muslim." At that point, all expressions of curiosity are quashed.[20] It's easy to see why strongmen who dispatch their agents to be trained in Israel, like Modi, Orban, and Bolsonaro—and would-be strongmen like Trump—feel envy, not to say admiration. Maybe even Recep Tayyip Erdoğan secretly feels a pang of jealousy.

Israel and the Khashoggi affair

On October 2, 2018, Saudi dissident Jamal Khashoggi, an exile living in Washington, D.C., was killed inside his country's consulate in Istanbul. Israel's media were soon buzzing about links between Israeli cybersurveillance companies and people around Saudi heir apparent and strongman Mohammed bin Salman (MBS), who was quickly suspected of having ordered the assassination. Along the way, some juicy tidbits came to light. For example, former Labor prime minister Ehud Barak revealed that an MBS emissary had offered to pay him to intercede with Israeli spyware companies. (Barak said he didn't accept.)[21]

Seven weeks after Khashoggi's murder, a team of *Haaretz* investigative reporters published details on the assistance that Israelis had given MBS in his sinister task. According to the newspaper, the NSO Group furnished Riyadh with a mobile phone hacking system a few weeks before November 2017, when the heir apparent launched a massive purge of rival Saudi leaders in order to consolidate his power. Initial contacts with the Israelis were said to have started in Vienna in February 2017, and continued in Limassol, Cyprus. The aim of these acquisitions was no secret, apparently. The Saudis wanted "to be able to hack into the phones of regime opponents in Saudi Arabia and around the world."[22]

That June, serious negotiations were held in a hotel in Vienna. Abdullah al-Malihi, known to be close to former Saudi intelligence chief Turki bin Faisal, was joined there by Saud al-Qahtani, then the number two man in the kingdom's intelligence service. The focus of the meeting was NSO's most sophisticated piece of spyware, Pegasus 3. On July 18, Shalev Hulio, NSO cofounder and chief executive, traveled to Riyadh, where he spent three days. The negotiations resulted in a $55 million order, and the material was delivered later that summer.[23] In November, MBS launched his campaign of massive arrests among the top circles of the monarchy. *Forbes* magazine and the Canadian research group Citizen Lab say that MBS's entourage spied on Saudi refugees, including satirist Ghanem al-Masarir, human rights activist Yahya Assiri, and blogger Omar Abdulaziz, now a refugee in Canada. The three men had been in close contact with Khashoggi. Abdulaziz has since brought suit in Tel Aviv against NSO and the Israeli defense ministry for supplying Saudi Arabia with the material that allowed his conversations with Khashoggi to be intercepted, and thereby helping plan his assassination.

Interviewed about NSO, Edward Snowden said, "They're the worst of the worst."[24] The famed whistleblower accused the company of always being ready to help and encourage regimes that violate human rights. In a videoconference broadcast in Israel on November 6, 2018, he added: "We aren't dealing with a cybersecurity company, but cyberinsecurity." Contacted by *Haaretz* for comment, NSO executives said exactly what American bankers hauled in front of congressional committees said after the 2008 financial meltdown: our work is subject to official regulation, we have never acted illegally, et cetera.

First the Palestinians, then Israel's dissidents

In a 2019 *New Yorker* article titled "Private Mossad for Hire,"[25] journalists Adam Entous and Ronan Farrow showed that some of the most experienced Israeli intelligence veterans have gone into the espionage and disinformation business once their military or intelligence service ended. For a price, they will spread distorted or false information to help clients undermine their rivals, whether political, economic, or otherwise. In short, they imitate at a smaller and local scale what Russia was accused of, namely helping Donald Trump during the 2016 presidential election.

The *New Yorker* article focused in particular on the activities in the United States of an intelligence and cybersecurity company called Terrogence. It was created by Gadi Aviran, the former head of research in IDF military intelligence, who spent time at Black Cube (in its literature, the company notes its founders' links to the Mossad and Unit 8200), and especially at Psy-Group, a private company that specializes in psyops, psychological operations designed to shape the behavior of targeted people and groups. Psy-Group, which has offices in London, Hong Kong, and Cyprus, specializes in using social media to delegitimize or smear a client's opponent during an election or a commercial competition, while guaranteeing that the identity of the person paying for its services will never be revealed.[26]

The Israeli police has since investigated Black Cube, which it strongly suspected of participating in a 2016 operation to smear Laura Codruța Kövesi, the former head of Romania's National Anticorruption Directorate, at the behest of unidentified, highly placed figures in the Romanian government. When the affair was revealed, Black Cube CEO Dan Zorella declared he had "learned a lesson" and that his company "has stopped providing services to governments or getting involved in politics in any way."[27] Many in Israel view Zorella's claim with skepticism.

The *New Yorker* article contains intriguing details about operations, but it's especially revealing about the Israeli specialists' state of mind. "Social media allows you to reach virtually anyone and to play with their minds," said Uzi Shaya, a former senior Israeli intelligence officer. "You can do whatever you want. You can be whoever you want. It's a place where wars are fought, elections are won, and terror is promoted. There are no regulations. It's a no man's land."

Tamir Pardo, the Mossad director from 2011 to 2015, is less enthusiastic. Using cybercapacity to influence the behavior of individuals and control populations "is a weapon," he said. "And we should find a way to control it, because it's a ticking bomb. Otherwise, democracy is in trouble."[28] He went on: "There are no regulations. That's the main problem. You can do almost whatever you want." Pardo is a man who believes in order. Like a number of spy masters who have returned to normal life, he is concerned about the potential negative impact that a lawless activity like cybercontrol might have on democracy's survival.

Gilad Erdan, who headed the Strategic Affairs Ministry under Netanyahu from May 2015 to May 2020, seemed less worried. His mission was to coordinate the fight against BDS and track Israelis opposed to the Palestinian occupation. In 2017, he created an initial secret list of those activists, as well as any ordinary citizens who may have expressed opinions he felt were "deviant."[29] Erdan freely admits that he drew up his list of potential traitors by rummaging around on social networks. Speaking anonymously, an official of his ministry justified creating the list by the fact that "many Israelis are encouraging the boycott against Israel and cooperating with foreign activists, against whom our ministry is supposed to act."[30]

In reality, only a tiny number of Israelis support the boycott of their own country. The anonymous official (possibly Erdan himself) was justifying the cybersurveillance of all "deviant" Israelis, whoever they may be. The Mossad and Shin Bet have mocked Erdan's incompetence, but Netanyahu did entrust him with coordinating cyberespionage and dirty tricks on social networks, to battle domestic enemies and the delegitimization of Israel. Sima Vaknin-Gil, a former IDF head of censorship who was Erdan's chief of staff, was once asked what exactly constituted this delegitimization. Her answer: "If you want to win this campaign, you have to do it with a great deal of ambiguity."[31] Not defining the ministry's targets allows it to select them as needed. The Foreign Affairs Ministry doesn't traffic in nuance, either. Any suggestion that Israel's policy toward the Palestinians is akin to racial or ethnic segregation comes under the heading of the delegitimization charge. Vaknin-Gil specified that "labeling products from settlements is the first step, a definite symptom of delegitimation." In other words, anyone who objects to the colonial occupation of the Palestinians will be charged as a delegitimist.

Tzahi Gavrieli, who runs the national campaign against delegitimization, says that anyone denying that Israel is "the national homeland of the Jewish people alone" is also open to the charge of delegitimization.[32] On that score, it's worth pointing out that Reuven Rivlin, founder of the Likud Party and the current president of the State of Israel, is a dangerous delegitimist, since he publicly criticized the nation-state law as segregationist.

The blacklist of people whom the ministry lumps under the heading of "delegitimizer" apparently continues to lengthen. Anyone opposed to Israeli colonial policy, including a few ardent Zionists, risks appearing on it. Cybersurveillance here reaches its ultimate goal. What started as a mechanism to control a native population under military occupation has extended its web to domestic dissidents, and to all those "deviants" who tomorrow risk having their telephones hacked, and their computers and entire private lives used to support charges of delegitimization.

It is no accident that Israel has emerged as a master of surveillance over an existentially threatening people (the Palestinians) as well as over internal dissent. Around the world, the country now embodies the promise of modern technology that allows governments to rule over people, preserve their power, and commit crimes beyond any civilian control. This is due to Israel's political leaders and a large share of its public's move to embrace a vision where might makes right, and where action is progressively freed from any moral constraint. Israel's commercial success in the particular area of cybersurveillance says a lot about the place it now occupies in the nebulous, growing international coterie of regimes in the Americas, Europe, and Asia, that share ethnic or religious identity politics and contempt for basic democratic values. Israel is a pioneer in the most highly developed techniques of secret control of populations and repression of human rights. At the same time, warns Israeli American anthropologist Jeff Halper, "the Israelization of governments, militaries, and security forces means the Palestinization of most of the rest of us."[33] The result? The Israelis' gradual submission to a security state in which they have given up—voluntarily or by force—everything that undergirds the rule of law.

6

The Shin Bet State Is Here

When people vote for authoritarian democracy

The moment an attack happens anywhere in the world, a swarm of Israeli "experts" pops up to criticize the "naiveté" of other countries, especially European ones, in the face of Islamic terrorism. After the 2016 Islamic State attacks in Brussels that killed thirty-four people, Israeli intelligence minister Israel Katz declared that "if Belgians continue eating chocolate and enjoying life and looking like great democrats and liberals, and not noticing that some of the Muslims there are planning terrorism, they won't be able to fight them."[1] Today, writes anthropologist Jeff Halper, Israel presents itself as the champion in the war on terror, and one that isn't too fussy about "democracy, due process of law, and human rights, all of which it considers liberal luxuries in a world awash in terrorism."[2] Israel is exporting the security state as a model for the future, and few other countries have invested so many intellectual, human, and financial resources in supporting it.

Israel extends its net from Palestinians to deviant Jews

The planning had been underway for a long time. Four years before seizing the West Bank, Gaza, and the Golan Heights in the 1967 Six-Day War, Israel was already considering what judicial norms should be enforced in conquered territory. In 1963, the IDF chiefs asked military advocate general Meir Shamgar (a future Supreme Court chief justice, 1983–95) to draw up a judicial code that Israel could apply in case it conquered new territory. In his book *The Six-Day War: The Breaking of the Middle East*,[3] Israeli historian Guy Laron writes that officers, officer cadets, and reserve officers were taught courses on applying military law in conquered territory starting in the summer of 1963. That December, the IDF appointed the former military intelligence chief Chaim Herzog to head a special unit designed to prepare for an eventual occupation of the West Bank (he would become its first military governor in 1967). From then on, the Israeli National Defense College included the management of occupied populations in its curriculum, and a booklet was printed for future administrators. Those booklets, writes Laron, "became part of a kit that all judges and prosecutors were to receive when the occupation commenced."

As a result of this planning, the original inhabitants of the Occupied Territories have been living under a special military judicial regime devised long ago and regularly "improved" on for more than half a century. During that period, democracy in Israel came in three flavors: guaranteed full rights for anyone of Jewish ethnicity; basic civil rights for Arab Israeli citizens, with a variety of discriminatory limitations; and an emergency military regime for occupied noncitizens. Given the length of the period in question, this amounted to an organized regime of discrimination. But for the last dozen years, a radical change has been promoted by an alliance of conservative and right-wing governments. The rule of law has been steadily undermined, even for citizens of the dominant ethnicity, those "bad Jews" who oppose the domination of one people by another, while the hunt for those holding dissenting views has been pursued with increasing vigor.

This rightward drift had been predicted from the very first days of the occupation by the Israeli scientist and philosopher Yeshayahu Leibowitz (1901–94), a pious and conservative Zionist of impeccable moral rectitude. He also anticipated a frightening development, the fusion of rabid Jewish nationalists with the messianic young members of the Bloc of the Faithful, whom he called "Judeo-Nazis." Leibowitz also inveighed against the Shin Bet, the domestic intelligence service that is deeply involved in controlling the occupied Palestinians: "A state ruling over a hostile population will necessarily become a Shin Bet state, with all that this implies for education, freedom of speech and thought, and democracy. The corruption found in any colonial regime will affix itself to the state of Israel."[4] Leibowitz said this at the very beginning of the occupation. Half a century later, *Haaretz* used his words as the headline on an August 2018 editorial, "The Shin Bet State Is Here." It warned that "the illusion held by many Israelis that persecution and silencing of others as practiced in the Occupied Territories would not trickle over the pre-1967 border, and would not hurt non-Arabs, is now shattering, and the last word has not yet been said."[5]

In fact, that history is still being written, a history of repressive new laws, decrees, bills, and regulations of all kinds being imposed on Israeli citizens with the assent or indifference of a large part of the public. The laws are multiplying so fast it could make your head spin. Their goal is the creation of a veritable thought police that penalizes any deviation from an approved ideological position on such subjects as the nature of the State of Israel, its history, or the history of Zionism. It is also designed to limit the activities of human rights organizations. A short but far from exhaustive list follows.

A 2011 law denies public subsidies to any K–12 school or municipal institution that commemorates the Naqba, which means "catastrophe." (Naqba is the term Palestinians use to refer to the mass expulsion they suffered at Israel's hands between 1947 and 1950.)

On July 11, 2011, the Knesset passed the Law for Prevention of Damage to Israel through Boycott, known as the Anti-Boycott Law. It punishes calls for boycotting Israel "or regions under Israel's control." It applies to a boycott of all Israeli institutions and settlements located in the Occupied Territories, along with the goods they produce.

In practice, these laws are hard to enforce, but they could be used, for example, to deny public funds to an Arab establishment that teaches the history of the Naqba, or to an Israeli theater troupe that refused to perform in a West Bank settlement.

A 2016 law requires human rights NGOs to state in their publications that they are "foreign agents" if more than half their funds come from overseas public institutions. This is very often the case, with substantial contributions from the United States, the European Union, Switzerland, and Scandinavia. By contrast, the law doesn't apply to extreme right-wing settler associations, which are heavily financed by private foreign Jewish and evangelical organizations.

Another 2016 law is designed to curtail action by Knesset members who are Palestinian citizens of Israel, and the Jewish members who are their allies. With a vote of three-quarters of the Knesset, the law can strip parliamentary status from any MK who expresses support for the national Palestinian fight, on the grounds that this constitutes "incitement to armed struggle."

A 2017 law supports barring entry into the country of supporters of organizations calling for a boycott of Israel, whether it's a boycott of the country as a whole, or only of goods from the Occupied Territories. The Strategic Affairs Ministry promptly bolstered the law by publishing a blacklist of twenty forbidden organizations and associations. These include BDS groups in the United States, France, Italy, Chile, and South Africa, along with Code Pink: Women for Peace, a major international organization; Jewish Voice for Peace; and the American Friends Service Committee. The latter is a Quaker humanitarian assistance organization that won the Nobel Peace Prize in 1947 for helping civilian victims during the Second World War, and in particular for saving Jews in Europe.

Even more revealing of Israel's increasingly authoritarian bent are various other bills introduced in the Knesset, some of which have already been voted on first reading. For example, a law proposed in 2017 by the Jewish Home Party, led by Naftali Bennett, would deny access to schools to any organization that criticizes conduct by Israeli soldiers. The bill is squarely aimed at the Breaking the Silence military reservists who condemn IDF abuses. The bill has not yet passed, but the then education minister Bennett applied it to public schools any-way. He did this by using Amendment 17 to the Public Educa-tion Law, passed in 2018, which denies access to high schools to "anyone outside of Israel who helps institutions that sup-port diplomatic measures that harm Israel." The amendment was specifically approved after B'Tselem director Hagai El-Ad addressed the U.N. Security Council.[6] El-Ad is now forbid-den from speaking in any school setting. In contrast, public schools generally welcome fanatical religious associations and settler activists.

Far more radical is the so-called loyalty in culture initia-tive, which has outraged any number of Israeli artists. Pro-moted by the then cultural minister, Miri Regev, it would allow the government to deny public funding to cultural insti-tutions that show "disloyalty to the state and its values." (The bill was voted on first reading in November 2018, but failed to gain traction and is currently in limbo.) Asked for a definition of such disloyalty, Regev gave the example of an artist "reject-ing the existence of Israel as a Jewish and democratic state."[7]

Regev's proposal joined a series of thought-police mea-sures designed to make official thinking mandatory. Already, the education minister has withdrawn a number of "disloyal" works. Dorit Rabinyan's novel *All the Rivers*, which describes a love story between an Israeli Jewish woman and a Palestinian Arab man, was eliminated from senior high school reading lists.[8] Dozens of other measures could be cited as examples, such as one by the former finance minister Moshe Kahlon to withdraw the tax exemption of NGOs that are critical of the state, notably the Israeli section of Amnesty International. Another: the education minister asked philosophy and linguistics professor Asa Kasher to prepare an "ethics code" for universities that would include creating an organization to regulate political activities on campus and stamp out deviant thinking.

But these proposals are trivial compared to those designed to hide IDF crimes against Palestinians and protect their perpetrators. Since November 2018, the ministerial committee for legislation has been weighing a bill proposed by two Knesset members, Shuli Mualem-Refaeli (ex–Jewish Home Party, now New Right) and Robert Ilatov (Our Home Party), who were in the coalition government at the time. The law would grant immunity to any Israeli soldier, police officer, or intelligence service member suspected of committing a criminal act during the exercise of their duties. This means that Elor Azaria, the soldier who cold-bloodedly killed a wounded, disarmed Palestinian teenager, would not be charged, because he was acting in accordance with his mission. The two MKs specifically referred to the Azaria case in arguing for their bill, whose initial text read as follows: "A member of the security forces shall not be held criminally liable, shall not be interrogated as a suspect, and shall be immune from any legal action for an act or order given while carrying out his job in the course of an operational activity."[9] In short, immunity under all circumstances. It's worth noting that the Israeli code of military conduct states that a soldier is allowed to refuse to obey a "clearly illegal" order. Under the proposed law, a deliberate killing would no longer be illegal.

But the booby prize definitely goes to that same MK, Robert Ilatov, who proposed a law outlawing taking pictures of Israeli soldiers in action. His bill reads: "Anyone who films, photographs, and/or records soldiers in the course of their duties with the intention of undermining the spirit of IDF soldiers and residents of Israel shall be liable to five years imprisonment. Anyone intending to harm state security will be sentenced to ten years imprisonment." Despite concerns over the bill's constitutionality, the legislation committee approved the bill in June 2018, with some wording changes.

To dispel any uncertainty about the real impact of a bill that Ilatov claimed would protect the troops' morale, he stressed the need to punish "pro-Palestinian" associations active in Israel. By this, he meant groups like B'Tselem, Breaking the Silence, Checkpoint Watch, Physicians for Human Rights, and Rabbis for Human Rights—NGOs that "delegitimize" soldiers' actions by publishing such images.[10] B'Tselem director Hagai El-Ad says the bill's intent is "to hide reality and achieve perpetual occupation of the West Bank without any accompanying condemnation."[11] In the vanishingly rare cases where soldiers are charged with crimes, the cases are always brought because their actions were filmed, says El-Ad, "even if they were all later released or given laughably light sentences."

In the Soviet Union under Stalin, photographs were often doctored to bring them closer to an idealized image or to official propaganda, which from the regime's point of view amounted to the same thing. The way ostensibly democratic Israel is going, displeasing images are no longer airbrushed; they're simply forbidden. The process is simpler, and actually more honest. In the ideal Zionist Israel, maintaining an ideological self-image as democratic and progressive required that the IDF be "the most moral army in the world" and that guardrails be built into legislation to maintain the fiction of Israel being "the only democracy in the Middle East." Today, those guardrails are falling away. People candidly admit that they can't wait for the chance to expel all the Palestinians. And they can also now outlaw anything that reveals what lies behind that state of mind. The vicious circle that Leibowitz predicted has been closed. The effects of colonization and occupation have become deeply ingrained within the psyche of the colonizing society itself, "with all that this implies for education, freedom of speech and thought, and democracy." The decay is so advanced that it is hard to see how Israeli democrats alone will be able to free their country from a security state that is growing more powerful by the day.

BtS, the enemy within

B'Tselem has long been a pioneer among Israel's human rights organizations, as well as the most reviled by the powers that be. Founded in 1989 against the backdrop of the First Intifada, it remains the primary source of information on abusive behavior by Israeli occupiers in the West Bank and Gaza. But two other organizations have borne the brunt of vindictiveness from the government and Israeli politicians: Breaking the Silence (BtS) and Boycott, Divestment and Sanctions (BDS).

Breaking the Silence members are Israeli military reservists whose goal is to expose the oppression of Palestinians through firsthand accounts of those who practiced it: the soldiers themselves. BtS was founded in 2003 by officers and noncoms who had served in the West Bank city of Hebron, the place where Israel's control is the most cruel, and also the most unusual. Since 1997, six hundred extremist messianic settlers, protected by about a thousand soldiers, have terrorized tens of thousands of Palestinians living in what is called the H2, the "Jewish" zone. That's the location of the Old City and the Tomb of the Patriarchs, which is sacred to both Jews and Muslims. On some streets, those Palestinians who haven't yet been driven out by the settlers' constant harassment live like caged animals, behind fencing they have erected to protect themselves. Settlers in the buildings above them constantly dump their garbage down into Arab houses, terraces, and courtyards. Their equally fanatical children throw trash and scrawl insults about Arabs and Muslims on walls.

In 2004, BtS organized its first exhibition of testimonies about the Arabs' daily life in Hebron. The authorities took note of the organization's initial publications about unpunished abuses committed by the occupying soldiers. Its leaders were invited to testify before the Knesset's defense committee. At that point, BtS was presented as the ultimate proof that Israel was a model democracy. But when its 2005 report on Gaza became public, the authorities' attitude changed. In the words of a number of elected officials, BtS became "an enemy of the State of Israel." In 2012 BtS published *Our Harsh Logic*, a book containing 145 soldiers' accounts of what they saw and did in the Occupied Territories.[12] All described how Palestinians were dehumanized, while young IDF soldiers were gradually groomed to accept their role in the repression. For eighteen- and nineteen-year-old recruits, it would take exceptional strength of character to resist going along with the program.

In an early attack on BtS, a law was passed forbidding the organization from speaking in Israeli schools. Hostility from the authorities and right-wing groups spiked after the organization's May 2015 publication of 111 eyewitness accounts by Silence Breakers about the reality of military operations in Gaza in summer 2014. The United Nations determined that in the course of the fifty-day intervention, 2,251 Palestinians were killed, the great majority of them civilians (of whom 551 were children) and tens of thousands wounded. On the Israeli side, seventy-three people died, six of them civilians.

On March 17, 2016, Israel's Channel 2 ran a completely fabricated piece claiming that Breaking the Silence was a threat to national security. Defense Minister Moshe Ya'alon called for an investigation of BtS, charging it with leaking classified documents. Breaking the Silence responded by suing the government for libel. The attorney general's investigation supported BtS's claims of fabrication on every point, and he concluded that there were no grounds for prosecuting the organization. But despite this important legal victory, harassment of BtS has continued.

Since its founding in 2003, BtS has published 1,200 accounts, an average of eighty a year. This represents testimony from 0.2 percent of the 40,000 annual male recruits. Or double that, actually, since not all recruits are assigned to Palestinian population control. But it's still a very small number.

"A new mood has settled on the country," says BtS director Yehuda Shaul. "Terms like 'occupation' and 'settlement' are being banished from people's vocabularies. Since those are exactly the things we're fighting, the initial sympathy that people felt for us has quickly turned into increasing hostility."[13] Think tanks such as the Jerusalem Center for Public Affairs, which is run by Netanyahu intimate Dore Gold, and the Zionist Strategic Center (ZSC) have set up websites like NGO Monitor that are dedicated to undermining organizations and initiatives trying to protect Palestinian rights. ZSC is also behind the Im Tirtzu ("If you will it") movement, which targets associations that oppose the occupation. Its director, Yoaz Hendel, used to be Netanyahu's director of communications. The biggest success of those think tanks and associations, says Shaul, "is that the very word 'occupation' has practically disappeared from Israeli political discourse. If you use it, you are immediately branded a leftist or a foreign agent, if not a supporter of terrorism." "When we try to find a hall to hold a public meeting, some mayor, minister, or MK will intervene to forbid it,"[14] and they are usually successful. BtS conferences are forever being canceled, Shaul says. Practically no school or city hall dares make an auditorium available, and even kibbutzim, who usually lean left, have turned them down. Finding a private venue is a near miracle.

In February 2017, Breaking the Silence organized an exhibition of photographs in a gallery in Jerusalem. When Culture Minister Miri Regev pressured the mayor to cancel it, two former Shin Bet directors, Ami Ayalon and Carmi Gillon, along with law professor Mordechai Kremnitzer, the deputy president of the Israeli Democracy Institute, arranged to find an alternate private space. Says Ayalon: "Incremental tyranny is a process which means you live in a democracy, and suddenly you understand it's not a democracy anymore."[15]

BDS, the strategic threat

Founded in 2005, the Boycott, Divestment and Sanctions (BDS) movement posits that the regime Israel has imposed on the

Palestinians fits the United Nations' definition of apartheid, as formulated by the International Criminal Court. Apartheid is "a crime against humanity...committed in the context of an institutionalized regime of systematic oppression and domination by one racial group over any other racial group or groups and committed with the intention of maintaining that regime."[16] In that context, specific acts range from murder, rape, and torture to legislative, administrative, and other means to prevent racial groups from participating in a country's political, social, economic, and cultural life, and to deprive them of fundament rights and freedoms.

According to its spokesperson Omar Barghouti, a Palestinian who studied engineering at Columbia University, BDS has three goals: end the military occupation of the West Bank and Gaza; have Israel recognize U.N. Resolution 194 on Palestinian refugees' right to return to their land; and ensure equal rights for Palestinian citizens of Israel. BDS has chosen not to get involved in the debate over the region's political future. Barghouti personally favors a single secular state shared by Jews and Arabs, but says most BDS activists prefer a two-state solution. Nor does BDS take a stand on boycott specifics. Target goods and services only from Israeli settlements in the Occupied Territories? Or everything from Israel as a whole? BDS leaves its supporters free to choose, which is a way of enlarging the movement's base. The vagueness allows it to attract people with different sensibilities but united in the goal of ending the occupation. In the United States this includes militant progressive Zionists, which would be hard to imagine in France.

For a long time, BDS remained marginal both in Palestine and the rest of the world. But in the 2010s, the movement's growing media stature drove Netanyahu to forcefully oppose it. Yet the tangible results of BDS's campaign are spotty. The boycott is somewhat successful, especially on American college campuses, but with nowhere near the scale of the boycott of apartheid South Africa. Divestment from Israel—and even just from its settlements—is tiny, and far less than the foreign funds they receive. As for sanctions, the people who suffer from them are the Palestinians, not the Israelis, because of pressure brought to bear by the Trump White House, which cut the American contribution to the United Nations Refugee Welfare Association, among others.

Still, BDS has scored a few symbolic victories. In November 2018, the Irish parliament passed on first reading a bill forbidding the importation and sale of goods and services "from illegal settlements in occupied territories," a formula indirectly aimed at the Palestinian Territories. On the same day, the Chilean Congress overwhelmingly approved on first reading a bill requiring the government to stop buying products from the Palestinian Territories. But a year later, the Israel lobby persuaded the Chilean controller to reverse the decision and forbid any boycott of Israel.

A few other successes have occurred at the local level. Urged by Jewish Voice for Peace (JVP), the state of Vermont and the city of Northampton, Massachusetts, abandoned plans to participate in antiterrorist training in Israel that was organized by the Anti-Defamation League. Since 2004, the league has sent more than four hundred high-ranking American police officials to Israel. JVP argues that the training promotes ethnic profiling and encourages American cops to practice it.

At the cultural level, the movement can boast of considerable support. The hundreds of artists and intellectuals who regularly or periodically back BDS's efforts include writers (Arundhati Roy, Eduardo Galeano), thinkers (Slavoj Žižek, Noam Chomsky, Judith Butler), musicians (Roger Waters, Brian Eno, Lorde), filmmakers (Ken Loach, Mike Leigh, Aki Kaurismäki), actors (Vanessa Redgrave, Julie Christie), and at least one fashion designer (Vivienne Westwood).

But in the political and economic spheres, BDS's successes over the last twenty years have been infinitesimal. No country, not even an Arab one, has responded to its appeal, and in many countries, including France and the United States, Israel has lobbied to get BDS condemned and its activities penalized. As for sanctions, Israel has thumbed its nose at the European Union, despite signing an agreement when it joined the EU in 2005 to identify the origin of its exports, so that products from settlements would not enjoy preferential tariffs. Israel has ignored the agreement, and the EU admits it is unable to enforce its own rule. In the United States, conservative senators have long argued that the U.S. should support the unrestricted sale of products from the Palestinian Occupied Territories. A high point was reached when Secretary of State Mike Pompeo, visiting an Israeli settlement after Trump's electoral defeat, called for products from the settlements to be labeled "Made in Israel."[17] In short, not only have calls for boycott not been widely persuasive, but in recent years Israel has scored antiboycott diplomatic successes on every continent.

For example, the multibillion pension fund of the United Methodist Church of America decided in 2016 to stop investing in Israeli banks that participate in colonization—which would mean all Israeli banks—but quickly reversed its decision the same year. In most cases, a well-organized Israeli lobby has managed to get players in the manufacturing, financial, and service industries to reverse their decisions to sanction Israel for its occupation over the Palestinians.

It's in the field of tourism that BDS briefly scored its most spectacular success, though it ultimately also ended in a fiasco. In November 2018, Airbnb announced that it would no longer carry listings for home stays in Israeli settlements. The company justified its decision by pointing to the case of Awni Shaaeb, an older Palestinian resident of the village of Ein Yabrud. Along with other local farmers, his land was seized in 1975 and given to a settlement called Ofra. According to the Israeli NGO Kerem Navot, a settler erected a building on Shaaeb's land in 2006 and listed it with Airbnb. Said the Palestinian: "For someone to occupy your land, that's illegal. For someone to build on your land, to rent it out, and profit from it—that is injustice itself."

But the BDS supporters' joy was short-lived. After an intense campaign by Tel Aviv and its intermediaries, especially in the United States, that accused Airbnb of anti-Semitism, the company caved in six months later. It resumed listing rooms in Israeli settlements in April 2019, while stating that all its profits would be given to organizations dedicated to humanitarian aid.[18]

Up to now, the BDS campaign hasn't yielded many effective results. So why has the Israeli government made the movement a primary target of its policy of shutting down opponents of settlement activities? It has gone so far as to create a Strategic Affairs Ministry with a hefty annual budget (a rumored 100 million shekels—about $29 million—but the official figure is secret), primarily aimed at tracking BDS militants. Many people, including some in Israel, think this a panicky reaction by an insecure country that gives BDS media exposure that helps, rather than hurts it. Barghouti often mentions the "priceless" help that the Israeli government unwittingly provides by raising BDS to the level of a "strategic menace."

It's worth asking the question: Is BDS so threatening that Israel had to hire the services of a huge Chicago law firm— Sidley Austin, with two thousand lawyers in twenty offices worldwide—to create files that might be used to incriminate BDS leaders? Journalists also wonder why the decision was kept secret, perhaps "to avoid the perception that [Israel] is interfering in the internal affairs of other countries."[19] And why make common cause with such dubious players as the extreme right-wing website Canary Mission, which compiles lists of faculty and students it feels display "hatred" of Israel in order to harass them and interfere with their job prospects? Especially since, to judge by BDS's growth on college campuses, this only strengthens the movement?

The international campaign to counter BDS activists is embodied by AMCHA (*amcha* means "your people" in Hebrew), which publishes a vast "interactive chart of the academic boycott." This lists all the university faculty and students in the United States who are seen as hostile to the continuing Israeli occupation of Palestinians, and portrays them as anti-Semitic. Since this obviously includes many American Jews, isn't that like shooting yourself in the foot with a cannon? That's the view of *Haaretz* columnist Anshel Pfeffer, who now refers to the Strategic Affairs Ministry as Israel's "Ministry of Silly Affairs." About its leader, he writes, "I hope that before Erdan moves on, the weedy online activists of BDS award him a special prize for serving as their greatest champion."[20] (Erdan is rumored to be the inspiration for "Eran Morad," the ridiculously self-abasing ex-Mossad colonel created by Sacha Baron Cohen in *Who Is America?*)

In reality, Israel's response to BDS isn't necessarily a strategic mistake. It's true that Israel's hounding BDS militants for their dissenting views makes American Jewish organizations very uncomfortable. But that doesn't mean the strategy is inept, because it responds to both an opportunity and an emergency. The opportunity: turning a small-scale organization into a "strategic enemy" helps further marginalize Palestinian political representatives, both the ghostly Palestine Authority, which officially runs the West Bank but has no decision-making power, and Hamas, which in Gaza rules an open-air prison. The emergency: the urgent need to head off a long-term danger far more serious than Palestinian demography or Iranian demons: the "delegitimization" of Israel.

According to Nathan Thrall, a senior analyst on Israel and Palestine with the International Crisis Group, BDS is the only movement that offers an alternative to the impasse created by the failure of the peace process after the 1993 Oslo Accords and the Second Intifada.[21] Unlike the First Intifada (1987–93), the Second (2000–05) led not to liberation for Palestinians but to a grave worsening of their plight. In the 1993 Israeli-Palestinian accord, the governing principle was summed up in the formula "land for peace." If the PLO signed a "just, lasting and comprehensive peace" with Israel, the Palestinians would get land of their own, and therefore a state. No peace meant no land. But BDS has reversed the formula by making the end of the occupation the first of its demands, without taking a position on the region's future. For BDS, it's "peace for land." If Israel evacuates the Occupied Territories and ends the occupation, then there will be peace—maybe not right away, but the conditions will be such that peace could come someday.

"The BDS movement offered an alternative," writes Thrall. "It rejected talk of fictive solutions, whether of two states or one. The most fundamental problem, in its view, was not in deciding what sort of arrangement should replace the current system; the problem was forcing Israel to change it at all"—precisely because Israel's policy is illegitimate.[22] BDS lets others decide whether a state that systematically commits illegitimate acts is itself legitimate.

To accomplish this, BDS has mounted an international campaign to force Israel to withdraw, and it no longer relies on the Palestinians' efforts alone. The movement realized that though the Palestinians lost the Second Intifada, Israel's image was seriously damaged in the eyes of the world. As David Kimche, a former diplomat and deputy head of Mossad, told me at the time: "Israel is spending thirty times more money and using thirty times more people in its communications than it did thirty years ago, yet it's thirty times less effective."[23] So where did Israel go wrong? wondered Kimche. The mistake, he concluded, was continuing the occupation.

The sight of a civic resistance challenging the democratic nature of the State of Israel, which has practiced ethnic segregation since its founding, is attracting a growing international audience. BDS is pushing the idea that Israel is not a democratic state that makes mistakes, but a state that "deliberately acts in violation of human rights," as former Palestinian MK Haneen Zoabi put it. That view is becoming more prevalent, and in ever-widening circles, and Tel Aviv's public diplomacy seems powerless to counter it. Israel then reverts to type, and starts hitting harder than ever: "If force doesn't do the job, apply more force." Thus the succession of bills and laws aimed at BDS and others, even though they can hardly ever be enforced. So journalist Gideon Levy, who makes no secret of his support for BDS, can title his *Haaretz* column "Hurray for Airbnb,"[24] yet neither he, his editor, nor the paper's owner have ever been charged. Which shows that up to now, these laws are mainly a way of staking out ideological positions. But the stage is being set for the day when their promoters will be able to enforce them.

The security state in action

Israel is constantly evolving as a security state, and moving in new directions. In the old days, the only activists to be interrogated and searched when they entered or left the country belonged to extreme left-wing splinter groups. Today, the Strategic Affairs Ministry concocts lists of people to be questioned and dispatches them to the appropriate authorities: interior, border security, immigration, and Shin Bet. If the targets are foreigners, they can be denied entry; if Israelis, they are admonished. The number of people put through this wringer is classified, but has risen so dramatically that well-informed travelers often arrive armed with the name of a local lawyer, just in case.

In December 2016, a professor from Malawi named Isabel Piri became the first person to be denied entry for being a BDS activist. But the anti-BDS measure only became law in March 2017. The Supreme Court later ruled that the law couldn't be applied retroactively, and reversed the exclusion decision.

In May 2018, Omar Shakir, the Israel director of Human Rights Watch (HRW), was given two weeks to leave the country because of his support for BDS. "This is not about Shakir, but rather about muzzling Human Rights Watch and shutting down criticism of Israel's rights record," HRW said in a statement. "Compiling dossiers on and deporting human rights defenders is a page out of the Russian or Egyptian security services' playbook."[25] The case went to the Supreme Court, which in November 2019 supported the expulsion. HRW responded that Israel had thus joined North Korea, Venezuela, Cuba, Sudan, and Iran as the only countries ever to expel one of its representatives.

The Palestinian American writer Susan Abulhawa was refused entry twice, when she arrived at Ben-Gurion Airport in 2015 and 2018 when traveling to literary festivals in the Occupied Territories. American student Lara Alqasem, whose father is Palestinian, was initially barred from entering in October 2018, despite having a visa issued by the Israeli consulate in Los Angeles and an invitation from Hebrew University of Jerusalem to pursue research there. She was held at the airport for two days before being admitted. Her lawyer noted that it was surprising to accuse her of boycotting Israel when all she wanted was to study there.

In late July 2018, the Iranian American writer Reza Aslan was detained at the border and quizzed about his political opinions. When he refused to answer, he was told "We can make it so you don't see your kids for a long time."[26] Israeli mathematician Daniel Kronberg was interrogated when returning from a trip and accused of being a BDS "delegitimization coordinator." In fact, he is a known activist with Ta'ayush, an Israeli Judeo-Arab association. Pacifist activist Tanya Rubinstein had the same experience on returning from a conference abroad, when she was questioned about her work on a film about the Gaza support flotilla.[27] The artist Yehudit Ilani was twice detained at the airport for the same reason.[28]

American millionaire Meyer Koplow, a major donor to Israeli schools and hospitals, was questioned merely because a brochure in Arabic was found in his luggage. Julie Weinberg-Connors, a member of an American Jewish peace organization and a recent immigrant who had come to study at a rabbinical school in Jerusalem, was asked what she'd been doing in the West Bank. When she said she had helped Bedouins resist expulsion from their village, Khan al-Ahmar,[29] she was threatened with deportation. It took the intervention of two Knesset members for her to be allowed to stay, and eventually to get Israeli citizenship.[30] American activists Simone Zimmerman and Abigail Kirschbaum were asked what they thought of Benjamin Netanyahu. Questioned about his contacts with the Silence Breakers, the Israeli American writer Moriel Rothman-Zecher was upbraided in what he called "difficult" terms, and warned against any "negative" activity during his stay.

Laura Mandel is a young Jew from San Francisco and a member of The Abraham Initiatives, a nonprofit dedicated to fostering tolerance between Jews and Muslims. After attending the ceremonies in Israel celebrating the thirtieth anniversary of her organization, she was questioned at the airport on departure. What did she do during her stay? Who did she meet? Was she involved in similar activities in the United States? At one point, the interrogator expressed surprise, asking, "Why would an American Jew be interested in relations between Jews and Arabs in Israel?"[31] Mandel was eventually allowed to board the plane, but without her luggage and personal effects. The Abraham Initiatives condemned the "humiliation" that Israeli officials had inflicted on its member. "Anyone who cares about equality and a shared life, and anyone who is in contact with Arabs—citizens or non-citizens—is tagged as a potential threat," it said. "It seems as if the security directives now include harassment not only of peace activists but also of those who act for a shared life between citizens of [Israel]."[32]

The case that proved the most awkward for Israeli authorities was the detention and questioning of Peter Beinart, a professor at the City University of New York who contributes to *The Atlantic* and *The Forward*. Beinart is one of those Jews who had always had warm feelings for Israel, but now feels increasingly out of step with it. In August 2018 he and his wife and children came to Israel for a few days. At the airport, an agent took him into a room used for interrogations. In an article in *The Forward*, Beinart describes what followed, a scene alternately dismaying and burlesque.[33]

"Then the political questions began," writes Beinart. "Was I involved in any organization that could provoke violence in Israel? I said no. Was I involved in any organization that threatened Israel's democracy? I said no." The questioner continued, but without a very clear plan. "What he did do was ask, again and again, for the names of objectionable organizations I was associated with. His definition of objectionable, however, kept changing." Beinart was asked about groups that incited violence, then groups that threatened Israeli democracy, then groups that promoted anarchy. "The man's imprecision was telling," he writes. "He established no consistent or objective standard for my detention. His standard was whether I planned to cause trouble—trouble meaning whatever he and his superiors wanted it to mean."

Unfortunately for Tel Aviv, Beinart is fairly well known, and word of the incident soon got around. Netanyahu was forced to apologize, calling the interrogation an "administrative mistake."

The fact is, this kind of mistake was bound to happen. When the law barring boycott supporters from Israel was passed in March 2017, MKs in the center and on the right who voted unanimously for it were full-throated in their support. "What does this law say, after all?" asked Bezalel Smotrich, the Knesset deputy speaker and an admitted racist. "A healthy person who loves those who love him and hates those who hate him doesn't turn the other cheek."[34] Roy Folkman, then a centrist Kulanu member, was more measured. "It's possible to feel national pride and still believe in human rights," he said. "This law represents [my party] as a nationalist, socially oriented party that believes in a balance between national pride and human rights."[35]

When former Shin Bet chief Ami Ayalon asked his old outfit for the reasons behind all the expulsions, detentions, and threats made against people holding dissident views, he received this statement: "All Shin Bet interrogations were carried out in light of suspicions of illegal and violent activity or in connection with terrorism that could harm state security."[36] Needless to say, none of the people stopped were informed of any suspicions or connections.

The repression campaign against confirmed or suspected BDS supporters went up a notch when the Israeli government made an unprecedented decision in mid-August 2019. At Donald Trump's request, it denied entry to two American congresswomen, Rashida Tlaib and Ilhan Omar, thereby preventing them from investigating the Palestinians' situation.

In this welter of expulsions and interrogations, the Israeli authorities' attitude is both confused and ridiculous. The most frequent motivation is suspicion of BDS support. We have seen how those suspicions can stem from so-called investigations by right-wing groups like Canary Mission, who aren't too concerned about factual accuracy. (Peter Beinart, for example, feels that Israel is practicing apartheid, but opposes BDS.) But that's not the heart of the matter. The authorities' behavior is now institutionalized, and reveals growing intolerance and an incomprehensible level of insecurity. In a given month, only about forty people from pro-Palestinian NGOs arrive in Israel to help with Palestinian rights. (Israel considers them all to be BDS supporters, which isn't always the case.) How can so few people constitute a threat to a society that has such crushing political, diplomatic, military, economic, intellectual, and technological superiority over its Palestinian adversary? In reality, Israel's behavior shows to what extent its leaders and their supporters stand mute in the face of growing charge of illegitimacy. This is close to the outer limits of the proposition that might makes right. The more Israel behaves this way, the more it strengthens the conviction that it is illegitimate. For a long time now, Tel Aviv's answer to any problem of whatever nature has been the use of force. As if it were second nature, intelligence and morality are yielding to muscle and invective.

7

A Species on the Verge of Extinction

Israeli civil society is suffering

Is Israel's anti-BDS detention policy stupid, evil—or both? That was the question that Israeli journalist Chemi Shalev pondered in a 2018 *Haaretz* article. He concluded that the policy gave the country's leaders a nearly infallible way of ruling through fear: "The more people who are stopped at the airport, the greater the international ruckus, the more dangerous BDS looks, the more the public hates it, the more the government can cast itself as a defender of the people, the more Netanyahu can agitate his base," and so on. "For Netanyahu and his partners, who wither when Israelis feel safe, and thrive when they feel threatened, isolated, and unfairly maligned, it's a virtual slam dunk."[1]

Who needs a Supreme Court anymore?

In such an atmosphere, the Israeli institution that most suffers from the public's support for the security state is the

Supreme Court. Israel doesn't have a written constitution, so its highest court operates as both a constitutional court and a court of cassation.[2] It is supposed to be the main bulwark of respect for democracy, and for a long time, the court was widely respected in democratic Israeli circles. But since 1996, when the extreme right began moving into important governmental positions, the court has been increasingly seen as an obstacle to be overcome in order to pass openly racist laws. Former justice minister Ayalet Shaked (right-wing colonial) made changing the rules for nominating justices to the court the centerpiece of her agenda. Candidates are currently chosen by a commission representing various interests, including the bar, and their names are submitted to the president of Israel for approval. Shaked wanted the candidates to be chosen by the government alone. After all, who needs the meaningless democratic veneer of a legal counterweight in a security-minded ethnic state?

Ever since its creation, the Israeli Supreme Court has constantly navigated between submitting to the state's essential norm—the primacy of the dominant Jewish ethnicity—and preserving the appearance of democracy (which it willingly abandons whenever Palestinians are involved). If you get right down to it, the court defends democracy only within Jewish Israeli society. For seventy years it has endorsed the notorious Defense Regulations inherited from British colonial rule. Among other things, these allow administrative detentions without stated grounds or time limit, based on the Shin Bet's mere word that a detention is necessary. These laws are only applied to Palestinians.[3] Similarly, the court long accepted the use of torture by the security services before rejecting it in favor of mere "moderate physical pressure," a phrase it has never deigned to clarify.

On November 22, 2018, the court rejected an appeal from the inhabitants of the Arab neighborhood of Sheikh Jarrah in Jerusalem, who had been served with an expulsion notice. Two days earlier, it had also dismissed an appeal from a Bedouin sheikh named Sayek Abu Madiam, who had been expelled from his property in the Negev, and spent ten months in prison as punishment for trying to return to it. Between the two, the court refused to take a case—and thereby let stand by default—involving the actions of Ateret Cohanim, a messianic Jewish association whose main goal is the "Judaization" of Jerusalem by expelling as many of its Palestinian residents as possible. In the case at issue, the group planned to expel 104 residents of the Silwan neighborhood bordering the Old City, for "unjustified" occupation of homes that had belonged to Jews before the 1948 war. (The expulsion had already been approved by the authorities.) In explaining its decision, the Supreme Court recognized that "evacuating people who have occupied the land for decades, some of them without knowing that the land belongs to others, creates great human difficulty, especially when it is done without compensation or any other solution."[4] Nonetheless, the court declared itself not competent to rule on the issue, thereby allowing the messianic organization to carry out the planned expulsions. In three days, in three cases opposing Jews and Arabs, the court chose the Chosen.

While this bias is of long standing, the Ateret Cohanim case is symptomatic of a profound change underway in Israel. Not only because the justice minister publicly favored the messianic organization. Or that the Palestinian residents who lost the case were forced to pay the winners' legal expenses, in addition to a large sum for the "unjustified" occupation of their own homes. But because the decision in the case set Israel's segregationist policy in stone.

To understand this change, it helps to know that thousands of Jerusalem apartments abandoned during the 1948 war are now inhabited by Jews. In some fashionable neighborhoods, the most elegant villas were given to deserving IDF officers. Can you imagine for one second the Israeli Supreme Court would now allow Palestinians to come back, evict the Jews, and recover the apartments, especially since said Palestinians had no connection with the former inhabitants? In matters of land and real estate, laws are applied very differently depending on whether you're a Jew or an Arab. And that goes to the heart of Israeli segregation, which was given the force of law in November 2018. "Greenlighting East Jerusalem eviction attests to revolution in Israel's Supreme Court," reported *Haaretz*.[5] That revolution led to the judicial validation of the new State of Israel, where ethnicity is now a keystone of the country's Basic Laws.[6]

In his 2018 book *The Wall and the Gate*,[7] Israeli lawyer Michael Sfard shows to what extent High Court justices have always tended to accept limitations on human rights where Palestinians are involved, be they residents of the Occupied Territories or citizens of Israel. In particular, arguments that raise security issues nearly always win out over ethical principles. Sfard shows how the Israeli judicial and juridical system has contributed to the colonization of Occupied Territories from the very start of the occupation, making the seizure of

Palestinian lands legally kosher at the highest level.[8] Since 1967, the Supreme Court has invariably endorsed the razing and expropriation of Palestinians' homes. Aside from a few very unusual situations, such as the victory by the Palestinian village of Bil'in in 2007,[9] it has always endorsed the route followed by the West Bank security wall (a route declared illegal by the International Court of Justice). For thousands of Palestinians, the wall made access to their land extremely complicated, if not impossible.[10]

For its part, B'Tselem in 2019 published *Fake Justice*, a harshly critical report on the Supreme Court's embrace of Israel's colonial aims.[11] It methodically demonstrates that while claiming the ethical high ground, the court has served as a fig leaf covering policies involving the military occupation of foreign territory that are contrary to international law. For fifty years, with rare exceptions, it has ruled in favor of the IDF and the settlers, often accepting without demur judicial decrees recognized only by Israel that have no validity at the international level (the invented distinction between "legal" and "illegal" settlements, for example). In addition, it has dispensed starkly unequal justice between settlers and Palestinians. In fifty years, not a single appeal to the Supreme Court challenging the demolition of a Palestinian house has succeeded. To the contrary, the court has resorted to any number of dubious devices to legalize Israel's seizure of half the West Bank. Land designated as "state property," "security zones" around settlements, or IDF "training zones" almost invariably winds up in settlers' hands. *Fake Justice* concludes that for half a century the Supreme Court has given legal cover to the progressive ruination of the Palestinians, with a spinelessness and accommodation that the report calls shocking. To B'Tselem, the High Court's respect for democratic norms suggests a Potemkin village, in which Palestinians are "compelled to take part in a charade, for appearance's sake, as if they were playing the part of extras in an Israeli propaganda film."[12]

The Supreme Court has also supported the security state against the demands of NGOs. For example, it upheld the legality of government regulations decreed at the start of the Second Intifada that were designed to curb "nationalist disturbances of public order," in other words, the mobilization of Palestinians. Those disturbances were defined as "activities in the area of public order, which are carried out by a group or an individual for subversive ideological motives on a nationalistic basis, which could harm national security."[13] Nowhere is it stipulated that these activities need be illegal or violent. You can be thrown in jail simply for having certain opinions, without having committed any crime. To legal scholar Mordechai Kremnitzer, these regulations endorsed by the High Court "belong to the repertoire of dark regimes."[14]

But the court's most revealing recent decision was the one it rendered in April 2015, which de facto—or ad absurdum— validated the Israeli colonization of Palestinian territories. By a vote of 5 to 4, the justices upheld a decree stipulating that a boycott of Israel was a civil tort punishable by money damages. The court defined boycott as "harm to the State of Israel by means of economic, cultural, or academic boycott of a person or any other entity, merely due to its connection to the State of Israel, one of its institutions, or an area under its control."[15] By penalizing mere support of a boycott, the court recognized that it was imposing a restriction on free expression, but judged it acceptable if it was "proportional" and done advisedly. Hanan Melcer, the justice who wrote the decision, argued that in some cases calling for a boycott was "political terror." But the main point lies elsewhere, in the six words taken from the decision: "or an area under its control," a euphemism for the occupied Palestinian territories. With those six words, the Supreme Court endorsed the government's position that boycotting products from the Occupied Territories was equivalent to boycotting the State of Israel. Paradoxically, the court thereby proved BDS's point: Israel was behind the colonization, so it couldn't try to avoid being a target of the boycott. In effect, the court itself made an equivalency between Israel and the Palestinian territories it occupies. The decision, wrote Lara Friedman of Americans for Peace Now, was "a boon to Israeli settlers and…a gift to activists worldwide who support the Boycott, Divestment and Sanctions (BDS) movement against Israel."[16]

The very next day, the court ruled in favor of a long-held demand of the settler movement and accepted the government's extension of the absentee property law to Arab property owners in East Jerusalem. The 1950 law authorizes the state to seize land and property belonging to "absentee" owners, namely Palestinians who became refugees and whom Israel won't allow to return. The law specified that whoever held property in Israel without living there could be considered absentee and have their assets confiscated. At the outset, the law was widely applied to buildings and land owned by Palestinians who "voluntarily" left. After conquering the West Bank and Gaza in June 1967, Israel quickly annexed East Jerusalem and its environs. Ever since then, the settler movement has

lobbied to have the absentee property law applied to East Jerusalem, so as to further its Judaization. The law faced a number
of challenges, but in 2013, Israel's attorney general formally
endorsed its application.[17] By endorsing the law in 2015, the
Supreme Court was authorizing property theft, pure and simple. Let's say you're a Palestinian living in a village a mile or
so outside the Holy City who owns property in East Jerusalem
but who doesn't reside there. It can now be seized, and—for
instance—legally acquired by an American in the United States
who has never set foot in Israel, who can then financially support Jewish Israeli tenants moving into an Arab neighborhood.

Lower courts in Israel have taken a similar path, and often
a more radical one than the one trod by the Supreme Court.
The case of Dareen Tatour, a little-known Palestinian poet
in her late thirties from the Nazareth area, is instructive. In
2015 she posted a poem on YouTube titled "Resist, my people.
Resist them" that included these lines: "I will not succumb
to the peaceful solution / Never lower my flags / Until I evict
them from my land." For this, Tatour was sentenced to more
than two years' house arrest without a cell phone or Internet
access, plus an additional five months in prison for "supporting a terrorist organization." In May 2019, her conviction for
the poem was overturned, but her conviction for other social
media posts was upheld. Leaving aside the issue of free artistic
expression, law professor Kremnitzer notes that no equivalent
punishment has ever been handed down for settlers' innumerable paeans to the "heroism" displayed by settler Baruch Goldstein when he committed the mass killing at the Tomb of the
Patriarchs in 1994. Likewise unpunished is Rabbi Yitzhak Shapira for writing the *Torat Hamelech* (The King's Torah), which

endorses killing non-Jews who threaten the lives of Jews, especially if they are Arabs. This includes babies, he writes, because as they grow up, their intrinsically evil nature will lead them to harm Jews. "These rabbis' influence over their flock is immeasurably greater than that of an Arab poet whose public standing, before her trial, was rather limited," says Kremnitzer, and they continue to expound their terrible doctrines.[18] But the judge who sentenced Tatour said that "it was enough for her to have possible influence on one individual."

Likewise, the military tribunals in the occupied Palestinian territories represent fifty years of sham justice. They are a law unto themselves, and they apply it accordingly. "Military law defines the struggle against the occupation as a crime," writes Amira Hass. That means *any* struggle, regardless of the form it takes. "There has not been, nor will there be, a serving Israeli judge, military or civilian, who will say that throwing stones or shooting at a military vehicle that is protecting the theft of water and land is justified self-defense," she writes.[19]

"A Palestinian brought before the tribunal in Ofer prison north of Jerusalem has no chance of obtaining even a simulacrum of justice," writes Michael Sfard, who speaks from experience.[20] "In these tribunals, the rate of convictions [of Palestinians] is above 99 percent. The hearings are held in Hebrew, which the defendants often don't understand, and members of the intelligence services regularly testify in secret—the accused and their defenders don't have access to their testimony."

Haaretz recently asked Leah Tsemel, a famous Israeli lawyer who has been defending Palestinians for nearly fifty years, if she had seen a transformation of the judicial system. "Yes, both in the prosecutors and in the judges," she said. "We are not on the same plane at all. At one time it was possible to understand one another…Today even that is gone. And no one is ashamed of it. You see it in the judgments but mainly in the 'music' [of the trials]."[21]

The situation is no better when it comes to the police. Yesh Din, Michael Sfard's human rights organization, studied 1,163 complaints brought to the Israeli police between 2005 and 2017 by Palestinians who said they were the victims of violent aggressions by settlers. The share of complaints referred for prosecution was a mere 1.9 percent, and 91 percent of the investigations were closed without any charges being brought. In short, of 1,163 Palestinian complaints filed, just three went to trial.

The civic opposition in disarray

Given the Supreme Court's willingness to accommodate Israel's embrace of identity politics, why does the country's extreme right wing want to further clip its wings? It's because they are tired of the hypocrisy of keeping up democratic appearances. They want to be free to openly piss in the pool from the diving board, legally establish the segregationist state, and make the rest of the world accept it. Here's an example. For decades, the Supreme Court has allowed hundreds of municipalities to forbid Arab Israeli citizens from settling there. It has used all sorts of administrative quibbles to accomplish this, but has not permitted the larger position to be inscribed in the nation-state law, because at that point segregation would be made part of the law. And that's exactly what the Israeli right wants: to give segregation the force of law. When the government introduced a bill that would allow a simple majority of Knesset members to circumvent Supreme Court decisions, David Shulman could see what was coming: "If the bill passes, it will enshrine a tyranny of the majority and undermine the very concept of inalienable rights."[22]

In Israel today, when the dominators and the dominated meet in legal combat, the government, the military, the judicial system, and the police all rush to help the villains—when they belong to the right ethnic group. Of a thousand abuses committed against Palestinians, maybe one case will come to trial, as if to maintain the fiction of democracy. It has gotten so bad that many Palestinians have given up filing complaints. They have no hope that the police will even register the complaint, much less follow through. Witness this headline on a 2018 *Haaretz* story: "Hasidic Jews attack Palestinian teens in Jerusalem; police arrest Arab who called for help."[23]

For citizens trying to resist the security state, the task becomes almost insurmountable. Opponents of the Palestinian occupation and their NGOs say they are acting because they have no choice, because their self-respect is at stake. Observing and doing nothing feels like cowardice, and is unacceptable. More than anything, theirs is a moral stance: to the banality of evil they respond with the banality of good. But they are now confronting an unprecedented system of control and repression of opinion. True, the surveillance that the Israeli security state exercises against these domestic opponents is less constant, forceful, and cruel than that suffered by the Palestinians. But it has lately become much more pervasive. And it starts with social pressure, the pressure to conform to the huge majority of society that takes its cues from the security establishment.

"For a long time I used to walk around Tel Aviv with a T-shirt that read FREE GAZA," the psychologist Kim Yuval told me. "I got some nasty remarks, but nothing happened. Today, that's all over. If I wore that shirt now, I'd be lynched."[24] Yuval works with African immigrants these days, but he used to work for Palestinian rights. "Fifteen years ago, Israeli Jews would deliberately mix with the Palestinians during demonstrations, to protect them. The army wouldn't dare shoot. Nowadays, that's all over. The army doesn't give a damn."

For mathematician Daniel Kronberg, the hardest thing is dealing with the "mental imprisonment" so many Israeli Jews display. "Nowadays, the word Zionism just means supporting Israel's policies under all circumstances," he says. "The moment you're not a 'Zionist,' your opinions don't matter: you're an enemy, and that's it." This tendency has always existed in Israel, but it has gotten much more intense in the last fifteen years. The worst, says Kronberg, "is when you say to people, 'You're being racist,' and they answer, 'Okay, I'm a racist. So what?'"[25]

People like Kronberg report a feeling of growing isolation from their surroundings, of alienation mixed with fear, while they struggle not to be dragged into the abyss along with the rest of society's racism and security madness. Opponents of the occupation form a kind of countersociety that is increasingly out of step and retreating into self-censorship, says filmmaker Erez Pery, who has headed the film department at Sapir Academic College.[26] So far, the Culture and Education ministries and the IDF's attempts to cancel the contracts of certain teachers or funding for programs they deem subversive haven't succeeded, says Pery. "But professors are starting to worry about expressing so-called deviant opinions, and their assistants, who have less protection, even more so. An academic institution should be a place for open debate. Instead, it is increasingly conforming to the dominant ideology. We'll see what happens with the law on 'cultural loyalty,' but we can already expect an increase in self-censorship." Like other people, Pery admits that he is starting to watch what he says. "A single word can make you the target of a hateful campaign from the extreme right," he says. An organization like Im Tirtzu specializes in drawing up "traitor" lists. "Using the word 'traitor' has become a standard way to attack anybody on the left," says Pery. "And Facebook is a favorite venue for denunciation."[27] Sigal Naor Perelman, a poet who teaches at the University of Haifa, agrees. "I'm careful about what I say now. We feel so isolated. In class, I no longer read the poems of Yitzhak Laor," a radical critic of the occupation.[28]

Hostility toward dissident thinkers is taking root in a variety of institutions. In 2015, a Tel Aviv teacher named Herzl Schubert was seen at a demonstration against settlement. The Education Ministry ended his teaching career, over the protests of the school's principal. Ronen Shoval, the president of the right-wing association Professors for a Strong Israel, put out a statement titled "Don't fire the teacher. Jail him."[29] When a student accused Adam Verete, a teacher of Jewish philosophy in Tivon, a northern township, of having participated in an "anti-Zionist" demonstration, he was fired, then reinstated, then fired again. Even though his school admitted that Verete had not taken part in the demonstration, keeping him on would have been a "distraction."[30]

"In Israel today, making a false accusation can help get rid of an undesirable person," says mathematician Kobi Snitz.

"It's informer season."[31] For a long time, teachers in Israel's Arab schools had to be vetted by Shin Bet in order to exercise their profession, he says. Under the Rabin government (1992–95), the Education Ministry ended the practice. "Today not only is it back, but now the teachers in Jewish schools have to pass a conformity test as well."

Israel as it existed until about twenty years ago still defined itself as Jewish and democratic. In reality, as the Palestinian MK Ahmed Tibi likes to joke, "It's democratic toward the Jews and Jewish toward the Arabs."[32] Since then, democracy has begun to shrink for the Jews as well. Ami Ayalon, a former Shin Bet head himself, condemns the rise of the security state. "We're not on a slippery slope anymore, but a very steep one. Israel's domestic security agency is becoming a problem for democracy."[33]

What characterizes what Israel has become? The gradual abandonment of democratic values, with the overwhelming approval of its Jewish population. This acceptance of the primacy of security norms, which was already at play in the treatment of Palestinians, has widened to include that segment of Jewish society condemned as treacherous by its own for trying to preserve its share of humanity. In 2019, the Israeli singer and actor Dudu Elharar called on the authorities to be firmer: "The time has come to limit the freedom of expression of singer-songwriters and all those representatives of the Israeli artistic world who go around the world slinging mud at the State of Israel."[34] Elharar was reacting to a call by Israeli artists and filmmakers to boycott the Israeli film festival that the country had organized in Paris. He didn't say exactly how much that freedom would have to be limited.

"A straight line of evil and racism runs from the Gaza border to Tel Aviv."[35] That sentence is from an April 2018 article called "It's not Netanyahu, it's the nation," by *Haaretz* columnist Gideon Levy. The problem, he says, is that most Israelis don't see Palestinians or Black Africans as human beings. "Opposing all this evil there are, of course, other Israelis as well," Levy writes. "There is no reason not to label them by the right name: better, more humane, compassionate, conscientious, moral leftists. They are not a negligible minority, but the war waged against them by the majority and its government has paralyzed them...This camp is defeated. They are a species on the verge of extinction."[36]

Thirty or forty years ago, journalist Uri Avnery, historian Zeev Sternhell, deputy Jerusalem mayor Meron Benvenisti, and others in Zionist circles all denounced the perils threatening Israeli society. At the time, there were fewer of them than the people who today are horrified by the direction their country has taken. But they were more integrated into Israeli society, and their voices carried further because they were perceived as legitimate. Today, NGOs and their members fighting the occupation are ostracized and feel marginalized.

"The big change," says BDS director Yehuda Shaul, "is that I grew up in an atmosphere where we aspired to live in a liberal democratic society, and that aspiration has disappeared. More than 80 percent of Israelis today have only known an occupation over another people. They can't imagine a different Israel. Meanwhile, the settlers, even though they're a minority, have captured the state. They've done it in a methodical, organized way. Respect for the law has been gradually abandoned. In 2015 the Israeli government even created a position of settlements advisor, and gave it to a leading representative of the settlers themselves. The Supreme Court had become useless, and the law no longer mattered."[37] Or rather, the only law that counted was that exercised by the strong.

As often happens in such situations, artists, intellectuals, and scientists are suffocating as they see their society adrift, finding themselves isolated as a result. "Pretty soon, even moderate Zionist voices, like [the late writer] Amos Oz or David Grossman, will be inaudible and maybe forbidden," says mathematician Kobi Snitz.[38] The pedagogue Yaniv Sagee, a leftist and fervent Zionist, is a founder of the Givat Haviva Center for Shared Society. When he came back after a long family visit in the United States in 2018, he admitted he didn't feel at home in his own country. "For the first time in my life, I feel a genuine threat to my life in Israel," he says. "This isn't an external threat from Iran and certainly not from Hamas. It is an internal threat from nationalists and racists."[39]

As also often happens in such situations, the people who feel smothered go into exile for shorter or longer periods—if they can. That's the case of filmmaker Nadav Lapid, who calls Israel "an uninhabitable country."[40] Asaf Avidan, probably the best-known contemporary Israeli musician worldwide, says "I don't consider myself Israeli."[41] He tells people that he is "from Israel" but not Israeli.

The actor and director Itay Tiran, probably his country's biggest theatrical star, is thoughtful and straightforward about his political views. "BDS is a perfectly legitimate form of resistance," he says. "And if we want to preach for a certain kind of political discussion that isn't violent, we must strengthen these voices, even if it's difficult...A normal political left should support BDS."[42] Tiran said this in an interview with *Haaretz* on the eve of his departure for Stuttgart, where he had been invited to act and direct. "If the nation-state law is the reference from which you calculate where Israeli society is, then clearly it's a racist, non-egalitarian law." When the left was in power, Tiran says, Zionism tried to hide its colonial aspect under a show of being progressive. Israel's Declaration of Independence speaks of the values of equality. "But the right's justifiable counter-argument is, 'Hang on, there's the law of return. Why is it that only the nation-state law drives you crazy?'"

Incorporated into Israel's Basic Laws in 1950, the law of return offers automatic Israeli citizenship to any Jew who wants to settle there. Tiran calls the law unjust, since Palestinians expelled from their homes have been collectively denied the right to return to their country after the 1948 war.

The interviewer pressed Tiran on this. "So you're saying that Zionism equals racism, no matter what?"

"Yes."

"And that Zionism equals colonialism?"

"Yes, exactly. So we all have to look at the truth, and then take a side."

Needless to say, Tiran represents an infinitesimally small group that is swimming against the current of Israeli society. But he's typical of people who find themselves oppressed by the way their society and its leaders are going, and what they do in response. They can't breathe, so they try to escape.

8

Hitler Didn't Want to Exterminate the Jews

Netanyahu, fake history, and his anti-Semitic friends

We now begin the most astonishing chapter in Israel's right-ward drift: the change in the way conservative Israeli leaders relate to extreme right-wingers who show occasional flashes of anti-Semitism, and to regimes and national leaders that practice identity politics while displaying unmistakable anti-Semitic leanings.

Here's one example among many. Soon after Donald Trump was elected president in November 2016, he made Steve Bannon his main White House strategist. Bannon, the former executive chairman of *Breitbart News*, the alt-right's most important media outlet, planned to attend the annual gala of the Zionist Organization of America, a right-wing group led by Morton Klein. This caused an uproar among major Jewish American organizations, because Bannon was accused of making anti-Semitic statements. He didn't attend, but by the time the annual ZOA gala rolled around in November 2017, things had changed. Bannon had left the White House, and the big Jewish organizations had watched Netanyahu forge a tight connection with Trump. So Bannon was no longer persona non grata. In fact, he was seated at the head table along with such ex–White House luminaries as Sean Spicer and Sebastian Gorka. Spicer was the press secretary who famously claimed that Hitler "was not using the gas on his own people the way Assad is doing."[1] Gorka, a Hungarian American Trump advisor, was known to have ties to Hungary's anti-Semitic Jobbik movement. So what made these right-wing anti-Semites welcome at Morton Klein and ZOA's table? Their unwavering friendship with the State of Israel. And Klein isn't alone. Netanyahu and his entourage think the same way.

How in the world did Israel ever come to this?

Did the mufti of Jerusalem instigate the Holocaust?

On October 20, 2015, Netanyahu astonished the delegates to the thirty-seventh World Zionist Congress when he announced that "Hitler didn't want to exterminate the Jews at the time, he wanted to expel the Jews."[2]

Wiping out the Jews of the world wasn't Hitler's idea, claimed Netanyahu, but it was suggested to him by Haj Amin al-Husseini, the grand mufti of Jerusalem. (The mufti was a former leader of the so-called Arab revolt, an anti-colonial Palestinian rising against the British between 1936 and 1939 that Her Majesty's army brutally repressed with the help of Zionist militias.) As his audience gaped in astonishment, Netanyahu went on to describe a dialogue between the Nazi and the mufti: First Hitler says he plans to expel the Jews from Europe.

"If you expel them, they'll all come here [to Palestine]," replies the mufti. "So what should I do with them?" "Burn them."[3]

This totally invented conversation supposedly occurred during an actual meeting between the men on November 28, 1941, that lasted all of ten minutes. This was five months after Germany invaded the Soviet Union, by which time Nazi *Einsatzgruppen* had already begun the mass murder of Jews, eventually killing between 1 million and 1.5 million.[4] Meanwhile, construction of future death camps was already underway in Belzec and Chelmno in Poland.

Internationally, people were aghast at Netanyahu's statement. Jewish groups were dumbfounded. Historian Christopher Browning called Netanyahu's claim "a blatantly mendacious attempt to exploit the Holocaust politically," adding that "Husseini was not the instigator of the Final Solution but rather the target of Hitler's attempted manipulations."[5] Dina Porat, chief historian of the Yad Vashem Holocaust Center, said Netanyahu's statement was "completely erroneous, on all counts."[6] The mufti may have hated the Jews, wrote Israeli columnist Anshel Pfeffer, but it is absurd "to maintain that al-Husseini, who was [in 1941] a powerless exile, had a pivotal role" in the genocide.[7] But Netanyahu persisted, and Browning understands why. "His extraordinary exaggeration of Husseini's complicity, and by implication that of the entire Palestinian people, is a blatant attempt to stigmatize and delegitimize any sympathy or concern for Palestinian rights and statehood."[8]

Portraying Palestinians as anti-Semitic is an age-old tactic. From the early days of Jewish settlers' move into Ottoman-ruled Palestine, some of them dismissed the locals' hostility as reactionary anti-Semitism, much like that of muzhiks in the czarist empire they had fled. It saved them from thinking too hard about the fact that they were colonizers.

It's true that al-Husseini was the first to be stigmatized as a Nazi by councilors of the Yishuv, the Jewish community in Palestine before 1948. But several Israeli historians argue that the mufti sided with the Germans less from ideological conviction than anti-British nationalism. Nonetheless, after World War II and the Holocaust, people fell into the habit of treating any regional leader hostile to Israel as a reincarnation of Hitler. Egyptian leader Gamal Abdel Nasser was the first to be so stigmatized, and so, briefly, was Anwar Sadat.[9] Yasser Arafat got the full treatment. When in June 1980 the Europeans adopted the Venice Declaration that called for the PLO to be part of peace negotiations for the first time, Likud leader and prime minister Menachem Begin snapped, "It's as if they're asking us to negotiate with Hitler." Later, Iran became the new existential threat, and Mahmoud Ahmadinejad inherited the bogeyman role. During his 2005–13 presidency, some Israelis dubbed him "Mahmoud Hitlerinejad."

Equating every evidence of hostility to Israel with a resurgence of Nazism is nothing new. In fact, when Israel is the first to use force against an adversary, it's essential that the target somehow be painted as a Nazi. On June 5, 1982, when Prime Minister Begin announced Israel's invasion of Lebanon to expel the PLO, several ministers in his cabinet expressed reservations. Begin responded, "Believe me, the alternative is Treblinka, and we've decided that there will be no more Treblinkas."[10] During the Second Intifada, when the IDF captured its leader, Marwan Barghouti, at home in Ramallah, Knesset member Zvi Hendel (right religious colonial) boasted that they had arrested "the reincarnation of Eichmann."

Paradoxically, Israel's leaders have turned the annihilation of Europe's Jews into an essentially ahistoric crime, the memory of which occupies a cardinal place in the national ethos while becoming an object of breathtaking banality in everyday life. About the institutionalized legacy of the Jewish genocide, Gideon Levy writes that "it solidified nationalism and validated militarism instead of shaping humanism, justice, morality and compliance with international law, which in 2019 Israel are considered treason or weakness...After the Holocaust, we are permitted to do anything, and of course, only with force."[11] Levy adds that the "distorted lessons" of the Holocaust were learned only by nationalists. "There is no universal conclusion or moral lesson. It didn't have to be this way." Thousands of young Israelis are taken to visit the death camps each year, he says, but "we've yet to see a school whose pupils came back from Birkenau straight to the Gaza border, saw the barbed-wire fence and said, 'Never again.' The message is always the opposite. Gaza is permitted because of Auschwitz."[12]

In daily life, on the other hand, it's a rare Israeli politician who at some time hasn't been smeared with nicknames or epithets drawn from the anti-Semitic lexicon. The most common is *yehudon*, or "little Jew," with the pejorative connotation of "little kike." Usually slapped on anyone who expresses pacifist ideas, *yehudon* has come to mean "Jewish wimp." The Israeli extreme right has called Henry Kissinger, American ambassador Daniel Kurtzer, and many others Jewish wimps for not kowtowing to the Jewish state. In Israel, you can be called a Nazi or a kapo[13] the way you might be called an ass-hole anywhere else. When Ariel Sharon evacuated the Gaza settlements in 2006, some of the crazier settlers put on striped concentration-camp pajamas. Today, this kind of demented linkage isn't unusual. The singer Dudu Elharar, a heartthrob of the racist right, has said, "I'd be happy to sit on the roof of Treblinka and see Amos Oz going up in smoke through the chimney."[14] I guess he was just kidding...Oz, who died in December 2018, was Israel's most famous writer and a spokes-man for the Zionist left that Elharar abhors.

On the settler right wing, hatred of any critical voice can take sometimes unbelievable forms. Benny Katzover is the chairman of the Samaria Citizens Committee, an important settler organization. In 2015 he posted on YouTube a video titled *The Eternal Jew*. It was inspired by a notorious 1940 film of the same name made in Nazi Germany that portrayed Jews as depraved deviants with hooked noses and shifty eyes. The characters in Katzover's video display the same grotesque features, except that now they are identified as the leaders of NGOs defending Palestinian rights and the peace process. Katzover stands by the point made in the film. He says Israeli and Jewish doves—wimps, in his eyes—"are upset because they don't like what they look like in the mirror."[15]

After the 1993 Oslo Accord, Israeli nationalists paraded images of Yitzhak Rabin and Shimon Peres in SS uniforms and sporting Hitler-style mustaches, while Ariel Sharon and Benja-min Netanyahu looked on. Israel must be the only country in the world where calling a political adversary a Nazi is so fright-eningly banal. It stems from Israeli society's unfathomable and paradoxical ignorance about the Holocaust. The country has world-class research institutes on the subject, but for most Israelis, Nazism just comes down to the death camps, the end result of two thousand years of Jewish suffering. How did the Nazis come to pursue the annihilation of an entire people? What kind of racial ideology was involved? How did its regime function? On these questions, most Israelis are totally clueless. For them, Nazism just means anti-Semitic madness. Since any adversary of Israel is necessarily anti-Semitic, it can legitimately be called Nazi.[16] "So for the general public, all those who oppose Israel are anti-Semites, Jews included," says filmmaker Erez Pery. "And all those who support Israel are kosher."[17]

Netanyahu's claim about the grand mufti fits this environment of generalized ignorance and the instrumentalization of Nazism and the Holocaust. It sparked outrage among scholars and part of the educated public, but was shrugged off by most everyone else. It didn't cost the prime minister a single point of his favorability rating in the polls. During the three electoral campaigns in 2019 and 2020, none of Netanyahu's opponents brought up his line exonerating Hitler to hurt him politically. His statement provoked acerbic criticism from a number of representatives of the American Jewish community, but not in France, where CRIF chose to look elsewhere. (I will cover CRIF and other French Jewish organizations in the chapters that follow.)

Nonetheless, Netanyahu's rhetorical sally is significant, because his obsession with making the mufti the real instigator of the Holocaust is symptomatic of a dramatic shift. Netanyahu had already written about the Hitler-Husseini meeting in his 1995 book *A Durable Peace: Israel and Its Place Among the Nations*.[18] There he had the Führer say, "We both have a common target: to annihilate the Jews of Palestine."[19] Published before Mahmoud Abbas became president of the PLO, the book calls him "a direct successor to the Mufti's genocidal intentions concerning the Jews."[20]

The Holocaust was a crime orchestrated by Nazis, who were the leaders of a European people, and committed against Jews, who were people also living in Europe. So there can only be one explanation for Netanyahu's lies about history. By shifting the conceptual responsibility for the drive for extermination from the Nazis to the mufti, and thereby the Palestinians, he is making their world — Palestine, the Middle East, the Arab and Muslim streets — the real matrix of anti-Semitism.

This is obviously misdirection. In a setting of ignorance and superstition, anti-Semitism in the Arab Muslim world is becoming menacing. It has existed throughout history, but never became as extreme as on the European continent. Making Islam the crucible of anti-Semitism is counterfactual at best and a terrible manipulation at worst. The notion of "Christ killers" wasn't invented in Islam, but in Christianity. The Dreyfus affair didn't happen in Pakistan. *The Protocols of the Elders of Zion* wasn't written in Mecca, but by the czar's secret police agents. Kishinev, site of the famous 1903 and 1905 pogroms, is in Moldova. The list of European roots of the Holocaust could go on forever, unfortunately. With his attempted sleight of hand, Netanyahu is trying to divert attention away from white, Christian Europe to the dusky, Muslim Middle East. To cement his ideological alliance with identity zealots in Europe and the United States, he is exonerating them of their historic anti-Semitism, the better to share a common interest: defending the West against the invading hordes.

The cement of Islamophobia

The great crusade that now unites Israel and ethno-nationalists everywhere is a combination of general xenophobia and the new alliance's cement, Islamophobia. How else to explain Netanyahu and his fellows uncritically supporting Donald Trump after eleven Jews were gunned down at the Tree of Life synagogue in Pittsburgh on October 27, 2018? The president's first reaction was to lash out on Twitter against the "fake news media" and the press as "the true enemy of the people" for generating "divisions," "hate," and "great anger."[21] About the shooter's motivation, he said not a word. Fed on a diet of racism spread by "white" websites, killer Robert Bowers claimed the Jews were "bringing the invaders," those immigrants he despised. (It's worth remembering that the theme of Jews slyly working to defile the purity of the Aryan race appears very early in the Hitlerian playbook. In *Mein Kampf,* Hitler wrote: "It was and it is the Jews who bring the Negro to the Rhineland, always with the same concealed goal and with their clear goal of destroying, through bastardization, the white race they hate.")[22]

Some 35,000 Pittsburgh-area Jews signed a petition informing Trump that he was not welcome in their city. It read in part, "For the past three years your words and your policies have emboldened a growing white nationalist movement...Yesterday's violence is the direct culmination of your influence." The letter continued: "Our Jewish community is not the only group you have targeted. You have also deliberately undermined the safety of people of color, Muslims, LGBTQ people, and people with disabilities."

Ron Dermer, Israel's ambassador to Washington, leaped to Trump's defense, as did his colleague Dani Dayan, the consul general in New York. Dermer, who is close to both Netanyahu and the ZOA, justified the president's strategy of spreading the blame around equally.

This tactic had been used before. On August 11 and 12, 2017, American neo-Nazis paraded through Charlottesville, Virginia, chanting, among other things, "The Jews will not replace us."[23] They were expressing the same idea as the Pittsburgh killer's view of Jews playing a role in the "great replacement." On August 12, one of the neo-Nazis suddenly rammed his car into a crowd of antiracist demonstrators, killing a young woman, Heather Heyer. President Trump's reaction at a press conference: "You also had people that were very fine people, on both sides." In other words, neo-Nazis and antiracists balance each other out, leaving the truth somewhere in between.

Eager to make a point, the Israeli ambassador picked up the theme. The Pittsburgh killer might be a white supremacist, he argued, "but I see a lot of people on both sides who attack Jews."[24] On the left and the right, presumably. Then he shifted his sights to Ilhan Omar, a Democrat running for Congress from Minnesota who is very critical of Israeli policies. In other words, Dermer segued from a crime committed by a white neo-Nazi to a Democratic Minnesota officeholder: a Black and Muslim immigrant guilty of no crime whatsoever. That kind of thinking lies at the heart of America's alt-right, whose government Netanyahu had made his main ally in the United States. It is also at the heart of his phantasmagoria, in which the Jerusalem mufti somehow morphs into the instigator of European Jewry's extermination.

In the United States, Islamophobia oozes up wherever the Zionist right is active, namely within the minority Jewish fringe in far-right circles. These included Stephen Miller, who urged Trump to bar entry to people from seven Muslim countries; David Horowitz; Ben Shapiro; Joel Pollack; and Pamela Geller, who invariably called the previous president "Hussein Obama." These ardent Israel defenders and white-supremacy sympathizers built their media careers on Islamophobia. In 2016, Ambassador Dermer received an award from the Center for Security Policy, a far-right anti-Muslim American think tank that works to block the construction of mosques in the United States. Eva Borgwardt, the president of the J Street U National Board, a pro-Israel lobby that is hostile to the Israeli right, has studied Jewish organizations in the United States that finance both Israeli settlements and anti-Muslim organizations. These include the Helen Diller Family Foundation, which has funded the American Freedom Defense Initiative, and which is known for its slogan, "Stop Islamization of America." The Jewish Community Federation of San Francisco has financed both Canary Mission, which works to delegitimize the BDS movement, and Project Veritas, a disinformation activist group founded by the anti-Muslim crank James O'Keefe. The list goes on.

Jews for Jesus, and vice versa

The most intense relationship, however, is the one between the Israeli settler right and the American evangelical movement. The link began in the 1980s and was forged after the 9/11 Al Qaeda attacks. While reporting for *Le Monde* in 2002 during the Second Intifada, I covered the visit to Israel by a delegation from the powerful Christian Coalition of America. Founded by the right-wing pastor Pat Robertson, the CCA at the time was one of the biggest evangelical organizations in America, with two million members and fifteen million supporters. To say the delegates were paying a visit to Israel is actually incorrect, since they spent all four days in occupied Palestinian territory: one day visiting holy Christian sites in East Jerusalem, and the rest in ultranationalist religious Jewish settlements. They were escorted by CCA communications chief Ronn Torossian, an Israeli American who was also a ZOA leader. Their main Israeli host was Rabbi Benny Elon, a far-right Knesset member who has called for expelling the Palestinians.

At the end of their visit, I interviewed Roberta Combs, a recent past CCA president, and later Rabbi Elon. "What will happen to the Jews when Jesus returns to Earth?" I asked Combs. "They will recognize that Jesus was indeed the Messiah," she replied. And what about those who still don't recognize him? Combs sighed apologetically and launched into an explanation involving Gog and Magog, seven years of tribulation, the Apocalypse, and the final battle against the Antichrist. Sounds pretty bad for the Jews, I said. Combs agreed, and said "Gehenna"—meaning unquenchable fire. I then interviewed Rabbi Elon, who of course believes in the coming of his own Messiah. What will happen to his new Christian friends on that day? "Well, they will recognize that Jesus was a false Messiah." And what about the people who don't? I asked. They will go to Hell, of course.

So there you have it: evangelicals and rabbis united today, yet each convinced that their God will carry the day at the end of time. Elon explained the real basis of this new alliance in the meantime. Anti-Semitism had been essentially Christian for the last two thousand years, but an important change had happened with the rebirth of Israel. From now on, he said, "anti-Semitism is Muslim." This was the foundation of the alliance created between his "transferist" movement and the American evangelicals.[25]

That is how two Texas megachurch pastors, Robert Jeffress and John Hagee, wound up standing next to Donald Trump in Jerusalem on May 14, 2018. On the seventieth anniversary of Israel's founding, the president had come to inaugurate the transfer of his country's embassy from Tel Aviv to Jerusalem, a move condemned by the entire international community. The presence of the two pastors signaled the triumph of the evangelicals.

Jeffress is the head of First Baptist Dallas and a televangelist with a vast audience. He was also a member of Trump's evangelical advisory board, which advised the president on matters of faith. Over the years, Jeffress has railed against homosexuality and Islam. When asked what he thought of the Jews, he replied that "You can't be saved being a Jew. You know who said that, by the way? The three greatest Jews in the New Testament, Peter, Paul and Jesus Christ, they all said Judaism won't do it, it's faith in Jesus Christ."[26]

His fellow ecclesiast John Hagee is also a major televangelist, and the founder of Christians United for Israel, a group that includes Christian Zionists. This hasn't kept him from declaring that Jews "have everything but spiritual life."[27] Like Jeffress, Hagee believes in dispensationalism, the idea that humanity will pass through seven stages until the glorious day when Jesus Christ returns to Earth to establish his eternal kingdom. Before that happens, Jews will be confronted with a terrible dilemma: to convert and pave the way for blessed times, or refuse to convert, and go to Hell.

Robertson, Jeffress, Hagee, and many other of these pastors are classic Protestant anti-Semites, which makes them moderates, along the lines of the Ku Klux Klan, which hated Catholics a lot more than the Jews. But every one of them is also a militant Islamophobe.

The Islamophobia cement appears in all the connections that bind evangelicals to the Israeli right. In the United States, the Zionist right wing is always present at their sides in anti-Muslim demonstrations. This is also true of some ultra-Orthodox Jews who have also recently made common cause with evangelicals, with the Chabad (Lubavitcher) movement being the most notable example. In a straight line from the "clash of civilizations," Islamophobia is also the cement that connects all those identity zealots from American white supremacists by way of the Europeans to the thugs of the India's BJP militias.

Israel and its supporters do much more than simply add bricks to this edifice. For many, they are the shining beacon on its summit. At times, their slide into racism takes cartoonlike dimensions. In Germany, a small group called Jews for the AfD was formed in autumn 2018 to support Alternative for Germany (AfD), an Islamophobic and extreme right-wing party with known neo-Nazi connections. In Israel, it enjoyed the support of the late Rafi Eitan. That was a man to be reckoned with: in 1960, he planned and executed the capture in Argentina of Adolf Eichmann, a major organizer of the Holocaust.[28] Eitan later became a high-ranking Mossad officer. A year before his death in March 2019, he had the odd idea of supporting Alternative for Germany. Why? Because he felt it was the only party that understood the dire threat that immigrant Muslims posed to the future of Europe. In a video, Eitan congratulated the party's leaders, including Alexander Gauland, who once said that Germany should be proud of what its soldiers achieved in the two world wars. Said Eitan: "Alternative for Germany brings great hope to many people, not just in Germany but in Israel and other Western countries," since it worked to block "the dangerous and mistaken policy of open borders."[29]

So you can go from being a major Nazi hunter to hanging out nearly six decades later with immigrant hunters whose only virtue is that they hate Muslims. It's worth noting that Beatrix von Storch, the deputy leader of these Germanic xenophobes, never fails to express her admiration for Israel, that outpost of resistance to "rampant Islamism."

The alliance with Eastern Europe's age-old anti-Semitism

Even more astonishing are the alliances being made between Israeli right-wingers and the anti-Semitic Europe of old. European ethno-nationalists have an ideological connection with people like Netanyahu, who have been shaped by so-called Revisionist Zionism. This had its roots in the ethnicity-based doctrine at the heart of most forms of East European nationalism. It combined all the strands of Zionism from its very beginning, but occupies a dominant place in the nationalist right. This explains the obvious fascination that some of its adherents felt for fascism. Netanyahu's father Benzion Netanyahu admired Mussolini, for example.

Among the Jewish settlers in Palestine, a member of the Revisionist Party named Abba Ahimeir created a group called Brit HaBirionim ("Alliance of Thugs," or, in its religious sense, "Alliance of Zealots") in 1928. He was joined by Uri Zvi Greenberg, an ultranationalist militant for a Greater Israel who would become one of Israel's "national poets."[30] These so-called Revisionist Maximalists thought their party too soft toward the British colonial administration, and even more so toward the local Palestinians, whom they wanted to expel. In the meantime, they secretly stockpiled weapons with the idea of causing panic by throwing bombs into souks. Ahimeir developed a mystical and radical vision of the renewal of the Hebrew nation, based on the crucial importance of the "land of Israel." He published a series of articles called "From the Notebook of a Fascist" in the Revisionist daily *Doar Hayom*. When Ahimeir declared his support for Hitler, his organization fell apart, but before then, the Alliance of Thugs made quite a few converts within the party, and for a time greatly influenced its youth movement, the Betar. In 1933, Ahimeir explained that he supported Hitler because of his "anti-Marxist core." A hatred for Communism justified every alliance.[31]

In the history of Zionism, Ahimeir and his thugs were an epiphenomenon, brief but significant. Some of their equally marginal followers were prepared to make common cause with anti-Semites because of their shared ideological foundation. In the 1940s, these fascistic Zionist leanings surfaced in the Lehi Group (aka the Stern Gang), which combined imperial ambition (create an Arab-free Jewish state on both banks of the Jordan) with anti-imperialist terror tactics (drive the British out of Palestine).

I once knew a Betar leader who explained that he had belonged to France's far-right Occident movement in the 1960s, even though it was anti-Semitic, because it was "primarily anti-Arab and anti-Communist." As with Ahimeir, this was all that mattered. The anti-Semitic element, which he didn't deny, was secondary. Hitler and Mussolini are no longer with us, but Revisionism's spiritual community survives among those who today advocate for authoritarian, muscular governments that benefit "real" Americans, "real" Hungarians, "real" Poles, the "real" French, and in Israel, only the Jews. Above all, they share that core hatred of Muslims and—now that Communism has disappeared—of progressives.

But a monumental change has taken place in Israel and within Zionism. Unlike in the years between 1930 and 1940, cryptofascist Israelis are no longer marginal. They remain racists and ultranationalists, but they are now in governments, they head parliamentary committees and hold high positions in the military, diplomacy, administration, and academia. This is all new, and it feeds the closeness between Netanyahu and his entourage with more and more of the world's strongmen. They share certain preoccupations: the supremacy of their ethnic group, hatred of immigrants and minorities, execration of defenders of human rights and free media, and a desire for a submissive judiciary. That is also why these relationships have generated so little negative reaction from Israel's political class and public, except of course among those weakened few who try to oppose the occupation over the Palestinians.

The link between Israeli leaders and European identity zealots began to take shape when Netanyahu returned to power in 2009. On December 15, 2010, a delegation from the European Alliance for Freedom, which included members of far-right parties in the European Parliament, arrived in Tel Aviv as official guests of the government. The group included Heinz-Christian Strache (Austria), Geert Wilders (Holland), and Filip Dewinter (Belgium). Israelis, Wilders said on that occasion, "are fighting our fight. If Jerusalem falls [to Muslims], Amsterdam and New York will be next." Dewinter declared that "the Arab-Israeli conflict illustrates the struggle between Western culture and radical Islam."[32] The visit marked the start of a strategic rapprochement that would grow to encompass the Hungarian and Polish governments and such xenophobic leaders as Matteo Salvini in Italy and authoritarian and ethnic regimes in India, the Philippines, and Brazil.

All those leaders have traveled to Jerusalem and been welcomed at the Yad Vashem Holocaust Memorial, where they received what Daniel Blatman calls "absolution in the name of the Holocaust victims in exchange for their pro-Israeli votes in international institutions."[33] Blatman holds the chair in modern Jewish history and Holocaust studies at Hebrew University of Jerusalem. Forgotten is the fact that Jair Bolsonaro, who was baptized in the Jordan River in 2016, called Hitler a "great strategist"[34] and suggested that the Jews in the death camps actually died of hunger and cold. Forgiven is Philippine president Rodrigo Duterte saying in 2016 that "Hitler killed three million Jews. We have three million drug addicts. And I would be happy to kill them."[35] It could be argued that these benighted leaders are far removed from the Holocaust and Judaism, and that their pathetic pronouncements are explained by their obvious ignorance and fascination with brutality. But what about the Hungarian and Polish governments, who are perfectly aware of the history of anti-Semitism in their countries?

Historian Francesca Trivellato, whose book *The Promise and Peril of Credit*[36] deals with the anti-Semitic myths that Jews secretly control the world of finance, reminds us how widespread those myths were in the past, and how they endure today. She notes that the Hungarian prime minister Viktor Orban has called Jews shadowy, miserly figures, stealthily moving their pawns around. They are "not honorable, but unprincipled; they are not national, but international; they do not believe in work, but speculate with money; they have no homeland, but feel that the whole world is theirs."[37]

It's all there, the anti-Semitic cliché of the crafty cosmopolitan Jew, the speculator and evil genius. Orban, a Christian nationalist and ultraconservative, is also a great admirer of Miklós Horthy, Hungary's regent from 1920 to 1944, whom he calls "an exceptional statesman." Horthy was deposed by the Nazis, but he aligned Hungary with Nazi Germany and the Axis, and between 1920 and 1941 introduced anti-Jewish laws modeled on the Nuremberg Laws.

On July 18, 2017, Netanyahu traveled to Budapest to meet with Orban. Only a few days earlier, he had intervened to bring his envoy to Hungary to heel. Ambassador Yossi Amrani had publicly demanded that the Hungarian government stop its partisans' unmistakably anti-Semitic campaign against the Hungarian-born American Jewish financier George Soros. Said Amrani, "the campaign not only evokes sad memories but also sows hatred and fear."[38] Orban flatly refused. So what do you suppose Netanyahu did? He took a firm stance...against his own ambassador. In essence, he said, "Who told you to get involved with the domestic politics of the country where you represent Israel?" Through a spokesman, the Israeli foreign affairs ministry said, "In no way was the [ambassador's] statement meant to delegitimize criticism of George Soros, who continuously undermines Israel's democratically elected governments."[39]

Back in Israel, this generated sharp criticism from the people who deplore Netanyahu and his entourage's weaponizing anti-Semitism for base political motives, in this case erasing Orban's anti-Semitic leanings, the better to cultivate a political alliance with him. At Yad Vashem, scholars shared their varied reactions with journalist Matti Friedman:[40] Mixed feelings about "right-wing politicians who might stoke animosity to Jews and other minorities at home but who also admire the State of Israel." Cynicism about "the ways Yad Vashem is used by Mr. Netanyahu in pursuit of his foreign policy, and by canny politicians from the outside who grasp the value of a photo op here." And resentment: "Many of us see a collision between what we believe are the lessons of the Holocaust and what we see as our job, and between the way Yad Vashem is being abused for political purposes." But historian Daniel Blatman says there's nothing new about using the memory of the Holocaust for its "Zionist reading," in particular its "exclusive uniqueness solely to justify Israel and heightened nationalism."[41] Still, it has risen to new heights in the last decade.

The affair that sparked the sharpest criticism in Israel occurred in February 2018, when Poland's Law and Justice

Party under Jaroslaw Kaczynski proposed a "memorial law" that threatened to imprison anyone who suggested that the Polish state or nation had been complicit in the Holocaust. In its desire to exalt a spotless patriotic past, Law and Justice wanted to preserve an image of Poland and its people as mere victims during World War II. (In postwar France, Gaullists and Communists did much the same thing, promoting the idea that the whole country had been in the Resistance.) It's true that after Jews and Roma, Poles were among the greatest of the Nazis' victims. Still, can one absolve the Poles who collaborated with the occupying Germans of any responsibility for the Holocaust, given the dominant position of anti-Semitism in modern Poland?

Netanyahu's ongoing cooperation with the Polish regime outraged Holocaust historians. Yehuda Bauer, the best known of them in Israel, called the détente "a stupid, ignorant, and amoral betrayal of historical truth."[42] Meanwhile, demonstrations of anti-Semitism in Poland were growing, covertly assisted by forces connected to the regime. Netanyahu made no reference to them. Neither did he bring up the distortions of historical truth in Lithuania, where 95 percent of the Jewish population was exterminated during the war, and where local leaders closed their eyes to people's participation in the mass killings.

Netanyahu spent six months negotiating with Polish prime minister Mateusz Morawiecki over a compromise text of the proposed law that some historians called shameful. It would allow Poland to keep its principled position, while eliminating the prison terms for whoever might cast doubt on the Poles' collective probity during the war.

The controversy took another twist in February 2019, when the then foreign affairs vice-minister Israel Katz repeated a line made famous by former prime minister Yitzhak Shamir: "Poles suckle anti-Semitism with their mother's milk." This time, the outcry erupted in Warsaw. Morawiecki demanded that Netanyahu publicly apologize. Then he canceled his participation in a summit meeting in Israel between the Jewish state and the Visegrád Group (Poland, Hungary, the Czech Republic, and Slovakia), which is Israel's main conduit within the EU for blocking any initiatives contrary to its interests. This was a humiliating defeat for Netanyahu. "With Poland, Netanyahu discovers the limits of playing with history," wrote Anshel Pfeffer in *Haaretz*.[43] He went on to accuse the prime minister of whitewashing Poland, Hungary, and Lithuania's promoting a vision of the Jewish genocide that exonerated their nationals of participating in it. Netanyahu wound up paying a price, wrote Pfeffer, because the Polish government has now also made rewriting history to suit itself the touchstone of its policy. Ethnicist, meet a *real* ethnicist! If Israel can recast its history and ignore the crimes it committed against the Palestinians, if it can stifle all criticism of Israel by labeling it anti-Semitic, why shouldn't the Poles use the same weapons to protect their own past? And what gives Israel the right to bring up Polish crimes against anyone? In the end, Netanyahu bowed to the Polish demand and kept quiet.

Soros, Trump, and anti-Semitism

In the last decade, financier and philanthropist George Soros has found himself demonized in certain right-wing Western circles. He is cast as the incarnation of the cosmopolitan financier promoting subversive ideas like democratic rights, education, welcoming foreigners, and protecting minorities. In short, a dangerous Jewish hybrid of billionaire and progressive: Rothschild and Trotsky combined. This imagined alliance is not new. In their mythic iconography, the Nazis melded the images of the greedy Jewish financier and the bloody Bolshevik Jew in one person, thereby giving their brand of anti-Semitism terrific potential appeal.

Recent attacks on Soros and his Open Society Foundation in the United States were initially launched by TV personality Glenn Beck. In his eyes, Soros embodied the cosmopolitan speculator undermining the values of the Christian West and the American nation. From 2009 to 2011, Beck had a daily prime-time broadcast slot on the Fox News Channel. In November 2010, he went on a tear against Soros, saying "Here's a Jewish boy helping send the Jews to the death camps."[44] This launched the "Soros the Nazi collaborator" canard that still circulates in the alt-right today. In point of fact, Soros was only thirteen when the Nazis occupied Budapest. He and some of his family survived, hidden by Hungarian Christians.

At first, Fox defended Beck in the name of free speech, but once things quieted down, the network suggested he find work elsewhere. At that point, Beck decided to give himself a philo-Semitic makeover. He went on a tour of hardcore West Bank settlements, where the radical religious movement hailed him as a hero.

The settler movement, and especially the fringe that mixes ultranationalism with religiosity, is an important bastion in the international campaign against Soros today. This is a campaign where American evangelicals meet Eastern

European identity zealots, united in defending what they call Judeo-Christian values. The authorities in Hungary organized the anti-Soros campaign, where in October 2017 András Aradszki, a deputy of the majority Fidesz Party, proclaimed "the Christian duty to fight against the Satan/Soros Plan."[45] The campaign has since grown to include a number of other countries, in particular Poland, Slovakia, and Romania, and is everywhere spreading "fake news" and rumors with anti-Semitic overtones.

France hasn't escaped, though the anti-Soros campaign has had limited success there. The newsweekly *Valeurs actuelles,* which promotes links between the French right and the practitioners of identity politics, ran this on its May 9, 2018 cover: "The billionaire who is plotting against France: Revelations on George Soros, the global financier of immigration and Islamism." The stench of anti-Semitism is barely disguised. The article claims that the Hungarian-born Soros controls an "empire" and rules over a "galaxy" whose sole aim is to destroy the West and the white race. French Jewish leaders were unperturbed. CRIF, which is always quick to pounce on "Islamo-leftist" anti-Semitism, said not a word of protest about the miasmal article. As it happens, the article's author, the lawyer Gilles-William Goldnadel, regularly writes for *Valeurs actuelles* and is the president of the Association France-Israel and a fierce defender of Israeli settlements.

Donald Trump himself actively participated in Soros-bashing, but he usually did it by insinuation, leaving the more obvious anti-Semitic tropes to his supporters. In the 2016 campaign he regularly linked Hillary Clinton with financial power centers embodied by Soros and others, such as Goldman Sachs chairman Lloyd Blankfein and Federal Reserve chair Janet Yellen, both of whom are Jewish. When one of Trump's TV ads attacked the "global power structures" that "secretly control the levers of power" in Washington,[46] Soros and Yellen's names and faces appeared on-screen. Speaking to the Republican Jewish Coalition, he refused to disavow a spot showing Clinton against a background of dollar bills and next to a Star of David. Nor did he lift a finger when his supporters, parroting the far-right conspiracy QAnon, sent out messages describing Soros as a "puppet master" manipulating American institutions.

Three days after the murderous attack at the Pittsburgh synagogue, Wayne LaPierre, the NRA chief executive and gun lobbyist, accused three Jewish billionaires—Soros, Michael Bloomberg, and Tom Steyer—of promoting "socialism" and "social engineering," code terms that conspiracy theorists use to mean psychological manipulation. Trump, though he tweeted compulsively, never commented on those anti-Semitic effluvia.

In June 2020, Facebook took a stance against the bigotry of the Trump reelection campaign. It removed a campaign ad that featured an upside-down red triangle, a symbol once used by Nazis to designate political prisoners, Communists, and others in concentration camps. The Menlo Park company—which in the past had taken a hands-off position on such material—said that the ad violated "our policy against organized hate."

Is anti-Semitism an inevitable byproduct of the nativist conservatism that Trump promoted? wonders Peter Beinart. The answer is yes.[47] Studies by the FBI, the Pew Research Center, and the Anti-Definition League all show that violence against minorities and immigrants, along with anti-Semitic acts and expressions, rose sharply when Trump was in the White House, as if he'd opened the floodgates. Jewish cemeteries were desecrated in St. Louis and Philadelphia shortly after the U.S. inauguration. The massacre in Pittsburgh, which was unprecedented in American history, was followed by a shooting by another white supremacist at a synagogue in San Diego six months later. So how did Netanyahu's supporters in Zionist America react? ZOA president Morton Klein minimized the white supremacy connection and immediately shifted the focus to two Muslim Democratic congresswomen opposed to the Israeli policy toward the Palestinians, charging them with anti-Semitism. More globally, whenever the anti-Semitism of white supremacists is raised, representatives of the radical Zionist right respond that the worst anti-Semitism occurred when Barack Obama was president, because of his anti-Israeli policies (and, for conspiracy theorists, the fact that he's a secret Muslim). Really, there's no news like fake news.

The question remains: Was Trump an anti-Semitic president? It's hard to say, because the man has no ideology or morality other than protecting his own interests. His biographers say he learned this from two men: his businessman father, an admirer of the Ku Klux Klan who gave his son an anti-Semitic education at a time when this was common, even in New York City; and Roy Cohn, daddy's lawyer, a monomaniacal anti-Communist Jew who would become his mentor. It was hardly an accident that Trump chose "America First" as his 2016 campaign theme. The staffer who suggested it must have known it was the watchword of the America First Committee, an isolationist group in 1940–41 whose spokesman, aviator Charles Lindbergh, made no secret of his Nazi sympathies.

Trump maintained with anti-Semitism the same transactional relationship he had with every other ideology. He was an anti-Semite when it was useful: in appealing to the supremacist part of his base, for example. And when it didn't serve him, he wasn't. The result: vague attacks on Jews alternating with bouquets of flowers. On the one hand, he used to constantly remind people that his daughter converted to Judaism and that three of his grandchildren are Jewish. On the other, he spouted the vilest clichés about Jews. At a fundraiser with wealthy Jews, he once said, "You're not going to support me because I don't need your money."[48] On another occasion, addressing the Republican Jewish Coalition, he called Netanyahu "your prime minister," as if the people in the audience owed allegiance to a foreign government.[49]

Nor did Trump disavow the anti-Semitic websites that made vitriolic attacks on the (Jewish) journalist Julia Ioffe for the profile of Melania Trump she wrote for the April 27, 2016, issue of GQ magazine. Ioffe was barraged by emails and tweets, some of which adorned her with a yellow star and threatened to send her to the gas chambers. Similar comments were addressed to reporters at The Forward, and to Jonathan Weisman, a veteran editor at the New York Times. Weisman was once sent an image of the Auschwitz gate with the slogan Arbeit Macht Frei replaced with Machen Amerika Great. Trump was apparently unruffled by this. Yet when young Democratic officeholders criticized Israeli policies, the president accused their party of being anti-Jewish.

"Trump isn't specifically anti-Semitic," said the professor Dov Waxman in 2019. "But he is, in the sense that he operates with classic racist stereotypes about all non-WASPs," whether they're Blacks, Latinos, Italians, Irish, or Jews.[50] And he was probably less racist about Jews than about African Americans, toward whom he adopted his typically utilitarian position. He constantly mentioned his "Black friends" in the movie world, while feeding the ugliest anti-Black prejudices. But whether Trump is a compulsive or an occasional racist doesn't matter, or whether this confused and opportunistic man is an anti-Semite to the core or just on the surface. What matters is that while he was president, he legitimized the spread of racism, including anti-Semitism and xenophobia, which were essential weapons in his political arsenal. To think that Israeli governments once considered Trump their ideal, perfect ally says a great deal about the depths toward which Israel has sunk.

There you have it: a daisy chain linking Trump, Orban, Kaczynski, German neo-Nazis, white supremacists, identity zealots, and evangelicals. But so what? Responding to criticism of Israel's relations with antidemocratic and identity-based regimes in Eastern Europe and elsewhere, former Likud MK Anat Berko said, "They might be anti-Semites, but they're on our side."[51] That says it all. Berko is active in the campaign to condemn anti-Zionism as the modern form of anti-Semitism. Of course.

9

It's Not Necessary or Healthy
to Keep Quiet

The crisis in American Judaism

What happens in Israel affects a great number of Jews living elsewhere—at least those who identify as Jews. The two largest diaspora groups are in the United States and France, and they differ in important ways. The number of American Jews matches the number in Israel, approximately 6.5 million.[1] The French diaspora is a tenth of that size. Depending on criteria, there are 450,000 to 750,000 French Jews, with around 600,000 being the most commonly accepted figure. There are other differences between the two groups. Compared to what happened in Europe, American Jews have experienced relatively modest anti-Semitism from Christians in the modern era. By contrast, anti-Semitism has raged in France from the Dreyfus affair to the Vichy regime's collaboration in the Holocaust. American religious and cultural communities have a huge number of associations and media outlets. In France, Jewish community activities are much more limited. French Jewish cultural life has practically disappeared outside of community organizations, and is weak within them. The contrast also extends to the academy. Many American universities have independent Jewish studies departments, more even than in Israel. The French public university system has just four or five academic institutions, and France has a single premier Jewish cultural outlet, Akadem. Its intellectual offerings are quite diverse, but it is cautious and "politically correct" on anything related to the treatment of Israel, because it is supported by institutions that include the Representative Council of Jewish Institutions in France (CRIF).

Finally, the two countries differ dramatically in the structure of their congregations. In France, Jewish religious leadership is centralized under the Consistory, an institutionalized entity set up in Napoleon's time. In contrast, American Jewish congregations are as decentralized as Protestant churches, with independent synagogues spread among the three major denominations, Orthodox, Conservative and Reform. The latter is the most modern of the three, and is mainly found in North America.

Despite these differences, French and American Jews' relationship to Israel remained similar for a long time after the Six-Day War in June 1967. Among those connected with French Jewish organizations—who represent a little less than half of French Jewry—almost all strongly supported Israel politically and financially, and most of the others were sympathetic. But toward the end of 2000, with the surge of the Second Intifada, a dramatic shift began. The French Jewish community organized within CRIF, and the rabbinate continued its unshakable support for Israel's foreign policy and took a hands-off attitude toward its domestic affairs. But sharp divisions appeared in American Jewish communities. A large majority continued to back the Jewish state unconditionally, but an increasing number began to withdraw from it. Some even broke completely over what they felt Israel had become: an oppressive, segregationist colonial state. And those American Jews aired their criticism publicly. In France, criticism of Israel is weak, practically muted. When voiced at all, it is done quietly, and in private.

American Jews are turning their backs on Israel

David Rothkopf is a visiting professor at Johns Hopkins University, and a former editor at large for *Foreign Policy* magazine. A moderate progressive Democrat, he was deeply disappointed by the 2017 Knesset vote barring members of twenty foreign organizations that support Palestinians from entering Israel. He wrote about it in an article in *Haaretz* titled: "Israel is becoming an illiberal thugocracy, and I'm running out of ways to defend it."[2] After reminding readers that he had always supported Zionism and the State of Israel, Rothkopf wrote:

"The vote by the Knesset...suggests that in fact, both the basic facts and values underlying democracy itself are being repealed in the country. I have rationalized maintaining my support for the State of Israel on a few assessments. First, the creation of Israel was in my mind just and necessitated by history. Next, my sense was that the issue of the rights of the Palestinians would be fairly resolved over time via negotiation. Fairness would prevail because Israel was founded upon democratic principles. Banning those whose opinions are uncomfortable for Israel not only weakens the country but it suggests that the reasons for my defense of Israel are collapsing...Net-anyahu's administration has made clearer still the case that Palestinians have been making for decades, about the sham of Israeli democracy."

As a defender of Zionism, Rothkopf had hoped that Israel wouldn't take the path it has today. But given what the country has become, he no longer sees how it can change course. In despair, he refuses to go on defending it, because nothing in its actions makes it defendable. Moreover, he does this openly, unlike his French counterparts. And Rothkopf is hardly alone. The United States is witnessing a public withdrawal from Israel by Jewish personalities, including by some very well-known public intellectuals.

These include David Myers, a nationally renowned scholar and a professor of Jewish history at UCLA. In October 2018, Myers became president of the New Israel Fund (NIF), which finances social and humanitarian projects in Israel. Under Netanyahu, the NIF has been the subject of increasingly vitriolic criticism in Israel. The NIF has urged Israel to repeal the nation-state law, which the NIF's previous president, Daniel Sokatch, called "tribalism at its worst."[3] Myers is a practicing Jew and a lifelong Zionist, but he is also an independent thinker driven by his convictions and not by Israeli political interests. Myers has raised money for a Jewish organization called If Not Now, whose members oppose Israeli's current policy toward the Palestinians.

In November 2018, Myers sat for a long interview with *Haaretz* in which, among other things, he said this: "I'm a Jew with deep ties to Israel, but [one] who can't keep quiet and accept the community dictate that says you shouldn't voice criticism in public. First, I don't believe that it is necessary or healthy to maintain silence. Second, I reject the claim that somehow public criticism of Israel pushes you beyond the bounds of the community...I neither support BDS nor work with BDS groups. But I do have friends who support BDS. And they're not anti-Semites."[4] The NIF, Myers said, includes people who are as concerned with battered women in Israel, the environment, and religious pluralism as with Judeo-Arab cooperation. "How did it come about that NIF is the enemy?" he asked. "Clearly, there is [in Israel] a playbook of vilification—and NIF appears on page one...We will not stand down in the face of bullies and intimidation. Nobody's going to tell me that I am a traitor...It can't be that the State of Israel expresses responsibility and concern for the well-being of world Jewry and tells it what it should do. But on the other hand, diaspora Jews are not allowed to express their interests and concerns in Israel."[5]

After Netanyahu's electoral victory in April 2019, Sokatch wrote, "It is time for Israel's true friends to say, loud and clear, that an Israel that ceases to be a democracy, one that permanently disenfranchises and rules over another people, will lose the support of the American Jewish community, the family of democracies, and the Free World."[6] The Reform rabbi Rick Jacobs also condemned the Knesset vote: "The new nation-state law will do enormous damage to the legitimacy of the Zionist vision."[7] As he sees it, if Zionism winds up creating an ethnic state where Jews have full citizenship rights and Palestinians are noncitizens or citizens with lesser rights, its legitimacy and that of the State of Israel become open to question.

Such statements by Rothkopf, Myers, Sokatch, Jacobs, and a growing number of others reflect a change by a whole section of American Jewry concerned about the future of Israel, a state increasingly perceived as politically backward and ethically immoral.

They also reflect the unprecedented phenomenon of more and more Jewish organizations refusing to toe Israel's political line. One of these organizations is IfNotNow, whose website makes its goal plain: "We are building a movement of Jews to end Israel's occupation and transform the American Jewish community."[8] Typical is the path followed by Simone Zimmerman, an IfNotNow cofounder who in March 2019 became the director of B'Tselem USA. She went to Jewish schools before college and enjoyed Jewish camps and Jewish youth activities. At one point, she worked for AIPAC, the official pro-Israel lobby. She has often traveled to Israel, speaks and reads Hebrew, and has many Israeli friends. But when Zimmerman saw what the Palestinians had to endure, her objection to the occupation, which was initially moral, turned into political engagement. This trajectory isn't followed by most young American Jews, but it is becoming more and more common. IfNotNow doesn't support BDS, but defends its right to act. When Israel bombs Gaza, IfNotNow activists gather in front of Jewish institutions to read the Kaddish, the prayer for the dead. It has made connections with other progressive movements that support minorities. It doesn't take a position on the political future of Israel and Palestine. Its only concern is to help end the occupation over Palestinians and bring about parity of rights among Jews and Arabs between the Mediterranean and the Jordan. If the two-state solution disappeared tomorrow, J Street (the progressive pro-Israeli lobby) and Peace Now might disappear with it, but IfNotNow would go on fighting against injustice.

The move away from Israel also involves other rapidly growing organizations, such as Jewish Voice for Peace, which alone supports BDS, and T'ruah ("The rabbinic voice for human rights"). Hillel International, the main Jewish student organization active on American campuses, has experienced a schism, with some of its members denouncing its blind adherence to everything Israel now embodies. And there are other signs that support for Israel is plummeting among young American Jews.

Birthright Israel has long brought young people to Israel every year to see the country's successes without ever confronting the Palestinian reality, but finds its numbers falling alarmingly.[9] The organization's very name, the Birthright Israel Foundation, is a striking summary of what the new nation-state law of the Jewish people has now carved in stone. The moment any Jew, whether American, French, or Vulcan, sets foot in Israel, he or she acquires rights that are denied to a native-born Arab citizen who has lived there forever. These days, many Americans brought to Israel by Birthright are demanding that the Palestinian question be faced.[10] Much like IfNotNow, J Street has started arranging alternative trips, bringing young American Jews to places like Hebron to witness the occupation with their own eyes. The watchword of those trips is "Let my people know," a deliberate echo of the gospel hymn and the Hebrew slaves' appeal to Pharaoh. "Let my people know" also suggests that up to now, Jewish institutions have hidden the truth about the Palestinian occupation.

A study by *Middle East Eye*, published in March 2019 and including many personal accounts, describes what led many young Jewish Americans to distance themselves from Israel.[11] Almost every one of them mentioned the shock and chagrin they felt when they first encountered a fact, event, or statement that clashed with values they hold dear. For most, this happened during a visit to Israel. One person was stunned by the unexpected level of racism there. Another wondered whether the disproportionate brutality against Palestinians was necessary. Many said that their conscience was stricken by the massive 2014 bombing of Gaza. What often followed was a period of questioning, during which the picture-postcard image of Israel began to fade. And finally, a stage they all reported going through: after always being told that the Palestinians are the aggressors against a small country that is just defending itself, "they realize that a lot of Jewish institutions have lied to them,"[12] says Maya Edery, a Jewish Voice for Peace coordinator. Since then, these young Jews' view of the organized trips to Israel has changed. They will no longer stand for the fact that nobody they meet mentions the presence of the Palestinians. "It's like taking someone to the American South in 1954 and not talking about Jim Crow,"[13] said Alyssa Rubin, who went on a Birthright trip. With their consciences pricked, these young people then faced the decision whether to take action or not. It's a choice that some would make when they went to college.

Among Jews in American universities, polls show declining support for Israel starting in 2010, despite the resources and effort expended by the Strategic Affairs Ministry and U.S.-based organizations such as Campus Coalition, Canary

Mission, and others that create blacklists of anti-Israeli campus activists and try to undermine groups critical of Israel.

In New York, I discussed this with J. J. Goldberg, the former editor of *The Forward* and the author of the classic *Jewish Power: Inside the American Jewish Establishment*.[14] It was 2015, and I mentioned that BDS seemed limited to a few well-known campuses like Harvard, Berkeley, and Columbia, but was absent from the great majority of colleges. "You're mistaken," said Goldberg. "In the United States, the process is always the same. A movement starts at a few prestigious universities, and then spreads to three hundred of the top schools." Then he added, "Just as the right is clearly a minority in American Jewish society but dominates the discourse, the anti-Israeli left is a minority among young Jews, but it dominates the discourse there."[15]

Goldberg was right. BDS is now present on many American campuses, and half its members are Jewish. "We are seeing a huge number of young Jews abandoning unconditional support for Israel," said Dov Waxman, the author of *Trouble in the Tribe*, a book about the divisions in American Judaism.[16] Sociologist Todd Gitlin, a professor at Columbia, has an even more trenchant opinion: "On campus, more and more Jews are becoming anti-Zionists. The polarization is quick and strong. Those who are pro-Israel feel that they can no longer express themselves, whereas it's what they are saying that is unacceptable. For some young Jews, anti-Zionism is an identity whose stock is on the rise."[17] That statement may not apply to all of America's five-thousand-odd institutions of higher learning, but change has definitely spread beyond just a few prestigious universities.

Why is this change happening now?

Erosion of support for Israel among young American Jews began under Barack Obama, when it became clear that Netanyahu was undermining his efforts to reach an Israeli-Palestinian agreement. But it really picked up steam when Donald Trump entered the White House and developed a close, almost symbiotic, relationship with Netanyahu and his government. "For Netanyahu to be on the best of terms not only with Trump, but also with Putin, Orban, and the evangelicals drives most American Jews crazy,"[18] says Michael Walzer, a moderate leftist, committed Zionist, and coeditor of *Dissent* magazine. Adds Gitlin: "When they hear David Friedman, Trump's ambassador to Israel, declare that 'God is on Israel's side' in the conflict with Palestinians, most are dismayed, and young progressives are disgusted."[19] "Most American Jews are moderate progressives," said writer and diplomat Henry Siegman, the president of the U.S./Middle East Project, in 2019. "They can't stand Trump's racism, his lies, and his way of wanting to settle everything by force. American Jews hate Donald Trump more than any other community, except for Blacks."[20] In fact, studies show that three-quarters of American Jews rejected Trump, his policies, personality, ignorance, and vulgarity—and also his Israel policy, which had only minority support, despite the many "gifts" he gave Israeli leaders.[21] For American Jews, the fact that poll after poll showed the former president to be Israelis' favorite foreign personality was a source of deep embarrassment.

Their hostility to Trump is partly related to the closeness that Netanyahu developed with him[22] as a protector of white supremacists, a closeness many saw as "shameful," says Siegman.[23] Hence the demand by Pittsburgh Jews that Trump not attend the memorials for the victims of an anti-Semitic white supremacist, and also their rejection of the Israeli ambassador's statement. Likewise, while most Israeli leaders fervently admire the "big, beautiful wall" Trump tried to build to stop the "immigrant invasion," most American Jews clearly come down on the other side of the argument, a position that has endured for generations. When, in July 2019, Trump tweeted that four Democratic congresswomen with immigrant backgrounds should "go back" where they came from, hundreds of American synagogues rallied in their support. Not because the synagogues were taking a position hostile to Israel, but because they hate xenophobia. And when Trump sent agents on what he called "massive" immigration raids, synagogues across the country created a network to protect the undocumented.[24]

American Jews were deeply shocked by Israel's adopting the nation-state law. In an article called "Israel: this is not what we are," the World Jewish Congress president Ronald Lauder said the law "will heighten the sense of polarization and discord."[25] Rabbi Rick Jacobs, the president of the Union for Reform Judaism, said he was "vehemently opposed" to the law and vowed to "fight it aggressively."[26] The Israeli American actress Natalie Portman slammed it as "a racist law."[27] And fourteen large Jewish Zionist or pro-Zionist organizations published a statement that "the bill would eliminate the defining characteristics of a modern democracy."[28] Even the Anti-Defamation League, the leading organization fighting anti-Semitism in the United States and normally a staunch Israel supporter, declared its opposition to the law.

American Jews' disenchantment with Israel was further accentuated by Netanyahu's political maneuvering before the 2019 legislative election. The better to guarantee his majority, he brought the despised Kahanists back into Israeli politics. Restoring legitimacy to an aggressively racist movement alienated American Jews. It's one thing to have a fascist party enter the Knesset, said Yohanan Plesner, the president of the Israel Democracy Institute, and quite another to have the prime minister invite it in. New Jersey senator Bob Menendez is very close to AIPAC, and was one of only four Democratic senators to vote against the 2015 international nuclear agreement with Iran. But Menendez says that by making common cause with the Kahanists, "Netanyahu is aligned with the antithesis of American values."[29] Even AIPAC gingerly distanced itself from the prime minister's position.

Finally, there is one last reason why the Trump-Netanyahu alliance turned American Jews away from Israel: the relationship with anti-Semitism. They couldn't stand seeing the two men mixing with anti-Semitic leaders and regimes and giving their countries' anti-Semitism a free pass, while regularly charging their own opponents—usually progressives—with anti-Semitism. In 2016, the future ambassador David Friedman, a man quick to discern anti-Semitism in any criticism of Israel, said on a far-right settler website that Jewish liberals were "far worse than kapos."[30] The old tactic of calling any critic an anti-Semite—or a kapo, if Jewish—was once very effective. But it doesn't work with a growing number of American Jews, and younger ones find it reprehensible. Which is why Ben Rhodes, a close confidant of Barack Obama, predicted that the "anti-Semitic argument" would carry less and less weight in future debates over Israel.

The United States is at a tipping point, said Rhodes. "We are one moment away from this changing, when someone breaks through the fear factor."[31] The fear was always of being dubbed an anti-Semite when you criticized Israel. But today, the accusation is damnable when it's used to immunize Israel from criticism for its crimes, and now looks more like what it is, a manipulation. The tipping point has already been reached by American Jews, and not just the young. Rhodes says he doesn't see how this could fail to increase, despite maneuvers by Israeli representatives and the pro-Israeli American lobby to impugn Israel's critics. Said a Democratic Party staffer, "It may be painful for the party as we move in a more progressive direction. But we'll come out in a better place—a more moral and evenhanded place—at the end."[32]

Crisis in the Democratic Party

In dealing with the Middle East, the Democratic Party faces a crisis it has never experienced before. The great majority of American Jews have always been Democrats, and when Israel was created, the party emerged as the most supportive of the new Jewish state on the American political scene. That began to change during the Reagan administration. Influenced in part by anti-liberal Zionist intellectuals connected with *Commentary* magazine, some American Jews gradually began adopting positions that would later be called neoconservative. This brought them closer to the Republican Party. Since 1997, Israel has been led 90 percent of the time by increasingly extreme nationalists, and Democrats have slowly lost their status as Israel's main defenders. Israeli leaders have increasingly turned to the most reactionary American voters and leaders, evangelicals, and hawkish nationalists, like former national security advisor John Bolton. Since Netanyahu's return to power in 2009, this closeness has taken on the trappings of exclusivity. Today the share of American Jewish voters who are conservative is still small, but it has become politically and financially very powerful.

Most Democratic leaders continue to proclaim their love of Israel while also pushing the two-state solution to the Palestinian conflict. With Netanyahu as prime minister again, they have been largely ignored by the Israeli leadership, which wants no part of a discussion about a Palestinian state. As a result, the Democratic Party is now in a crisis. As Republicans become "the party of whites," Democrats present themselves as the "party of diversity." They claim to represent minorities whose members, whether African American, Latino, or of immigrant background, vote largely Democratic. But minorities with non-European origins are less attuned to Jews' past suffering, especially when Palestinians in the Middle East look more like the victims today. Supporters of Israel once called Black politicians like Keith Ellison and Hank Johnson anti-Semites for their pro-Palestinian positions. But since gaining a House majority in the 2018 midterms, the Democratic Party now includes representatives who are female and nonwhite—and not inclined to drop the Palestinian issue.

One group, dubbed the Squad, consists of four congresswomen: Ilhan Omar of Minnesota, a former Somali refugee;

Rashida Tlaib of Michigan, the daughter of Palestinian immigrants; Alexandria Ocasio-Cortez of New York, Puerto Rican; and Ayanna Pressley of Massachusetts, African American. They are members of the left wing of the Democratic Party, and they openly support the Palestinian cause.

After winning election in 2018, Tlaib chose to skip the traditional trip to Israel that AIPAC sponsors for all new members of Congress, where they meet Israeli movers and shakers but not a single Palestinian. Tlaib said she would arrange her own trip. Comparing the oppression of Palestinians to that of Black Americans facing racial segregation, she said, "I want us to see that segregation and how that has really harmed us being able to achieve real peace in that region. My delegation will focus on Israel's detention of Palestinian children, on education, clean water, and poverty." She wanted "to offer an alternative perspective from the one AIPAC promotes."[33] In an unprecedented step, Israel barred Tlaib and her fellow congresswoman Ilhan Omar from the West Bank.

The rise of these female politicians is due both to the decline in Israel's popularity within the Democratic Party (and in American public opinion generally) and the growing interest in the Palestinian question, especially among the party's ethnically diverse base. In both cases, the evolution came in reaction to the Trump administration's exclusive support of Israel's policy, and to the vilification campaigns waged against Tlaib and Omar by Trump and the Republicans. On March 8, 2019, Trump said that by accepting the women into their ranks, the Democratic Party was "anti-Israel" and "anti-Jewish."[34] Yet the Democratic leadership twice tried to muzzle them. It even briefly threatened to exclude Omar from the party.

First, it tried to portray Omar as anti-Semitic for making an issue of AIPAC's financial influence. But a wave of support immediately built, accompanied by testimony from former AIPAC operatives who confirmed that, like all lobbies, AIPAC uses its financial clout to help favored candidates get elected.[35] Stung, the Democratic leadership retreated. Then it happened again, when Omar said, in reference to AIPAC, "I should not be expected to have allegiance [or] pledge support to a foreign country"—meaning Israel—"in order to serve my country in Congress."[36] Trump had said she should be removed from the House Foreign Affairs Committee. The Democratic leadership tried to comply, but couldn't.

What explains these repeated failures? It's because the party is in a bind. On one hand, Trump and his fellow Republicans became undisputed in their claim to be Israel's best ally, and there was nothing the Democrats could do to change that in Israelis' eyes. On the other hand, Israel's image declined quickly within the Democratic Party. According to a January 2018 Pew Research Center poll, Democrats older than 65 very largely supported the Israeli point of view, while those 35 and younger supported the Palestinians. A year later another Pew poll revealed that young Democrats' support for Israel was in free fall. Among self-described progressives, support had dropped from 33 to 19 percent in a single year.

To the Democratic base, Israel's policies embody everything it rejects: colonialism, xenophobia, hostility to immigrants, and ethnic tribalism bordering on white supremacy. At the University of Michigan, Ann Arbor, a demonstration against the "apartheid walls" that enclose Palestinians was organized by Jewish students and the local branch of La Casa, a major Hispanic student association that opposes Trump's wall. As a La Casa member shouted, "We have the same goal: fighting white supremacy and xenophobia."[37] Such joint actions between organizations of progressive Jews and those of Blacks and other minorities are becoming more common. It may soon be that the majority of young, politically minded Jews will be in the left wing of the Democratic Party.

The dilemma facing the Democrats was simple: its leaders feared that by welcoming people with opinions strongly critical of Israel, the party would alienate moderate Democrats and many independents. But they also knew that if their candidates turned their backs on the growing share of the party that rejected unconditional support of Israel, they might have lost the critical youth vote, as they had in 2016. The result was a vacillating attitude that worked to the advantage of Democrats critical of Israel.

The *New York Times'* evolving coverage of the Palestinian question perfectly mirrors the changes at work among Democrats. The *Times* has traditionally been center-left politically, and it staked out a position strongly opposed to the Trump administration. Its writing about Israel's policies toward the Palestinians has undergone a parallel and highly visible change, as two instances will illustrate.

The first was a December 2018 *Times* editorial about the Israel Anti-Boycott Act proposed by two U.S. senators, Rob Portman, Republican of Ohio, and Ben Cardin, Democrat of Maryland, that would penalize companies that joined a boycott of Israel or of products from the Occupied Territories by allowing states to require that their contractors sign pledges saying they would not engage in such boycotts. The

Times editorialized that the bill "is clearly part of a widening attempt to silence one side of the debate. That is not in the interests of Israel, the United States or their shared democratic traditions…Many devoted supporters of Israel, including many American Jews, oppose the occupation of the West Bank and refuse to buy products of the settlements in Occupied Territories. Their right to protest in this way must be vigorously defended."[38]

(In France, CRIF has repeatedly tried to get legislation passed in a similar "attempt to silence one side of the debate." I don't know of a single major French press outlet that argues that BDS's right to protest "must be vigorously defended.")

Then in January 2019, the *Times* published a piece by Michelle Alexander, a newly hired African American columnist, called "Time to break the silence on Palestine."[39] Alexander began by referring to a famous speech that Martin Luther King Jr. gave against the war in Vietnam at New York's Riverside Church on April 4, 1967. In his entourage, most of King's friends had urged him not to give the speech. Moving from segregation against Blacks to the international stage by criticizing a war conducted by his country in Vietnam would weaken his position, they warned. He would be called a traitor, or a communist. In response, King said, "A time comes when silence is betrayal," and added, "That time has come for us in relation to Vietnam."

In her opinion column, Alexander argued that a time had also come today, where keeping silent about Palestine was a betrayal of fundamental American values. Yes, she wrote, some civil rights organizations had so far preferred to keep quiet so as not to be called anti-Semites, as yesterday the opponents of the war in Vietnam were called communists. Yes, she continued, many universities were afraid of appearing on the blacklists kept by Canary Mission and its ilk, who partner with Israel's Strategic Affairs Ministry to sabotage careers and discredit "deviant thinkers" in the American academy. But the time had come to share Dr. King's courage. To follow Rabbi Brian Walt, who after many visits to Israel and Palestine said that what he saw there caused him to abandon his faith in Zionism.

For an editorial writer on the staff of the *New York Times* to be a committed believer in the rightness of the BDS movement says a lot about the evolution of the paper and its readers. Likewise, the fact that the attacks on the *Times* have failed says a lot about the weakening of the pro-Israeli lobby in public opinion. It hasn't lost its dominant position, but it now faces a growing contradiction in the very setting that was supposed to sustain it: American Judaism.

In the United States, a challenge to Israel's status

When in March 2017 the Knesset passed the law denying entry to Israeli territory to anyone supporting a boycott of the country,[40] reaction from American intellectuals was quick in coming. More than a hundred scholars, including many well-known professors of Judaism, signed a petition that began as follows: "Among us are those who oppose the BDS movement, those who oppose BDS but support a settlement boycott, and those who support BDS. [But] in spite of our different views, we stand in strong opposition to the new law. It will be bad for

Israel, bad for the cause of democracy at this fragile moment, and bad for the principles of free speech and thought on which our scholarship is based."[41]

Among the scholars circulating the petition, one of the best known was Michael Walzer, from Princeton. A committed Zionist, he said, "I have been active in opposing BDS on campuses. I have been going to Israel every year starting from the '70s...I think Israelis have to worry that a government that is not willing to tolerate foreign visitors who are critical may not for long be willing to tolerate citizens who are critical."[42] Columbia's Todd Gitlin, who also signed the petition, put it this way: "Having frequently and publicly opposed the BDS movement for years, while advocating an economic boycott of settlement products and investments, I now see that the State of Israel has added me to its enemies list. For such an honor I'm not especially grateful. Nor do I rejoice at the spectacle of Israel walling itself off into a fortress of paranoia."[43] Said Hasia Diner, a historian who specializes in American Judaism, and who also signed the petition: "I'm against academic boycotts, but this could possibly tip me over to say, you know, BDS is in fact the only way"—meaning the only way to shake up a nation becoming flagrantly antidemocratic and segregationist.[44]

More and more young American Jews have the feeling that as time goes on, Israel and its Jewish population are headed for disaster, creating a society from which they must disassociate themselves for ethical reasons. This is something the Democratic Party leadership can't afford to ignore.

Today, more than twenty American states have adopted anti-BDS measures. But in the absence of serious peace negotiations between Israelis and Palestinians, the BDS campaign appears to be the only one that can make a dent in Israeli impregnability, as shown by the absurd lengths to which Israel goes in trying to crush BDS in the United States.[45] Todd Gitlin summed the situation up this way: "I am deeply hostile to BDS. But for years, I've found the policies Israel pursues depressing. Today, the most important thing is to oppose what Israel is doing, not to stand in BDS's way."[46]

Many American Jewish organizations, except those clearly dominated by the Zionist right, have mixed feelings about how to deal with BDS activities. The case of the Anti-Defamation League is typical. For now, it still supports penalizing BDS's work. But *The Forward* revealed that in 2016 the organization conducted an internal study on the question. It concluded that penalizing BDS would be "ineffective, unworkable, unconstitutional, and bad for the Jewish community."[47] One can imagine how much community pressure must have been brought to make the ADL change its position and call for prohibiting BDS's activities. "The problem isn't only that penalizing BDS is ineffective," says Dov Waxman. "It's that it mainly benefits BDS."[48] This international call for a boycott has met with very modest success in the United States, but its progress in people's heads has been spectacular.

When Airbnb originally announced that it was pulling out of the occupied Palestinian territories, Joshua Shanes, who teaches Jewish history at the College of Charleston, lamented, "Liberal Zionists faced a critical test with Airbnb. We flunked it."[49] His argument: Israel had established an equivalency between the State of Israel and the settlements on the one hand, and between Israel and the Jewish people on the other. In supporting Airbnb's decision to pull out of the settlements, progressive Zionists had the chance to show that you could be a Zionist and oppose the Palestinian occupation by making the point that boycotting products from Occupied Territories wasn't necessarily being hostile to Israel. Unfortunately, said Shanes, the B'nai B'rith, the large secular Jewish organization, saw the Airbnb boycott as "a discriminatory decision" and anti-Semitic. The Anti-Defamation League came around to the same point of view. Said Shanes, "If Jews and others are forced to choose between Israel with its settlements, or else to walk away entirely, liberal Zionists may not be so happy with the choice many make."[50]

10

"No! No! You can't quote me on that!"

The blindness of French Jews

Members of French Jewish organizations are only dimly aware of the internal debates within Judaism on the other side of the Atlantic. That's not news. But neither do they keep up-to-date on daily events elsewhere, even in Israel. Unlike those American Jews who are distancing themselves from Israel, French Jews are undergoing what historian Pierre Birnbaum calls "Israelization."[1] It should be said that the organization that speaks for them, the Representative Council of Jewish Institutions in France (CRIF), is spectacularly discreet about recent developments in Israel. For example, it said not a word when the nation-state law was adopted, making ethnic segregation part of the country's Basic Laws. When even President Reuven Rivlin expressed his strong disagreement with the law, that wasn't enough to spur the French Jewish establishment to voice the slightest criticism, much less open the matter for discussion. Nothing on Israel's adopting antidemocratic security laws, either. Not a peep about Netanyahu welcoming Kahanists back to the political scene, or conjuring up a Palestinian figure as the instigator of the Holocaust. Or telling his ambassador to quit pressing Hungary to abandon its anti-Semitic campaign against George Soros. Not to mention Netanyahu's electoral campaign calling for the annexation of Palestinian territories.

None of these topics sparked public debate or even comment within France's organized Jewish community. Whatever Israel does, whatever its leaders say and however its voters vote, Israeli policy is and must be endorsed by the French congregation—and no back talk. The leadership of both the French and American Jewish communities support Israel more or less unconditionally, but what is happening *within* those communities is very different, and the gap is widening. In the United States, criticism of Israel is getting louder. In France, it remains inaudible.

From *La Révolution* to right-wing Zionism

As in Israel, French Judaism today is more diverse than in many other countries, and comprises two main groups. The first are Ashkenazi Jews, from Eastern Europe. They were initially to be found in Alsace and Lorraine, two departments bordering Germany. Then, starting in the last third of the nineteenth century, they were joined by Yiddish-speaking immigrants from Eastern Europe, also Ashkenazi, who were fleeing the pogroms and misery that were their daily lot. Most went to North America, but a large share remained in Western Europe. In the interwar period, the Yiddish saying "As happy as God in France" described how the Republic welcomed these immigrants. Progressive politics produced the first French government led by a Jew, the socialist Léon Blum in the 1936 Popular Front. Until the 1960s, and despite the Holocaust's killing a third of France's Jews, the Ashkenazim were the main component of the Jewish community.

The second main group are Sephardim, who fall into three categories. First, a small number came from the Jewish presence all around the Mediterranean dating from well before the destruction of the Second Temple in 70 CE. A second wave brought Jews expelled from Spain and Portugal, starting in 1492 and continuing throughout the sixteenth century. For the next two hundred years, they were France's Jewish elite.[2] The third group, which is now the majority in France, are Jews who left the Maghreb, the three North African countries colonized by France: Algeria (conquered in 1830, annexed in 1848), Tunisia, and Morocco (became French protectorates in 1881 and 1912).

Some Maghreb Jews settled in France during the first half of the twentieth century, but their numbers swelled dramatically in the 1950s, when independence movements swept through the three North African countries. As France gradually withdrew, first from Tunisia and Morocco in 1956, then from Algeria, which won its independence in 1962 after eight years of battling the French army, the trickle of Jews leaving the Maghreb became a flood. Some 99 percent left Algeria, for example. Emigration from North Africa was complete with the Six-Day War in June 1967 between Israel and the Arab countries, ending the historic Jewish presence in North Africa. In 1954, there were 500,000 Jews in the Maghreb. Thirteen years later, after the Israel-Arab war, there were just 62,000, mainly in Morocco.[3] In the following years, most of those Jews left as well. Of these half-million people, about two-thirds settled in France, a quarter in Israel, and the rest in Canada, Argentina, and the United States.

The arrival in France of some 330,000 Maghreb Jews within a single generation profoundly transformed the Jewish landscape, says Charles Enderlin, the author of a book about contemporary developments in French Jewry.[4] The changes were not only numerical—the Ashkenazim now found themselves in the minority—but also cultural and political. In religious matters, Ashkenazim and Sephardim share the same general reference points, though their rituals vary, sometimes in striking ways. But in social, worship, and political matters, the North African Jews gradually put a new stamp on the French Jewish community.

Birnbaum has described the historical and structural differences between French and American Judaism in his 2012 book *Les Deux Maisons*.[5] France has a centralized state, he notes, with a strong and undivided national identity, as reflected in his coinage "Un État, une Église, une Synagogue" (One state, one church, one synagogue). In America, by contrast, the national structure is federal, and therefore weaker, but more tolerant of minority identities. Birnbaum feels that this makes the U.S. "more receptive to the flourishing of Judaism than the recognition of Jews solely as citizens."[6]

Birnbaum writes that French Judaism is marked by its desire to become part of the French nation, accepting the duties imposed by citizenship in exchange for the benefits that this affords. Jews formally became citizens in September 1791, and this was institutionalized under Napoleon, and settled during the Third Republic (1870–1940). Subscribing to the Republic's great principles—the French idea of citizenship and the separation between church and state—would serve as the roof beam atop the national structure to protect it against all storms. Yet the protection given to French Jews by the Republic vanished between 1940 and 1945 under the Vichy regime, which abandoned the Jews along with the idea of the Republic when it became "the French state" and collaborated with the Nazi occupation. It passed anti-Jewish laws that deprived French Jews of their full citizenship and legitimacy in society, then helped send them to the death camps.

What are the characteristics of this citizenship? Its first principle is that French citizenship is a unique identity that is uniform for everyone throughout the whole public space. "Ever since the Revolution," writes Birnbaum, "French society has demanded a single loyalty to the State, the Nation, and the Republic that excludes all forms of specific identities, even particular imagined self-identifications, and therefore, of necessity, multiple loyalties."[7] That exclusive French identity was famously defined by Count Stanislas de Clermont-Tonnerre in a speech to the National Assembly on December 23, 1789, supporting the emancipation of the Jews: "To Jews as a nation, all must be denied, but to Jews as individuals all must be granted...It is unacceptable for there to be a society of noncitizens within the state, a nation within the nation."[8] But that rule wasn't specifically aimed at Jews, writes Birnbaum. Emancipation gives access to citizenship for any minority that joins the French nation, whether Jews or Protestants, Bretons or Basques. Any individual identity apart from that of *Français* is excluded from the public sphere. In the United States, it's typical for people to be seen as WASP, African American, Chinese American, Jewish American, et cetera. But in France the very idea of multiple or mixed identities is not only indefensible, it is inexcusable. You are born or become French, and once you are, that's all you are.

Today that vision is in crisis, as globalization has rattled its frozen character, making it less and less well adapted. But it has greatly helped minority groups and immigrants become part of the nation. (France has long welcomed more foreigners than any other European country.) It has done so, says Birnbaum, by "trying to erase all forms of identity connections by relegating them solely to the private space, wiping out regional, cultural, linguistic, and corporate allegiances, and forbidding particular forms of action as attacks on the ideal of a militant citizenship aimed at universalism. The revolutionary contract is simple: access to citizenship brings the bestowal of all rights, and presupposes giving up all privileges and loyalties."[9] No privilege for any caste or group; only the nation counts, and therefore no loyalty to any norm other than citizenship.

Accepting the terms of this contract gave French Jews access "to the highest spheres, as deputies, senators, ministers and generals, judges and prefects," roles they cheerfully filled. In the First World War, "France had an army where Jews were well represented in the officer corps,"[10] including seven Jewish generals and hundreds of colonels and captains. This assessment is true in many areas: medicine, law, the arts, and politics. The republican contract, established by a strongly centralized state whose roots go back even before the Revolution, "opened the path of meritocracy to the Jews."[11]

Rejecting that contract by French anti-republican elites generated the deep anti-Semitism of the French Catholic right, from the Dreyfus affair to the Vichy government, a virulent anti-Semitism that would only begin to fade after the Holocaust.

In contrast, Jews in the Maghreb experienced a very different history. Of the three countries, the most striking case is that of the Jews of Algeria, who were brutally driven into exile to France in 1962, when President de Gaulle finally realized that the Algerians' drive for independence was unstoppable. When Algeria's revolt began in 1954, some local Jewish leaders tried to stay neutral between the French political authorities and the rebels. A few courageous Jews even joined the insurrection. But as armed clashes escalated, Jewish leaders were forced to choose. In huge numbers, they opted for the colonial side, that of *Algérie française*.

They chose that side partly out of gratitude for what they had been given. Like the British version, French colonialism worked to create local allies in the countries it conquered, dispensing privileges to favored minorities and not to all native inhabitants. In the case of the Maghreb, the French colonial authority bestowed French citizenship on the Jews of Algeria through the famous 1870 Crémieux Decree. With the wave of a wand, their status magically changed from *dhimmi* (protected, but under Muslim rule) to one of high privilege. Admittedly, French colonial society in Algeria was strongly anti-Semitic. Edouard Drumont, who wrote the famous anti-Semitic screed *La France juive*,[12] was elected as a right-wing deputy from Algiers in 1898, in the middle of the Dreyfus affair. But colonial society was far more hostile to the Arabs, a mass of people deprived of any political rights.

From 1870 until their departure, the France experienced by Algerian Jews (and to a lesser extent by those in Morocco and Tunisia) was not a France where citizenship for all implied equality of rights. It was a France where inequality was inherent in the colonial regime. In French Algeria, some people were fully citizens and others only partly so, and segregation was part of everyday life. Naturally, some Jews objected. But when it came to choosing between preserving the colonial status quo or fighting for the independence of colonized people, most chose the first option.

In 1961, when it became clear that France was going to give the Algerians their independence, some young Jews, especially in the city of Oran, which had the country's largest Jewish community, joined the fight led by the OAS (Organisation Armée Secrète, Secret Army Organization). A terrorist group of extremist colonials, it was created in hopes of blocking Algerian independence. It hardly mattered that within the organization those Jews were now fighting shoulder to shoulder with many extreme anti-Semites who twenty years earlier had enthusiastically supported the anti-Jewish laws for the Algerian territory that were passed by the Vichy government (whose first act was to revoke the Crémieux Decree granting French citizenship to Jews).

From 1961, when they realized that the war was lost, to 1963, those Jews washed up on the French shores of the Mediterranean. But this was no longer the France that had greeted their Ashkenazim coreligionists a half-century earlier, the country where you were "as happy as God." For these 110,000 Jews, along with the million others fleeing French Algeria, France was the country that had betrayed and abandoned them. They arrived not full of hope, but defeated and full of bitterness. Like their repatriated fellows, many vowed eternal hatred for de Gaulle, who had "ditched" them. And many maintained a colonial viewpoint mixed with hostility toward Arabs and Muslims that ranged from the casual prejudice common in Algerian colonial society to its most radical fringe's hateful and vicious racism.

In his 2020 book *Les Juifs de France entre République et sionisme,* Charles Enderlin writes that for those Maghreb Jews, the Israeli army's crushing victory over its Arab enemies in June 1967 felt like sweet revenge after their recent suffering and defeat. Before the Six-Day War broke out, those North African Jews were in the front ranks of demonstrations supporting Israel. The slogan they tapped out on their car horns sounded exactly like the ones they had honked a few years earlier in Algiers. The rhythm of "Is-ra-el will win" was "Beep-beep-beep beep-beep"—exactly matching "Al-gé-rie fran-çaise" or "O-A-S will win," which they had shouted during their demonstrations in Algeria. They joined a colonial thread expressed by a large swath of the French extreme right, whose leaders mostly supported Israel against "the Arabs" in that war. Francois Brigneau, the editor in chief of the fascist paper *Minute,* wrote that the Jewish fighters in the OAS "were battling the same enemy five years earlier." In other words, he was drawing a parallel between Israel's fight against the Arab world in 1967 and that of the OAS against Algerian independence in 1962. Raymond Aron, the great French (and Jewish) political thinker, noted that supporters of the Israeli cause included "people who were continuing the Algerian war in the Middle East and seeking revenge by way of the Israelis."[13]

Maghreb Judaism produced a powerful movement that would profoundly change Judaism in France. "Today, Sephardim dominate French Jewish institutions, both demographically and politically," says Enderlin.[14] Not that those Maghreb Jews suddenly all became Muslim haters or fanatically pro-Israel. But those who still clung to the old colonial vision two generations later, even though they are a minority, have seized the political and religious reins of the community. They have likewise become the most unconditional supporters of successive Israeli governments. In January 2003, when the Palestinian Second Intifada was raging, they relished the book published by historian George Bensoussan (writing under the pseudonym Emmanuel Brenner) that claimed that "Muslim immigration…comes from a cultural world that has long been at war with the West, from the Crusades to the extreme violence of decolonization conflicts," and that this Muslim world is characterized by "violent anti-Semitism fed by propaganda spread from the Maghreb and the Middle East [that is] genocidal in nature."[15] This kind of thinking stems from the joining of right-wing Zionism's historic ethnocentrism and the colonial attitudes that some Jews from North Africa still cling to.

CRIF: Community organization or pro-Israeli lobby?

Among French historians, Birnbaum is surprised to see how deeply Jewish institutions in France are attached to the Republic and to the notion of citizenship.[16] He thinks this explains why there is so little discussion of Israeli politics. You're a French Jew, now and forever. It's a little like those French citizens from Morocco or Algeria who don't follow what's happening back in their home countries. Birnbaum's explanation is well founded, but it doesn't tell the whole story, because CRIF never hesitates to take a position when it comes to defending Israel's interests, including on matters that involve French policy. By contrast, discussions and even polemics occur within U.S. Jewish organizations in part because of the different and diverse way Judaism was organized in America from the very beginning. It's also due to the fact that there is a confusion of purpose in France that doesn't exist in the United States.

In America, two leading Jewish organizations coexist, and they have very different functions. One is the Conference of Presidents of Major American Jewish Organizations; the other is the American Israel Public Affairs Committee (AIPAC). There are many connections between the two, but their functions are separate. The first represents American Judaism in all its diversity. The second lobbies to support the Jewish state and defend its interests.

In France, CRIF combines both of these functions. Officially, it represents French Judaism, but in fact it's a lobby for a foreign country, and it sees itself that way. Reading its daily newsletter makes this clear. Its denunciation of the "Iranian menace," for example, repeats the talking points of Israeli diplomacy verbatim and gives the matter an importance out of all proportion to its place in domestic French politics. Here is another example. When the Israeli Supreme Court endorsed the expulsion of Omar Shakir, the Israel director of Human Rights Watch in 2018,[17] CRIF immediately published Israel's argument in support of the decision, without mentioning any dissenting Israeli voices.[18] People in the know describe CRIF as essentially a full-time pro-Israeli lobby. It does manage a few community activities, but pays them little attention, much less than do some of its affiliates, like the Unified Jewish Social Fund, the Consistory, or the Universal Alliance Israélite, which have much less political clout at the national level.

This confusion of roles is extremely damaging. First, it suggests that France's Jewish community is entirely of one mind when it comes to Israel. Worse, it shows that "CRIF leaders don't have a vision of what a plural Judaism in France should be," says Pierre Saragoussi, the first director of France's Holocaust memorial foundation.[19] That attitude "keeps the CRIF from investing in the development of Jewish youth, who might think about having a future as Jews in France," he says. "Our Jewish schools only prepare young people to make *aliyah*.[20] Personally, I want to keep a European Judaism alive." By positioning itself as an Israeli lobby, says Saragoussi, CRIF "fails as a place for reflection about both Israel and French Judaism."[21]

Historically, this wasn't always the case. The current situation only began to take shape with Israel's 1982 war against the PLO in Lebanon. This was the first war seen as nondefensive, and therefore harder to justify in the eyes of the world. The tendency to unconditionally support Israel under all circumstances was reinforced when the Second Intifada erupted in Palestine in late September 2000. Since then, CRIF has embraced its unofficial but very real role as a lobby, largely at the expense of its community responsibilities. It is especially vigilant that no criticism of Israel should arise from Jewish organizations. As Jean-Christophe Attias, the chair of medieval Jewish thought at the École pratique des hautes études, puts it, "the cord with Israel has become an umbilical one."[22]

From CRIF's point of view, the results speak for themselves. You practically never hear the slightest public criticism of Israel from its members. A few associations might be unhappy about Israeli settlements or the so-called Middle East peace process, but the criticisms are rarely made publicly. Sacha Ghozlan, the president of the Union of Jewish Students of France, explains this phenomenon by the feeling of danger he says French Jews have been living with since 2000. "The fear is that if Jews publicly criticize Israel, it will legitimize anti-Semitic attitudes. Whereas if we stand like a solid, monolithic block, we better guarantee our safety."[23] Ghozlan admits never hearing a single debate in the community after the nation-state law was adopted, despite its segregationist content and the controversy it sparked in Israel. Within his own organization, the subject never came up for discussion. The law was passed. Time to move on.

This is a strange notion. Is denying Israel's crimes against the Palestinians and its embrace of segregation really the best way to guard against anti-Semitism? Because that's what's involved here. What would people say if a French Arab who identifies with Islam or his ethnic roots argued that we should keep quiet about crimes committed by Assad, al-Sisi, or the Saudis, so as not to stir up Islamophobia or hatred of Arabs? We know that some people think that way. But all that the Jews, Arabs, and others accomplish by muffling crimes that "their people" commit is to increase racism against their communities. Jews are dominated by fear, as Ghozlan freely admits. But what they really fear isn't anti-Semitism, but isolation, being excluded from their community. "People prefer to hush up disagreements because they're afraid of being called traitors," he says. "Admitting Israel's misdeeds would be giving in to its accusers. When you point out that this is a position of weakness, that admitting certain things would be proof of strength, it doesn't fly."[24] I got the sense that Ghozlan himself would also choose silence. In the old days of Communism, it was said there was no future outside the party. As an organization, it functioned like a closed countersociety, where any dissidence was betrayal.

One of the most striking results of this enforced unanimity is the drastic impoverishment of Jewish cultural life in France. The Jewish press there is "collapsing," says Meir Weintrater, the longtime editor of the now-defunct community monthly *L'Arche*.[25] The radio broadcasts used to be politically more diverse, with four of them sharing the same FM frequency. They are now down to two, it's hard to tell them apart, and most of their content is religious. As for CRIF itself, "the intellectual deficit there is enormous," says Jean-Yves Camus, an independent scholar specializing in the far right who watches developments in French Judaism.[26] The debate forums within France's Jewish community have become so anemic, they let CRIF announce the order of the day, defending Israel on topics that are all set in Jerusalem: the anti-Iran obsession, the international effort to outlaw and punish BDS, the casting of anti-Zionism as the modern incarnation of anti-Semitism, and finally the constant instrumentalization of the memory of the Holocaust to fit the ethnocentric vision developed in Israel, where the Jews' past suffering is used as a shield against any accusation of crimes being committed in the present.

On all those points, CRIF-as-lobby tries to impose its views on the French political authorities and public discourse. A few recent affairs will illustrate how CRIF acts as a weapon in the hands of the Israeli embassy in Paris.

On October 11, 2018, the television program *Envoyé special* (on the public broadcasting network France 2) ran a trailer for an upcoming news report called "Gaza, une jeunesse estropiée" [Gaza's youth: crippled]. Its subject: the weekly demonstrations that had been taking place at the Gaza border every Friday since the previous March 30, which Palestinians call "Land Day." Each week, Israeli snipers killed several young Palestinians and wounded hundreds of others, while they themselves were in no danger.[27] This had been going on for six months. Israel's ambassador Aliza Bin-Noun demanded that France 2 cancel the broadcast, on the grounds that showing the images would "feed anti-Semitism." Embassy staffers admitted they hadn't seen the images or heard the accompanying narration before asking that they be censored, but accused the report's producers of being "accomplices of Hamas."[28] CRIF promptly chimed in, repeating well-rehearsed talking points. Meyer Habib, a National Assembly deputy representing the overseas French in the Middle East, said that airing the report would "set the stage for future anti-Semitic violence, if not attacks."[29] In other words, censorship was being requested in the name of fighting anti-Semitism. That's a peculiar way of thinking. Just imagine if an Arab country, with the support of a group of American imams, demanded that a PBS *Frontline* report on crimes by the Assad regime in Syria or the Saudi-led war in Yemen be suppressed, on the grounds that it would increase Islamophobia and anti-Arab sentiment in the United States.

There are people who confuse Israelis with Jews in general, whether from ignorance or narrow ethnic bias, and have their old or newfound anti-Semitism fed by the crimes committed by Israel. That's nothing new. The same is true for Islamophobia. To the people who mix up Muslims, Islamists, Arabs, and jihadists, every horrible act committed by one of them reinforces the notion that Islam is a criminal religion and that Arabs are born barbarians, the way other people think Jews are born deceitful and rich. But as Lao-tzu said, "When the wise man points at the moon, the fool looks at his finger." It's not the reporting of crimes perpetrated by Al Qaeda, Bashar al-Assad, or Mohammed bin Salman that contributes to Islamophobia or anti-Arab racism, it's the crimes themselves. Racists instrumentalize the horror of those crimes to project their collectively targeted hostility at a whole group of people—Arabs or Muslims. In the same way, showing images of young Palestinians being killed isn't what feeds anti-Semitism, it's the killings themselves. As if they were in a shooting gallery, Israeli snipers target despairing young Palestinians every week. Some people find that terrible, some are disgusted by the military's show of impunity, and some become racists.

Fortunately, France 2 doesn't take orders from CRIF. It went ahead and broadcast the program.

Three months later, CRIF was at it again. In December 2018, the CNCDH, France's national advisory commission on human rights, awarded one of its annual prizes to the NGO jointly representing B'Tselem in Israel and El-Haq in Palestine. The prize was to be given by France's minister of justice, Nicole Belloubet, but she begged off at the last minute, claiming illness. The diplomatic flu was no doubt brought on by the combined pressure of the Israeli embassy and CRIF, whose president, Francis Kalifat, called the CNCDH's position "incomprehensible." The prize wasn't withdrawn, but Belloubet's skipping the ceremony was approved by the French prime minister. In Israel, the awarding of the prize led the foreign affairs vice minister at the time, Tzipi Hotovely, to portray B'Tselem as an NGO that spread false information solely to harm its own country. Michael Oren, who was then the deputy minister for public diplomacy, said it "defends terrorism." Though unable to have the prize canceled, CRIF lobbying lessened its impact by getting the French government to distance itself from the ceremony. No one in the French Jewish community stood up to say that CRIF was making a mistake, that in the area of human rights B'Tselem in fact brings honor to its country, just as El-Haq brings honor to Palestinians. Also, that their cooperation is one of the few gleams of hope and dignity in the ocean of blood and tragedy that the conflict has generated for decades.

Those two interventions by CRIF are dismaying, but they are trivial compared to the way Israel protects its larger interests. This isn't 2016, when AIPAC managed to get the U.S. to increase its financing of the Israeli army by an extra ten billion dollars over ten years. But the interventions are symptomatic of how alarmed Israel is to see its image and policies increasingly challenged, and of its determination to not miss a chance to impose its vision of things. The fight against BDS that Israel launched is mainly a battle to keep what is really happening in Palestine from getting out. It is also a battle to mobilize Israel's supporters, Jewish and non-Jewish, around a common ethno-nationalist ideology. Thus, in December 2018 the Israeli government asked the German government to stop financing the Jewish Museum Berlin, because the museum gives exhibit space to Arab Jerusalem. In a Jewish museum, there's no room for anyone who isn't Jewish.

On December 3, 2019, CRIF—and by extension the State of Israel—scored a relatively inconsequential but nonetheless significant victory. With the passage of a bill by Deputy Sylvain Maillard, France's National Assembly joined some twenty of the world's parliaments in adopting the International Holocaust Remembrance Alliance's definition of anti-Semitism, which encompasses all criticism of Israel. The success of the pro-Israeli lobby in France was very limited. The resolution wasn't binding and was only voted on by a quarter of the parliamentarians (154 for, 72 against, and 43 abstentions, out of 577 members). More than half of the deputies had not participated in the vote. But this was also significant, because the refusal of members to vote reflected the lobby's pressure. They ducked the issue so as not to have to cast a public vote against a bill most of them didn't endorse.

Michel Tubiana, president emeritus of the Human Rights League of France, confronted the issue head-on. "To this day, the right of the Palestinian people to have their own state is being denied," he said. "The existence of Israel isn't being threatened by the Palestinians; the Palestinians' right to exist is being denied by an occupying power that receives support ranging from active financial support, I refer here to the United States, to a cowardly complicity, by which I mean the European Union, including France. So it would be somewhat incongruous to want to legislate on this topic while no one is thinking of incriminating those in Israel and in France, including their national representatives, who challenge the right of the Palestinians to have their state or even go so far as to deny their existence!"

Ethnic separateness and the burden of cowardice

I met with a variety of Jewish French personalities in writing this book, and I always mentioned that the U.S. petition concerning BDS had been signed by more than a hundred leading Jewish American intellectuals. They had deep differences about BDS, I said, but they agreed on the basic democratic need to respect the legitimacy of an appeal to boycott Israel. So why, I asked, is such a thing impossible in France? In answering, almost everyone I interviewed stressed the big difference in the way the law treats freedom of expression in France and the United States. An antiracist law like France's Gayssot Law[30] would be unthinkable in America, they said, where the First Amendment protects free speech—all speech.

The Reform rabbi Delphine Horvilleur explained the difference by the fact that French Judaism is "heir to a tradition that is Catholic (the Vatican) and centralizing (Napoleon), where dissidence means heresy."[31] Lawyer Arié Alimi stressed the difference between American Jews, who are almost all Ashkenazi and therefore heirs of the Enlightenment, and French Jews, most of whom are more culturally Sephardic, "a tradition closer to ethnocentrism than to the Enlightenment."[32]

When I asked my interviewees if they themselves would sign such a petition, the answer, with very few exceptions, was no. Journalist Meir Weintrater, the president of J Call, a leftist Zionist organization, said that he wouldn't sign such a petition because "those in favor of BDS include people who oppose Israel's right to exist."[33] Sacha Ghozlan, the student union president, said that he wouldn't sign either, "because boycotting Israel is not an opinion." When I asked him if calls to boycott Franco Spain, Soviet Russia, or apartheid South Africa were legitimate, he said yes, but that Israel was different. Why? "Well, it's still a democracy."[34] Even after adopting a segregationist law on the nation-state of the Jewish people?

One well-known French Jewish intellectual I interviewed embodied the malaise you encounter among people who like to think of themselves as open and progressive, but who go into lockdown the moment Israeli policy comes up. When I told him about U.S. Jews signing the BDS petition, and how that seemed impossible in France, he first reeled off a series of historical explanations. Then he said, "Do you think I don't realize that wanting to punish a call for a boycott of Israel is stupid?" Then, seeing me taking notes on what he'd just said, he froze. "No! No! You can't quote me on that!"

All right, but it begs the question. Beyond the carefully framed explanations about the distinct historic relationship of the Americans and the French with democracy and the state, which makes their Jewish populations so different from each other, shouldn't we consider a more ordinary factor among contemporary French Jewish intellectuals, namely the burden of cowardice?

In the United States, IfNotNow cofounder Emily Mayer puts it this way: "When my generation looks to Israel, what we expect to see is the same commitments we have at home: equality, dignity for all, and justice."[35] Israel's segregation of the Palestinians is a problem for Mayer, and she says so. Isn't there a single French Jewish intellectual who dares to say the same thing? "Where are France's Vidal-Naquets today?" wonders the New York journalist and Francophile Adam Shatz.[36]

One of the most interesting figures in modern French intellectual life, Pierre Vidal-Naquet (1930–2006) was a scholar of ancient Greece and a protean author. He studied Jewish topics, though he wasn't a dyed-in-the-wool Jewish intellectual.[37] Immediately after the June 1967 conquest of the West Bank and Gaza, Vidal-Naquet predicted that unless Israel gave up those territories, it would inevitably sink into no-exit colonialism.

Today, a number of progressive Jewish intellectuals in France are dismayed by the path Israel has chosen. Some are even disgusted. But they remain silent because they think they can't be heard, out of cowardice, or because they feel it's too hard to make their voices heard in the tension gripping French Jews, or because it's still too soon. But the main reason is the fear of finding themselves excluded from the community, blacklisted, deprived of their circle of friends, robbed of a protective cocoon. Unfortunately, this lets CRIF lobbyists upstage them, and they wind up marginalizing themselves a little more every day, not to mention yielding influence to those ever-more-numerous Jews who gladly side with Israeli leaders, whomever they happen to be. Those followers illustrate the overall movement of supporters of French Jewish institutions in two ways. One is the political shift to the right that studies and polls have noted over the last two decades.[38] The other is a turn inward accompanied by a strong upswing in religiosity that hasn't been much studied yet.

When I put the BDS question to sociologist Michel Wieviorka, he pointed to recent changes in the French Jewish community. "In the years between 1960 and 1980, an intellectual in the organized community like Richard Marienstras[39] would certainly have signed a petition like the American one. But that's not possible these days. We immediately excommunicate deviant thinkers."[40] As we saw in the last chapter, some American Jews are breaking free of Israel's tutelage. In France, supporters of Jewish institutions are moving in the opposite direction, and now follow Israel's lead exclusively.

For a long time, French Jews ranged politically from the center to the far left. When they were on the right, they were moderate, like Simone Veil.[41] But in the 2007 presidential election, they voted in large numbers for Nicolas Sarkozy, the conservative candidate. The shift has often been attributed to the blunders committed by Lionel Jospin, the Socialist candidate. He was prime minister in 2000 when the Second Intifada broke out, and he failed to grasp the wave of anti-Semitism sweeping the low-income housing projects in the suburbs. As an explanation, that's a bit thin, and it overlooks something essential. The move to the right by French Jewish communities makes no sense unless you consider the "umbilical cord" that CRIF has tied to Israel and its policies. Israel has been ruled by the nationalist right for forty of the forty-four years since it first came to power in 1977, and its extremist colonial wing has played an increasingly larger role in those governments. CRIF has mandated unconditional support for those governments, so the dominant political outlook in Israel has also become dominant within French Jewish circles, at least among those who monopolize the microphone.

Israel's drift to the right and the continuing rightward colonial movement I've described help explain what is happening to French Jews affiliated with Jewish organizations. You would be amazed if you heard how people talk on Jewish radio in France—not just occasionally but every day—and the call-in shows are even worse. The level of free-ranging Islamophobia and anti-Arab hate speech is frightening, on par with the most vicious French ethno-nationalist websites.[42] The talk mirrors the anti-Semitism that is on the rise in the housing projects, with this difference: French society today is much more tolerant of Islamophobia, whereas the authorities usually react very quickly to expressions of anti-Semitism. And the anti-Muslim and anti-Arab talk doesn't just link Islam to anti-Semitism. It often spills over into a rejection of immigration and decent treatment of immigrants. Historians Esther Benbassa and Jean-Christophe Attias agree: "What's being rejected isn't just the critique of Israel, but the whole progressive idea: egalitarianism, anti-racism, and welcoming immigrants."[43] More generally, the French Jewish radio broadcasts provide an outlet for an ethnocentrism and colonialism that is a carbon copy of what you can hear and read on any day in Israel, with one notable difference: in Israel, critical voices can be heard, even if they are marginalized; in France they are nonexistent. Most French Jews don't hold reactionary views, but those who do are the most active in Jewish institutions, and their numbers are growing. That they represent ideas almost universally held in Israel itself allows them to impose their viewpoint a little more every day.

This situation is most apparent among Sephardic Jews, whose relationship to Israel is "like revenge for *dhimmitude*,"[44] notes scholar Jean-Yves Camus. That's a concept developed by the polemicist Bat Ye'or around the concept of *dhimmi*, a state of protected inferiority that traditional Islam ascribes to Christians and Jews.[45] For Bat Ye'or, *dhimmitude* is the driving force in a Muslim religion that she considered dominating, barbarous, and anti-Semitic. This attitude is especially shared by young people outside the organized Jewish community who are now passing on a family memory in ideological form. Camus says their position is basically "You Arabs screwed us in Algeria, so we're going to get back at you through Israel."

"One thing about Israel that fascinates young French Jews is the Tzahal,[46] the fact that Jews there carry weapons and impose their will" on Muslims, says Jean-Yves Camus. "For some, that's a tangible sign that these are messianic times. They get all their information from Jewish radio programs and websites, and become blindly infatuated with Israel because it's successful in so many areas, real and imagined. But what mainly drives them is a fascination with its strength."[47] "What we're witnessing in France isn't a renewal of traditional cultural Sephardic Judaism, but a revival of bigoted religiosity," says lawyer Arié Alimi. "Within it, connecting with Israel is more important than connecting with Jewish culture. When the president of the World Jewish Congress opposed the nation-state of the Jewish people law, those French Jews were horrified and baffled, because they actually agree with the law."[48]

A fascination with strength, a circling of the wagons around a communal ethnic core—we are now at the very heart of Israeli society's drift. Why should we be surprised that this is accompanied by a determined search for separateness, both in France and Israel? It leads French Jews to move into neighborhoods where many of their own kind live, and if possible are the majority. There, they have practically everything they need, from the kosher deli to the Jewish day school by way of the synagogue. They rarely leave the neighborhood, and they avoid mixing with "the French." In this atmosphere, "French Jewish institutions cultivate a pro-Israel exclusivity and a separateness that mirrors what Muslim institutions do,"[49] says historian Benbassa, who is also a senator. The education provided in France's hundred-odd Jewish schools, especially in the religious establishments, is largely unrelated to the demands of national education. In Créteil, a large town southeast of Paris with a big Jewish community, the Ozar Hathora day school belongs to the same network as the one in Toulouse where Mohammed Merah committed his massacre.[50] "The people who send their children to school there have lost touch with the Republic," says Benbassa. They've created a ghetto for themselves, and live as if under siege, she says. "During the memorial services commemorating the Vel d'Hiv roundups [that occurred under the Vichy regime], they speak about today's France as if we were still in the same situation."[51] (On July 16–17, 1942, 13,152 Paris Jews, almost all of them non-French refugees, among them 4,115 children born in France and therefore French citizens, were rounded up at the Vélodrome d'Hiver by the French police under Nazi orders, and were sent to Auschwitz.)

France's Jews are increasingly self-enclosed, if they aren't actually leaving for Israel.[52] For those who choose to live hermetically that way, Netanyahu is their hero. This can lead to shameful behavior, like the spectacle they created after the 2015 shooting attacks on *Charlie Hebdo* and the Vincennes kosher supermarket. Immediately after the attack, Netanyahu spoke in Jerusalem, and called on French Jews to emigrate to Israel. Two days later, he attended a memorial service at the Great Synagogue of Paris led by Haïm Korsia, the chief rabbi of France, in the company of President François Hollande and Prime Minister Manuel Valls. Netanyahu was hailed with incredible fervor by his fans, who chanted "Bibi, King of Israel!" at the top of their lungs. This turned a moment of reverence in memory of the seventeen victims, in particular those from the attack on the Jewish store, into a political rally for an Israeli prime minister on the campaign trail back home.

Rabbi Korsia, clearly concerned that more and more French Jews were wrapping themselves in rigid identity zealotry, tried to repair the image created by the evening by declaring that "the words from the French Jewish community are words of trust in France. France needs *fraternité*."[53] But in the new urban Jewish ghettos popping up around the country, his calls for trust and fraternity may be a dead letter. If necessary, the Israeli government and CRIF will make sure of that. And within institutional French Judaism, no one will speak up to oppose what is happening.

11

I Am Exhausted by Israel

A schism in Judaism?

An evening of satirical sketches called *Queen of a Bathtub* by Hanoch Levin made a splash when it was produced in Tel Aviv in 1970. The title sketch involved a family that welcomes a boorish cousin into their home. He turns out to be the kind of slob who doesn't dry himself off after showering and tracks water all over the apartment. Eager to get rid of their ill-mannered guest, they start closing off rooms one after another to keep him out. Eventually the family finds itself locked in the bathroom, with the toilet. When one of the kids says, "It stinks in here!" a parent answers, "Maybe it stinks, but it's home."

Levin, who died in 1999, was his country's most caustic playwright. Fifty years ago, he could already see the path Israel would take in its pursuit of ethnic separateness.

Which Israel do you support, exactly?

Just how far can triumphant ethnocentrism carry Israeli society? There is no shortage of ideas to further reinforce the authoritarian state. Waiting in file cabinets are draft bills to consolidate the segregation put in place by the nation-state law. To legalize "residential separation" between Jews and Arabs, for example. Or to tighten the screws on human rights defenders. Bills to exclude Arab members from the Knesset, on the pretext of forbidding their expressing certain opinions, have already come before the Committee on Legislation. In 2017, MK Oded Forer (Israel Our Home, right-wing secular) moved to strip the parliamentary status of any elected official who denied the state's Jewish and democratic character, or who defended opinions "that threaten Israel's security." Given its deliberately vague parameters, such a law could be used to rid the Knesset of its Arab members, no doubt as a prelude to purging its remaining deviant Jewish ones.

As for the future of the Palestinians, other bills are also waiting in file cabinets, ready at hand for possible scenarios, but the line has been drawn. Speaking at a settler forum in Samaria on July 10, 2019, Netanyahu explained what determined his West Bank policy. "I am guided by several principles when it comes to the West Bank," he said. "The first: This is our homeland. The second: We will continue to build and develop it. Third: Not one resident [settler] or community [settlement] will be uprooted in a political agreement. Fourth: Israeli military and security forces will continue to rule the entire territory, up to the Jordan Valley. Fifth: I am working to get international ratification of these principles. Look at what we did in the Golan Heights and East Jerusalem [with Trump's recognizing their annexation]." Without giving specifics, Netanyahu then added that "Israeli sovereignty will be gradually applied to territories in the West Bank."[1]

Just a campaign speech, some people will say. But a speech to fuel the hopes of the most determined segment of Israeli society. And more than that, a speech unchallenged by any contrary policy position. During the three legislative elections in 2019–20, the Israeli-Palestinian relationship option that Netanyahu offered wasn't debated, much less challenged, by the Blue and White or Labor opposition. The colonial right is split on the secularism issue, but it remains irrevocably hostile to any agreement that would create a Palestinian state, as does the great majority of voters. In reality, writes David Shulman, "the costs of such an agreement are tangible, immediate, and perhaps overwhelming, involving the loss of territory, an end to colonialization, and potential political collapse, whereas the costs of maintaining the status quo are, for many Israelis, if unpleasant, eminently bearable."[2]

So if there is no peace and no returning Palestinian territories, what happens next? B'Tselem director Hagai El-Ad sees only two options. The first is to keep reinforcing the existing apartheid. "You make inroads wherever you can, and turn it into a fait accompli," he says. "You hope you'll never have to negotiate, but if that ever happens, at least you'll be ahead of the game. In the meantime you muscle your way forward, you expel people, you seize land, you oppress Palestinians in the hope of discouraging them." That plan has already been working for decades, he says; not as well as the governments might like, but it pays to be patient. "The idea is that if the Palestinians don't leave, their children eventually will." The second option is the one preferred by the ultranationalists, and "at least they're more or less open about it," says El-Ad. "If an opportunity ever presents itself, seize it. In Israel, the expression 'Another war, another opportunity' is being voiced publicly more and more often."[3] The opportunity in question would allow Israel to create an ethnically pure state, rid of the Arabs. The idea has spread, if sometimes by implication, to the benches of the Knesset. "Its partisans are encouraged by the social, ethnic, and religious drawing inward now happening in the U.S., Europe, and elsewhere," he says.[4] Having long been out in front, its partisans feel that the world understands them better now.

The ultras have made a lot of headway in the fifty years of occupation, and while they aren't yet dominant in Israeli society, they are its most determined segment. Spread among the various rightist parties and within religious Zionism, they represent the biggest share of public opinion in favor of annexing the West Bank. "They see themselves as the party promoting apartheid from the Mediterranean to the Jordan," says Breaking the Silence director Yehuda Shaul, "while they await the blessed day when Israel will be rid of its native inhabitants."[5] Theirs is the first of what Shaul considers the four major factions dividing Israel today.

He calls the second faction "the party of domination." The largest group numerically, it includes people ranging from moderate Likud members through Blue and White centrists to Laborites on the left. They don't hold a mystical view of the land; they just want to continue dominating the Palestinians and undermining their national identity. For that reason,

THE STATE OF ISRAEL VS. THE JEWS

they don't see formal annexation as necessarily useful. "They might go so far as to consider a Palestinian state if necessary," says Shaul, "provided it always remained a rump state over which Israel could maintain absolute mastery."[6]

Ethnic separation is essential to the third faction, represented by Avigdor Lieberman. This group doesn't care about land, it just wants a state free of Arabs—period, paragraph. If the conditions were very favorable to Israel, it might consider exchanges of land and people. Shaul says that this faction views the 1.8 million Palestinians with Israeli citizenship as "a threat just as dangerous as those in the Occupied Territories."[7] It wants to establish Israeli sovereignty from the Mediterranean to the Jordan, and to balkanize the Palestinians, who would be given a kind of autonomy like that of South Africa's former Bantustans. Within a Greater Israel, the Palestinians would be clumped in tiny pockets of autonomous territory around their cities, which they would administer under supervision. (In Israel this is derided as the "Arab Emirates of Palestine" scheme.)

The fourth faction, Shaul's own, which he calls "the party of parity," is for opponents of the occupation. "In this party, people like me argue for the existence of two sovereign states side-by-side. Others want a single state: one person, one vote. But both aim for equality for the people of both population groups."[8] This faction has the support of the great majority of Palestinians who are citizens of Israel, and a tiny minority of Jews. "It's very weak," says Shaul, "but the other three agree in wanting to make it disappear."

Shaul is describing a society blindly turning inward as it drifts toward disaster. Israel seems to have no sense of what within it could avert that disaster, or who would do it. You have to wonder: Does Jewish Israeli society have what it takes to resist the current that is carrying it? The answer has to be no. Nothing will happen in the Middle East unless an international coalition of major powers (the United States, Europe, and Russia, at the very least) forces Israel to give up its domination over the Palestinians. It won't be accomplished by a change of government in Israel, or even by a new American president. Unless great pressure is applied, Israel won't change. Things could conceivably happen under new circumstances, but right now it's hard to imagine. On the other hand, nothing says the U.S., Russia, and the Europeans in their wake will maintain the same relationship with Israel that they have up to now.

The question of Israel's "right to exist" will soon no longer be rhetorical or ideological. Israel exists, a fact recognized by every nation on Earth. The question will be asked from a purely practical standpoint. Israel has been instituting a system of apartheid in daily practice. Once that system is firmly entrenched as a matter of settled law, writes columnist Gideon Levy, the liberal democracies that have led the West since the end of World War II will have to answer this question: "Which Israel do you support, exactly?"[9] A disembodied Israel whose practices you choose to ignore, or a real Israel that is every inch an authoritarian ethnocracy? Sooner or later, that's a question that Jews living outside of Israel will also have to ask themselves if they don't want to be sucked into the wake of Israel's closing in on itself, which can only end in bitterness.

That's the weakness that will bring us down

Paradoxically, anxiety about the country's future is emerging from Jewish Israeli society, in the form of a deeply felt pessimism. Not only because tens of thousands or maybe hundreds of thousands of Israelis have tried to get European passports. "You never know what tomorrow could bring," says filmmaker Erez Pery. "Despair among young Israelis is much more widespread than people imagine."[10] The insecurity primarily stems from Israel's policy of force, which mainly generates more fear. This is what French political scientist Bertrand Badie calls "the impotence of power."[11] Today, it looks likely that Israel will become an ever-stronger segregationist state, given how far the balance of power over all comers is tipped in its favor. Yet Israelis live in a state of permanent anxiety, because they sense that the situation is far more precarious than it appears. Regardless of the balance of power, however sophisticated or brutal the methods used, and even if a massive expulsion of Palestinians occurs—maybe especially if it occurs—there is no guarantee that the Israelis can ever escape the trap they have set for themselves. Like the family in Hanoch Levin's sketch, they have locked all the doors. In Israelis' eyes, the fear of the slightest failure becomes the risk of a defeat from which they won't be able to recover. As if pulling a single stone from the edifice they've built would threaten the whole thing with collapse.

In January 2019, two notable Israeli figures retired within six days of each other. General Yitzhak Brick had been the Defense Ministry's longtime ombudsman. Benny Morris was the first historian in Israel to search the archives and reveal the truth about the Palestinians' expulsion in 1947–50; he later supported the idea of a new expulsion. Both men gave long interviews on the eve of their departures, and both expressed a dark vision of the future.

"Israelis are living on the *Titanic*," said Brick, who warned that if Israel faced a real war, its ground troops are so unfit that only its air force would be operational.[12] "There is a steady drop in professional knowledge of some reserve units in the ground forces," he said. And counting on the air force alone is a "disastrous conception" for the future. Brick didn't spell it out, but his thinking was clear: assigning generations of young soldiers to low-level police operations in the Palestinian occupation instead of training them for war hurts the troops' capabilities. So the general worries about hitting an iceberg up ahead.

Benny Morris sounded equally pessimistic, but in a different way. He regretted that Israel didn't carry out a complete ethnic cleansing of Palestinians in 1948, and now felt his country's situation is hopeless. It is no longer a matter of getting rid of 800,000 Palestinians, as in 1948, but nearly 3 million people living between the Green Line (the 1967 borders) and the Jordan River, not counting an additional 3.7 million in Israel and Gaza. And unlike in the Naqba period, Israel would be expelling them before the cameras of the world. In territory dominated by Israel, there are already as many Arabs as Jews. "The whole territory [between the Mediterranean and the Jordan] is unavoidably becoming one state with an Arab majority," said Morris. "Israel still calls itself a Jewish state, but a situation in which we rule an occupied people that has no rights can't last in the twenty-first century."[13]

Morris grimly foresaw what would happen to a single state containing both groups. "As soon as [the Arabs] have rights, the state will no longer be Jewish," he said. "The Arabs will demand the return of the refugees. The Jews will remain a small minority within a large Arab sea of Palestinians, a persecuted or slaughtered minority...Those who can will flee to America and the West...The Palestinians have no reason to give in, because the Jewish state can't last. They're bound to win. In another thirty or fifty years, they will overcome us, come what may."[14]

Given the current imbalance of power, such an apocalyptic vision of the future seems improbable, but it speaks to a well-founded fear. If the State of Israel wants to survive without fundamental changes, it will be forced to gradually enforce a totally structured, codified apartheid. Such a state could last for some unknown period of time. The Palestinian occupation has already lasted fifty years—who would have imagined it?—to the point that people like Hagai El-Ad find it wrong to use the word "occupation," as if it were still something temporary. But such a state clearly won't endure forever, just as segregating a population deprived of rights is eventually bound to fail. Before that happened, Israel would probably strengthen its ties with the world's ethno-nationalist regimes, and in so doing further isolate itself every day. Whether they deplore or cheer this future, many Israelis are already starting to feel it coming.

The late Haim Gouri, the last of Israel's "national poets," talked to me about this feeling of being at an impasse during a long interview in January 2006.[15] He had been an ardent Zionist, then believed for a while in the emergence of the "new Hebrew" emancipated from diaspora Judaism. After the June 1967 conquest he briefly caught "Greater Israel" fever, before, as he put it, "discovering" Palestinian nationalism. In 2016 the Culture Ministry wanted to award him the Zionist Work of Art Prize. He turned it down flat,[16] later telling me that he couldn't stand the government's "ultranationalistic ideology and messianic fervor."

I first met Gouri in the living room of his little Jerusalem apartment, sitting with his wife. He was eighty-three, and initially seemed a little distrustful. Later, after our conversation, he explained that he'd been afraid I wouldn't understand him. But a feeling of trust gradually developed. Gouri's memory was sharp, and he expressed himself wonderfully, in simple, well-chosen words.[17] He put up with three hours of my questions, until his wife finally reminded him that he shouldn't tire himself.

Gouri had concluded that the Zionist ideal, which he said was "founded on the idea of seizing land by force," had been a failure. "The confrontation with another people living here makes it impossible," he said. He compared Zionism's fate with that of Communism: two ideologies founded on a seductive idea of emancipation, but which had sunk into the mire of brutal oppression. All that was left of Marxism, in what was called Soviet "real socialism," was a horrible totalitarian oppression of peoples and individuals. In the same way, said Gouri, all that remained of theoretical Zionism and "real Zionism" was a new apartheid.

Brick, Morris, Gouri…Starting from different premises, these three visions, born in the heart of historic Zionist thought, had reached similar conclusions as to the impossibility of today's Israel enduring. They are shared by many people engaged in the fight against the occupation. "Israeli civil society is terribly weak, and it's full of lies," says Hagai El-Ad.[18] "Once every ten years, a soldier is arrested and charged, and that passes for democratic respectability. The crimes are real, but the investigations are fake. The trials where Palestinians are convicted are fake too, but the expulsions are real. The laws authorizing all this are real, but the justifications are fake. How long can this mystification be maintained? A long time? Yes. Forever? I don't think so. And that's the weakness that will bring us down."

The vague awareness of that mystification, and the impossibility of breaking out of it for fear of what could happen next, is what makes so many Israelis feel that their situation is precarious, despite looming like a superpower over their adversaries. That is also what has allowed their leaders to stay in charge. They systematically showcase the might that Israel has achieved, while constantly feeding the fear in which their Jewish citizens live.

Diaspora renewal in the United States

The solid establishment of state apartheid doesn't only impact Palestinians and Israelis. It is being increasingly rejected by international institutions, and even more so by civil society abroad. Will diaspora Jews gradually emancipate themselves from a thug nation that claims that it alone can speak in the name of Judaism? The signs of a possible divorce are already starting to appear. Israel is adopting an exacerbated racist attitude with politics that borrow the worst tendencies of white supremacy. The more it does this, the wider the disconnect between Jews and the Jewish state in a place where one might least expect it: the United States.

Michael Walzer, Dov Waxman, Henry Siegman and others... All these observers of American Judaism confirm that the United States is undergoing what they call a "diaspora renewal." This is the emergence of an American Jewish culture and experience that hews strongly to Judaism while being constructed at a remove from Israel, and in some cases, in opposition to it. What makes this phenomenon new is that since the Six-Day War in 1967, the diaspora communities' institutional Jewish identity—to the extent that one can be clearly defined—was built around support for Israel. This was true both in the United States and in France. Israel embodied contemporary Judaism: it was the beacon toward which all Jewish eyes were supposed to turn. Except for a few Haredi sects and those many Jews without a connection to organized Judaism, no Jewish culture could develop in the diaspora without a connection with Israel. In parallel, Zionism and the State of Israel developed an ideology that was both hostile and contemptuous of "diaspora culture," which it reduced to the supposedly congenital weakness of "little Jews," exiles unable to defend themselves.

One scene from Isy Morgenzstern's 1996 documentary about the writer Isaac Bashevis Singer says everything about Zionism's dim view of the Jewish diaspora.[19] I'll describe it from memory. The year was 1978, and Israeli prime minister Menachem Begin was in Washington, DC, when Singer received the Nobel Prize in literature. Begin decided to go to New York to congratulate him. In the filmed scene, the two men naturally speak Yiddish, their mother tongue. But Begin soon gets annoyed, and says something like "Why do you write in Yiddish? It's a dead language. A language of the

THE STATE OF ISRAEL VS. THE JEWS

dead." At first Singer tries to explain, but Begin presses him, arguing that Yiddish embodies the Jews' inability to defend themselves. Then he abruptly says, "I mean, you can't even say 'Attention!' in Yiddish." A bit exasperated, Singer marshals his famed wit and says, "You know, if you can say 'Achtung!' in German, you can just as easily say it in Yiddish. But I'll grant you this: Yiddish isn't a language that was invented for generals." The anecdote sums it all up: Zionism's hostility to Yiddish culture, and its overall relationship to the diaspora and the contemptible "little Jew," whose weakness was the cause of their extermination.

If you believe the Zionist caricature, diaspora Jews are so weak and submissive that they go missing in action during their own history, all the way from the destruction of the Second Temple to the resurgence of Jewish nationalism in the nineteenth century. Their story is reduced to two millennia of suffering and impotence. A pair of important and very different books show how far that is from reality.

The first is *The Story of the Jews*, by British-born historian Simon Schama, and especially its second volume, *Belonging (1492–1900)*.[20] Without neglecting the tragedies, Schama shows how diverse, rich, and often glorious Jewish history in the various diasporas was. The second is *The Jewish Century*, by the University of California, Berkeley, historian Yuri Slezkine,[21] which posits two archetypes, the Mercurian and the Apollonian. He masterfully portrays the diaspora Jew as the embodiment of the Mercurian type—a cosmopolitan trailblazer, urban, mobile, innovative, and transgressive, a vector par excellence of modernity and globalization. This type is the complete opposite of the Apollonian, who lives with his feet in the mud, clinging to his piece of territory, hostile to change and suspicious of anyone not of his tribe. Coming from a shtetl in the Russian Pale of Settlement, most Jews eager to escape the ghetto chose a Mercurian path, and usually some version of socialism. So did those who would go on to build transnational financial empires. The socialist and capitalist impulses were both born of ambitions oriented to the universal. Zionism also sought emancipation, but it followed the Apollonian vision instead, with its freight of ethnic nationalism and walled tribalism.

From its very beginning, the founders of the State of Israel were heirs to that kind of nationalism, and Netanyahu and his entourage have embraced its most radical, ethnocentric form. So they aren't shocked by the narrow, nationalistic thinking of an Orban or a Kaczynski. It speaks to them; they're comfortable with it. That's also why Israel's priorities have led its leaders to make a strategic alliance with American evangelicals and nationalists. This is partly cynical realism, since those groups are ten times bigger than the U.S. Jewish population. But it is also because ideologically, the Israeli leaders have much more in common with those various Apollonian types than with liberal American Jews, three-quarters of whom are hated Mercurians.

In a contrary trend, American Jews are rediscovering the diaspora, says Henry Siegman: "A self-sufficient Judaism that no longer needs Israel to exist. In their eyes, Israel should be 'the light of nations,' and here it has become an object of shame, the light of the worst regimes."[22] Thus the growing confrontation between American Jews, who are nearly all Mercurians, and Israelis, who are Apollonians. Unlike other large Jewish communities (in France, Britain, and Argentina), the American one is big enough to be comfortable with confrontation. There are about as many Jews in the United States as in Israel. And what America's influential Jewish university departments teach "is very different from what is taught in Israel," says Dov Waxman. "It is much more focused on the history of the diasporas and less on the centrality of the Promised Land."[23] The United States diaspora is also the only one to have created its own distinct body of literature. Israel has some first-class writers, but American Jewish novelists, for example, work on a broader and more ambitious canvas. The same is true of American Jewish filmmakers.

Above all, American Jews have created a religion and a ritual all their own: Reform Judaism, which is not recognized by the rabbinical authorities in Israel, has become the largest Jewish denomination in the United States.[24] At its core is a key concept, *Tikkun olam*. That is Hebrew for "repairing the world," in a biblical and literary sense, which is closer to the ideas of redemption and improvement. *Tikkun olam* doesn't refer to improving just the Jews' condition, but to the role Jews can play in the improvement of humanity.[25]

The foundations of American Reform Judaism were laid in 1885, in the Pittsburgh Platform.[26] In its eighth and final point, it stressed the concept of social justice as the ideal of Jewish law and the essential goal of *Tikkun olam*. The Pittsburgh Platform worldview was at the origin of Jewish liberalism in the U.S., embodied most visibly in the alliance of Blacks and Jews that fought for civil rights from the 1950s to the 1970s. It was also behind some Reform Jews' early ties with various brands of socialism. These nearly disappeared for a time, but are now enjoying a resurgence. That liberal outlook shows up today in the fight against racism and sexual discrimination, support for immigrants' rights, and outreach to Muslims, whose importance was already written into the Pittsburgh Platform.

This attitude is the antithesis of the dominant one in Israel, and makes the widening political and cultural gap between Israeli and American Jewish life increasingly stark. In September 2018, *The New Republic* published a special issue, "A Diaspora Divided," that was entirely devoted to the ongoing schism. It contains articles that would have been hard to imagine in such a mainstream intellectual magazine just a few years earlier.

Yehuda Kurtzer, the president of the Shalom Hartman Institute–North America, a major private educational institution, begins his article, "The Deep Sources of a Great Divide," by observing that "American and Israeli Jews do not share most elements of culture."[27] The opposition is between Israelis' fierce ethnocentrism and American Jews' preference for a more diverse, mixed society. The things that characterize Israel today—the lack of cultural pluralism, its treatment of the Palestinians, and its international alliances—"contribute to American Jews' alienation and anger," Kurtzer writes. Thus the emergence of "an alternative—the possibility of going it alone," if not against Israel, at least without it. Kurtzer dreams of a development that would give American Jews a choice: "Neither abandoning the project of Israel, nor slavish loyalty to it." But when he observes what is happening to Israel, he feels that hope may be vain.

In the same issue, novelist Jacob Bacharach argues that American Jews should simply turn away from Zionism. "I am exhausted by Israel," he writes in "A Homeland in America."[28] He knows his exhaustion is trivial compared to the Palestinians' humiliation and oppression, but it "is difficult to escape when every conversation about what it is to be a Jew, regardless of your faithful observance or lack thereof, whether you keep the Sabbath or barbecue pork in the backyard on a bright Saturday afternoon, returns to the question of Israel, this distant, foreign country, a lodestar to some of us and a millstone to others, but either way a central and immediate concern to our Jewish lives." How nice it would be, he writes, to just live life as an American Jew without constantly being asked by Jews and non-Jews alike to define himself in relation to Israel—from which, he is happy to note, so many young Jews are now breaking away.

Bacharach writes that the question now is "How do we create an authentic and enduring Jewish community in America? This is a far more existential question to American Jewry than the question of whether the Hamas charter recognizes Israel's 'right to exist.'" He concludes that "our real obligation [is] not to carve out a Jewish home abroad, but to defend the home that we've built right here."

Bacharach is articulating a trend that is growing in the United States, but which remains totally embryonic in France: a confident, coherent, and vigorous diaspora Judaism.[29] It insists on living a Jewish life unconnected from the terrible burden of Israel, which it sees as backward-looking and walled within its colonial beliefs, where racism shows through at every step. Bacharach dreams of being able to declare "I'm Jewish and Israel doesn't concern me." He also dreams of being able to lead the fight against racism, as well as against the revival of anti-Semitism in the United States, without being subject to the manipulations that Israel imposes on that struggle.

One of the intellectual spokesmen for this American diaspora renewal is Daniel Boyarin, a world-renowned scholar of religion who teaches the culture of the Talmud at UC Berkeley.[30] Like the late Israeli philosopher Yeshayahu Leibowitz, Boyarin doesn't mince words in describing what is happening in Israel and Palestine. "More piercing to me is the pain of watching a tradition, my Judaism, to which I have dedicated my life, disintegrating before my eyes," he wrote in 2006. "It has been said by many Christians that Christianity died at Auschwitz, Treblinka, and Sobibor. I fear—God forbid—that my Judaism may be dying at Nablus, Dheisheh, Betein [Beit El] or El Khalil [Hebron]."[31] Those words were considered blasphemous when they were published, but more and more American Jews agree with them today.

Toward a schism in Judaism?

A majority of Jews in the United States don't subscribe to the diaspora discourse, vigorous though it may be. Some benevolent critics of Israel point out that it lacks a truly popular dimension. "It's true that we're witnessing a revival of interest for diaspora Judaism," says Yehudah Mirsky, who teaches Near Eastern and Judaic studies at Brandeis, "but it's limited to intellectual, artistic, and university circles. If the diaspora renewal consists in saying 'I'm American and I don't need Israel to be Jewish,' I don't think it will succeed. I'll believe it when I see Jews organizing to demand that Congress stop financing arms sales to Israel. We're not there yet."[32] Mirsky probably represents majority Jewish thinking. But Michael Walzer, who criticizes Israeli policy but remains a fervent Zionist, says he is concerned about the rapid drop in support for the Jewish state that he sees among his students. "What worries me the most aren't the young Jews who support BDS; there aren't that many of them. No, it's the disaffection for Israel by a great number of my Jewish students. They're not interested in what's happening there, and they don't want to talk about it."[33]

In the United States, the future of a revived Jewish diaspora diverging from the line taken by Israel is being debated in the public square. Journalist Jonathan Weisman states his prediction as if it were established fact: "American Jews and Israeli Jews are headed for a messy breakup."[34] To young American Jews, he writes, Israel no longer looks like little David threatened by fierce Goliath, but like a bully, heavily armed and indifferent to the suffering it inflicts on another people. Michael Siegel, a leading Chicago rabbi and ardent Zionist, speaks of a gulf that can't be bridged."[35] The thought is echoed by Rabbi Steven Wernick, the former head of the United Synagogue of Conservative Judaism, the second-largest U.S. denomination. When a Conservative rabbi was detained by police for performing a wedding in Israel (where the Orthodox totally control family law), Wernick wrote an open letter to the Israeli government in which he said "I do not believe we can talk about a 'gap' between Israel and the diaspora. It is now a 'canyon.'"[36]

Haaretz correspondent Chemi Shalev wrote in 2018 that Israel's irreconcilable differences with American Jews and the Democratic Party would lead to divorce. "The gap between self-absorption and willful blindness and the basic tenets of enlightened liberals will soon become unbridgeable," he wrote.[37] In the end, "Israel will ultimately pay a steep price for its foolhardy neglect of the liberal world" and its norms, which prevailed at the country's founding.

The reality of those "liberal norms" is debatable, but the future that Shalev predicts is a plausible one. The American diaspora renewal is happening within a time frame that the Israelis don't understand. A 2018 *Religion Watch* survey that studied the 350,000 Jews in the San Francisco Bay Area[38] found that, as a group, they are becoming increasingly hybrid. Among people 65 and older, 42 percent were in mixed marriages, where one partner is Jewish and the other is not; among those 35 and younger, the figure was 66 percent. A quarter of those families included a partner who was Hispanic, Asian, African American, or from some other minority group. Yet the overall total Jewish population isn't falling. In the mixed couples group, the number of Jews who move away from Judaism is matched by the number of non-Jews who embrace it. The study found that, as a result, the educational programs of some Bay Area synagogues now teach "that there are many types of Judaism, all of them normal." As is often the case, California is leading the way. By its very nature, this growing trend in American Judaism rejects ethnocentrism. To these new diaspora Jews, what Israel has become seems not only foreign but repellent. Writes Jonathan Weisman, "Many American Jews, especially young American Jews, would say, 'Israel is Israel's problem. We have our own.'"[39]

What does Israel think of all this? In general, Israelis have never shown much interest in other Jews, except to encourage them to come live in Israel. Nor has Israel been especially interested in American Judaism beyond the financial and political support it could provide. So it's naturally quite hostile to the change within Judaism in the U.S. Many Israelis see American liberalism and variety of religious practices as a new "Hellenization" of Judaism. Between the third century BCE and the second century CE, Judea and the Jewish communities along the Mediterranean were exposed to a strong Greek and, later, Greco-Roman influence. This was systematically resisted by the Zealots, who fought to keep the Jewish faith free of outside interference. Israelis fear that what is happening in U.S. Judaism today will inevitably lead to assimilation, with all those "reformed" Americans shedding their Jewish identity.

Most American scholars hesitate to predict the future of the diaspora renewal in the U.S., but Eva Illouz, a French Israeli sociologist who teaches at the Hebrew University of Jerusalem and the School for Advanced Studies in the Social Sciences (EHESS) in Paris, is convinced that the process now underway is irreversible.[40] She thinks the split might be as significant for Judaism as the one between Catholics and Protestants was for Christianity. American Judaism, says Illouz, "is founded on two pillars: tolerance and pluralism. The movement has generated Jewish thinking that is intrinsically emancipated from its solely theological dimension. This has allowed many Jews to remain within Judaism. The idea of diversity, including religious diversity, is essential in America, whereas in Israel the reverse has happened. There, a single Jewish way of thinking has been imposed, and any dissident interpretation is repressed. This wasn't foreordained at the beginning, but it happened. And the split is now abyssal."

Israel today embodies values contrary to those held by Jewish communities ever since the Enlightenment, in the name of which Jews have tried to be model citizens. "Israel has chosen to wall itself off," says Illouz. "For Jews, the choice now is between clinging to an ethno-tribalism that rejects modern Judaism's tradition, or joining a Judaism embodied by a group that is renewing it." In the United States, she thinks that Israel will eventually lose the battle. "A minority of American Jews will stick with tribalism, but the majority will choose the side that defends universal values." As evidence, she cites the Jews of Pittsburgh and their collective rebuff to Trump after that city's synagogue shooting, compared to the support he received from Israel.

Could this diaspora renewal spread beyond American Judaism—to France, for example? There, Illouz is more cautious. The "Islam question" is a major obstacle in France, whereas she says it remains marginal in the United States. (Islamic anti-Semitism has not been significant in the U.S., where violent anti-Semitism is almost the exclusive province of white supremacists.) By contrast, the eleven hate killings of Jews in France between 2006 and 2017 were all committed by Muslims, a situation unique to Europe. This naturally inclines French Jews to close ranks with their own tribe.

Rabbi Delphine Horvilleur, the bearer of American Reform Judaism's ideals in France, is even more dubious. "Ever since Napoleon, French Judaism has been very conservative in matters of religion," she says.[41] This would impede any potential move by the organized French Jewish community to break with Israel. For different historical reasons, Pierre Birnbaum also thinks a diaspora renewal among French Jews is unlikely.

If anything, he is witnessing what he calls their rapid "Israelization."[42] Almost alone in French academia, historians Esther Benbassa and Jean-Christophe Attias teach a Judaism free of Israeli ideological tutelage that might embody a philosophy supporting diaspora renewal in France, and even they don't think it possible.

Yet a diaspora renewal movement has existed in France, and not that long ago. Between 1980 and 1990 the magazine *Combat pour la diaspora* published some thirty issues. Its guiding light was the great Shakespeare specialist Richard Marienstras. He and historian Pierre Vidal-Naquet founded le Cercle Gaston-Crémieux, whose goal was to "promote a Jewish diaspora existence that was not subject to synagogue or Zionism." But this Jewish tradition has completely disappeared in France in recent decades, says sociologist Michel Wieviorka.

I doubt that this disappearance will be permanent. True, the number of Jewish voices in France that are publicly critical of Israel can be counted on one hand. But if the future that Israel offers the Jews of the world remains the current one, I don't think Jewish diaspora communities, including France's, will remain forever indifferent to developments in the United States. To varying degrees, those communities are experiencing the same socio-demographic changes as those occurring on the other side of the Atlantic.

12

The Last Goddamn Thing We Need

After Trump

Donald Trump is gone, leaving in his wake a field of ruin in the country and the world. In the Middle East, as pledges to his most loyal supporters—ultranationalists and evangelicals—Trump spent four years showering Israel with diplomatic and military "gifts." At the end of his term, three things involving the Israeli-Palestinian conflict occurred almost simultaneously that illustrate the stakes now facing President Biden. On January 18, 2021, the Secretary of State nominee Antony Blinken outlined his Middle East strategy for the Senate: renew negotiations between the Israelis and Palestinians over a peace agreement that would create, in the hallowed formula, "two states side by side," while he cautioned that the prospect remained a distant one. On January 12, B'Tselem, the Israeli human rights association, published a report titled *A Regime of Jewish Supremacy from the Sea to the Jordan River: This Is Apartheid.*[1] Between those two dates, the Israeli army redoubled its bombing of Iranian military sites in Syria. So in just six days, the future stakes in the Middle East were set: a yawning gap between the new American administration's view of the Israeli-Palestinian conflict and the reality on the ground, matched by Israel's unrestrained use of force.

The Donald's deplorable legacy

The United States' withdrawal from the Iran nuclear deal in 2018[2] was the crudest example of the Trump administration's contempt for international law and institutions. His decision was greeted with enthusiasm by the Israelis, for whom disregarding international norms they dislike is a permanent feature of their behavior. This was accompanied by the many gifts to Israel, all designed to remove management of the Palestinian conflict from United Nations auspices and impose by force what Israel hadn't been able to acquire by law.

The list of these gifts ranges from the recognition of Jerusalem as the capital of Israel to public support of its wholesale annexations in the West Bank. It includes recognizing the annexation of Syria's Golan Heights, eliminating the word "occupation" from the American diplomatic vocabulary, affixing a "Made in Israel" label to products from Israeli settlements in the Occupied Territories, closing the PLO offices in Washington, canceling USAID subsidies to Gaza and the West Bank, canceling American support of UNRWA, the U.N. agency that helps Palestinian refugees, signing a presidential decree making criticism of Israel and Zionism the equivalent of anti-Semitism...and the list goes on. As William Burns, Biden's choice to head the CIA, has written: "In all my time as a diplomat, I never saw an American president concede so much, so soon, for so little, with so much potential for collateral damage."[3] It's no surprise that the Israelis feel bereft at Donald Trump's departure.

Leaving aside Trump's political blunders and the damage he wreaked throughout the Middle East, he must be given credit for a political success few would have expected when he entered the White House. True, nothing remains of his "deal of the century," the vaporous plan he had offered the Palestinians. Trump's idea of peace in the Middle East was born of his typically Mafia-like reasoning: join disproportionate pressure — we're talking a horse head in the bed, à la Don Corleone — with the hint of financial benefits for the Palestinians if they were willing to knuckle under and give up all their political rights. Based on the alliance of power and money, the dream shared by Trump, Netanyahu, and Mohammed bin Salman consisted in getting the Palestinians to agree to a quasi state split into multiple enclaves, where their sovereignty would be limited to handing out traffic tickets. If the trio could also find a Palestinian quasi dictator to impose order on his population in the style of Israel's new friends, the Saudi MBS, the Egyptian Sissi, and the king of Bahrain, the plan would be perfect.

As we know, that approach was a failure. But Trump may still leave one political legacy in the Middle East: the alliance he helped forge between Israel, Egypt, and the Gulf monarchies. It could endure because it makes practical political sense. Those countries share a common interest in confronting Iran's regional ambitions, and each offers unprecedented advantages to the others. Thanks to their connection with Israel, the Arab states can hope to see political and financial doors opening to them, in particular in the United States.

They can also benefit from Israel's cybersurveillance capabilities in controlling their own people, whom they fear more than anything. Israel in turn can expect this alliance to help it undermine any nuclear agreement with Tehran, while giving it access to important regional markets. Better yet, Israelis might hope for a significant and perhaps permanent loss of interest by Arab states in the Palestinian question.

The Palestinian cause has already lost some of its impetus, partly because of exhaustion and partly because of developments in the Middle East: the rise of Iran, the American war in Iraq, the various Arab Springs, and the civil war in Syria. Other developments, such as the waning importance of the region's energy reserves, have also pushed the Israeli-Palestinian conflict further down on U.S. diplomacy's priority list. In addition, more and more American and international leaders have come to agree with the radical conclusion that "Oslo is dead." The idea of negotiations between Israel and the Palestinians that would lead to a permanent peace agreement and a two-state solution is seen as pointless. In a way, all Trump did was to provide a stronger foundation for that belief. The Israelis certainly don't want to see a true Palestinian state emerge. And the Palestinians no longer have a convincing strategy for their liberation.

In diplomatic circles today, no solution appears to be currently viable. But while Oslo may be dead, no one has yet come up with an alternative approach. Some in the United States feel that the Palestinian question has been permanently marginalized. Others imagine that a new generation of Palestinians might yet strongly resurrect it. The dominant sense today is drift. The result? As Barbara Leaf, the National Security

Council senior director for the Middle East and North Africa, put it, "the Biden administration does not intend to invest great effort for now in renewing the Israeli-Palestinian peace process."[4]

Biden's challenge: dealing with an apartheid state

The report published by B'Tselem a week before Biden's inauguration stands as a milestone in the history of Israel. For the first time, a major Israeli NGO stated that the entire territory under Israeli authority, "between the Mediterranean and the Jordan," is being governed by "apartheid," described in this case as a "regime of Jewish supremacy." What makes it apartheid? Because, says the report, "Israel accords Palestinians a different package of rights in every one of the units [where they live] all of which are inferior compared to the rights afforded to Jewish citizens."[5] The report details this statutory inferiority in managing the Palestinians ("Divide, Separate, Rule") in four specific areas: immigration, taking over land for Jews while crowding Palestinians into enclaves, restriction of Palestinians' freedom of movement, and denial of Palestinians' right to political participation. In each instance, it highlights the evidence of discrimination suffered by Palestinians. The report is short and direct, and is summed up with this sentence: "A regime that uses laws, practices and organized violence to cement the supremacy of one group over another is an apartheid regime." That, it adds, is the definition of apartheid in international conventions.

In Israel, calling the situation in the Occupied Territories "apartheid" isn't new. Shulamit Aloni, a minister in various Labor governments, used the word when talking with me when the Second Intifada erupted. In February 2002, I also interviewed Michael Ben-Yaïr, who was the attorney general during Yitzhak Rabin's second government. A longtime Zionist like Aloni, this distinguished, thoughtful jurist said how terribly worried he was. "I feel I have to cry out: 'We must save Zionism!'" said Ben-Yaïr. "The object of Zionist thinking was never the domination of another people...We are committing crimes that fly in the face of international law and public morality. 'Targeted liquidations' is state terrorism. The moment a power establishes two different legal systems, one democratic and liberal, and the other repressive and cruel, that's when apartheid starts. When two peoples have neither the same status nor the same rights, where an army defends the property of the one and destroys that of the other, where a settler has a right to much more water than a native, where segregation is inscribed in the law, there is no other term to define the situation except apartheid. And don't tell me that the Palestinians exercise their own power in Zone A! Since 1967, no decision has ever been adopted in their territories without Israel's consent."[6] Last but not least, in the United States, former president Jimmy Carter chose to call his 2006 book *Palestine: Peace Not Apartheid*.[7]

So what led B'Tselem to enlarge the use of the word "apartheid" from the Occupied Territories to the whole Israeli-Palestinian reality? To the NGO, the establishment of apartheid was a long process that was cemented when the nation-state law was passed. "The Nation State basic law, enacted in 2018,... permits institutionalized discrimination in favor of Jews in settlement, housing, land development, citizenship, language and culture. It is true that the Israeli regime largely followed these principles before. Yet Jewish supremacy has now been enshrined in basic law, making it a constitutional principle—unlike ordinary law or practices by authorities, which can be challenged."[8]

In one sense, B'Tselem's decision is problematic. If all Palestinians between the Mediterranean and the Jordan are living under the same regime, the question of "the end of the occupation" for Palestinians in the West Bank and Gaza no longer arises. All Palestinians are in the same boat. Which I think is a mistake. But at the same time, B'Tselem's logic is irrefutable. Because Jewish supremacy is now inscribed in the state of Israel's Basic Laws and applies to its entire territory, from the Mediterranean to the Jordan.

Now that he is president, is Biden conscious of the reality of the Israeli apartheid that both B'Tselem and Jimmy Carter have pointed out? Does he understand that the old American orthodoxy that he plans to revive after the four-year Trump interregnum fails to take the urgency of that reality into account? That the orthodoxy denies reality? Trying to resurrect the logic of Oslo nearly thirty years later is worse than illusory, it's blindness. Reverting to the idea of a negotiation between two parties seen as equal, who would sign a dignified peace without powerful external interference, can only lead to repeating the deterioration since Oslo, but to an even greater degree, given the shift in the balance of power between Israelis and Palestinians. It would guarantee the perpetuation and worsening of Israeli apartheid. If Biden doesn't understand that, or if he understands it but can't or won't draw the necessary conclusions, he will fail to end the Israeli-Palestinian conflict, just as his predecessors have failed. And the Palestinian question will continue to fester.

Without intense outside pressure, why would the Israelis voluntarily abandon an apartheid that gives them so many advantages? Their refusal to find a truly equal compromise with the Palestinians is understandable, because it's human. It's in the nature of all dominant groups to preserve their domination and fear what might happen if they lose it. There is no reason for the Israelis to spontaneously start weighing the idea of compromise and that of parity in rights and dignity between the two peoples. The only way they would do that would be if the absence of such a compromise were perceived as more dangerous than the fear it inspires. And the Israelis are a long way from that.

"The strategy is: go fast, be bold."[9] That's what Biden's future national security advisor Jake Sullivan told the *New Yorker* journalist Evan Osnos a month before the Democratic candidate's victory. That's a fine ambition. But in dealing with the Israeli-Palestinian conflict, speed and boldness were quickly forgotten by the new administration. In his Senate confirmation hearing, Antony Blinken not only argued for the return to negotiations for "the so-called two-state solution," but added, "I think realistically it's hard to see near-term prospects for moving on that."[10]

One would be tempted to smile if it weren't so tragic. Not only because Blinken didn't mention Israel's embrace of apartheid, while continuing to act if Israel was "the only democracy in the Middle East." Blinken's statement was tragic because the Oslo Accord had anticipated five years of negotiation.

The phrase "Palestinian state" doesn't occur anywhere in the Accord, but the Palestinians understood that it tacitly stipulated that their state would come into being within five years. That was nearly thirty years ago, and Blinken today isn't even suggesting a possible quick conclusion of new negotiations. This is a way of telling the Palestinians that after thirty years of fruitless waiting, they will probably have to wait another thirty years to achieve an independence that daily becomes more evanescent. As the Israeli joke has it, "Netanyahu loves peace so much that he will be happy to discuss it for the next fifty years."

To no one's surprise, Israel warmly embraced Blinken's nomination to the State Department. Even Dore Gold, a colonial-right ideologue who is very close to Netanyahu, said he was "reassured." After Bill Clinton, whom the Israeli right opposed, and Barack Obama, whom it despised, the nomination makes Biden appear more understanding. Where a fringe of the Democratic Party is moving away from the "unbreakable link" with Israel, Blinken embodies the traditional American position on the Israeli-Palestinian conflict. This attitude has always been favorable to settlement supporters. In fact, ten days before Biden entered the White House, the Israeli government announced the construction of eight hundred new homes in the West Bank.[11] It also hinted at a future renewal of construction in the E1 Zone of a project historically opposed by the Bush and Obama administrations as well as the Europeans because it would destroy the West Bank's territorial integrity. This was the Israeli leaders' way of telling Trump's successor, "A word to the wise."

Summing up, Blinken assured the Senate that he expected to reengage with Iran, preserve Israeli interests as they saw them, and bring MBS and Saudi Arabia to heel. That may be a communication policy, but it's not coherent diplomacy. Because if Biden's primary aim is to restore and enlarge the scope of the nuclear accord with Tehran, he will necessarily have to impose his will on Jerusalem and Riyadh.

The Iran wager

Israel and the Gulf monarchies are all too aware that the signing of a new international accord limiting Iran's military nuclear program would be a serious setback for them. Especially because it would involve this major unknown: What implications would it have for the region, and in particular for the Israeli-Palestinian conflict, our area of concern? Before speculating about the future, we should note that when he took office, Biden appeared determined to revive the Iran nuclear deal. On December 1, 2020, he gave an interview to the *New York Times* columnist Thomas L. Friedman. In international affairs, Biden felt that the most crucial issue facing the U.S. was to reconfigure its relationship with China. The situation was complicated, he said, and would take time. On the other hand, he said the relationship with Iran was a pressing issue. Biden planned to return to the terms of the Iran nuclear deal. He hinted that he favored a quick return to the application of the accord by both parties, which would imply the canceling of sanctions on Iran imposed by Trump. But Biden especially wants to reduce and control the Iranian ballistic arsenal.

But wasn't Biden moving too quickly without sufficient guarantees? wondered Friedman. The president-elect shot back: "Look, there's a lot of talk about precision missiles and all range of other things that are destabilizing the region." But the fact is, "the best way to achieve getting some stability in the region" is to deal "with the nuclear program." If Iran gets a nuclear bomb, he added, it would put enormous pressure on the Saudis, Turkey, Egypt, and others to get nuclear weapons themselves. "And the last goddamn thing we need in that part of the world is a buildup of nuclear capability."[12] In taking that position, Biden was repeating the (unstated) reasoning behind the earlier negotiation: Iran was already a "threshold power" with nuclear capability, but it hadn't built an atomic bomb, so the real reason to negotiate with it is to avoid nuclear proliferation. Without an accord, if the pressure on Iran continues, it will eventually build a bomb—and at that point there will be nothing that anyone can do anymore.

The paradox of the September 11 attacks—committed by radical Sunni jihadists, almost all of them Saudis—was that when neoconservative ideologues invented the "Axis of Evil" thesis without any geopolitical coherence in order to get rid of "America's enemies," they wound up defining Shiite Iran as the primary menace threatening the "free world." And Israel played a major role in that shift. It already had atomic weapons, wasn't a signatory to the International Non-Proliferation Treaty (INPT), and wasn't about to share its deterrent capacity with anyone else in the Middle East. When Tehran was initially approached on the nuclear issue in 2003, Prime Minister Ariel Sharon reacted virulently. After him, Benjamin Netanyahu repeatedly claimed that any negotiations with Tehran were doomed to failure. In his eyes, negotiation itself was unacceptable. So when Trump unilaterally withdrew the United States from the Iran nuclear deal, he was applauded more loudly in Israel than anywhere else in the world. And Netanyahu found himself at the apogee of his career.

For a long time now, a number of people have felt that Netanyahu has turned Iran into a boogeyman to keep Israelis in a permanent state of existential anxiety that serves his political interests. So he greeted Joe Biden's victory the way one might expect: with contempt. Early in Trump's lame-duck period, Netanyahu declared that "there must be no return to the previous nuclear agreement."[13] Then, on November 27, the Mossad assassinated Mohsen Fakhrizadeh, Iran's senior nuclear military research engineer. Biden held his tongue, but some of his close associates aired their anger publicly. Ben Rhodes, an Obama-era deputy national security advisor, called the assassination "an outrageous action aimed at undermining diplomacy between an incoming U.S. administration and Iran." Former CIA director John Brennan tweeted that it was "a murder" and "an act of state-sponsored terrorism."[14] This impressed the Israelis not at all, who increased the tempo of their regular bombing of Iranian bases in Syria just before Biden's inauguration. And a week after the event, General Aviv Kochavi, Israel's chief of staff, told a meeting at the University of Tel Aviv that "a return to the nuclear deal, or even a similar deal with some improvements, is bad and wrong." Under his command, he added, "the IDF is revising its operational plans for thwarting Iran's nuclear program."[15]

So Biden knows what to expect. After all, he was vice president when Netanyahu publicly humiliated President Obama on March 3, 2015. It was on that day that he addressed a joint session of Congress and criticized Obama's Iran policy, to frantic applause by Republicans and many Democrats. The invitation to speak to Congress had been concocted by the Israeli embassy and Republican Speaker John Boehner without informing the White House. Biden knows that if he really wants to succeed with Tehran he can't avoid a confrontation with Israel regardless of its government, given the Israelis' sense of both impunity and being under siege.

In the future, Israel won't hesitate to activate all its lobby's influence to thwart a new accord with Tehran. And Saudi Arabia, the Gulf monarchies, and Egypt will be applauding from the wings. The Iranian negotiators—once burned, twice shy—will be even more cautious than last time. As Biden told Friedman: "It's going to be hard, but yeah."[16] That's putting it mildly.

But like Obama, Biden may succeed. The new U.S. president briefly bared his fangs at the Israelis (and the Saudis) when he named Robert Malley to be his special envoy to Iran on January 29, 2021. The news dismayed the Israelis. Since the aborted Camp David negotiations between Israelis and Palestinians in July 2000, Malley, who was Clinton's special assistant for Israel-Palestinian affairs, has been seen in Israel as the most pro-Palestinian of American experts. When he was nominated, he was the president and CEO of the International Crisis Group, a progressive think tank specializing in conflict resolution that is largely financed by the liberal magnate George Soros, the bête noire of American and Israeli right-wingers alike.[17] But the Israelis may realize that they will probably be no more able to stop Biden from working on the Iranian case than they were with Obama. On the very day Malley was nominated, an Israeli general was quoted in *Haaretz* as saying (on background): "The Americans will sign the agreement with Iran in any case, with us or without us."[18]

If a more or less intense confrontation with Israel is inevitable, the question becomes: To what point? Under some circumstances, it could turn pretty rancorous. "Every year between 2009 and 2013, Israel considered an independent attack on Iran. Ultimately, Prime Minister Benjamin Netanyahu did not implement the plans," mainly because of Washington's strong opposition.[19] Joe Biden seems determined to go down in history as the man who avoided nuclear proliferation in the Middle East. But we can't disregard the fact that Israel might be tempted to prevent him from this by attacking Iran independently, thereby forcing America's hand. That scenario seems unlikely today. What is more likely is that Biden, like his predecessors, will avoid or minimize confrontation with the Jewish state as much as possible. But if an accord with Tehran is signed—and its results better guaranteed than the first time—this will lead to profound, region-wide upheaval, by the mere fact of reinserting Iran as a legitimate party to the discussion.

To accomplish this, the United States may have to pay a steep price to buy Israel's official or tacit acquiescence. What kind of price? At worst, the first victims could be the Palestinians and the recognition of their future rights. But if Biden is bold enough, he might also use the atmosphere around an accord with Tehran to play on the Israelis' short-term political weakness and finally force them to end their occupation of the Palestinian territories. To box Israel in, Biden could be led to change the relationship between the United States and Israel for the first time in a very long time. He would have to end Israeli impunity, quit systematically vetoing any Security Council resolution unfavorable to Israel, and seek an accord with the European Union, Russia, and China to impose on Israel a proper solution to the conflict with the Palestinians, leading to the end of the occupation of their territories. If Biden could do all this, the Israelis would find themselves in great difficulty. They would view the dismantling of their domination of the Palestinians as a terrible political defeat. But it could open the path to a more peaceful future.

Is such an option improbable today? Certainly. Is it highly unlikely? Yes. But is it unthinkable?

Conclusion

"Israel vs. the Jews"

Tony Judt, in memoriam

In October 2003, when the Second Intifada was underway—and being met by Israeli repression of unprecedented violence—the late, great English-American historian Tony Judt published an article in the prestigious *New York Review of Books* called "Israel: The Alternative."[1] It caused an outcry, and earned Judt innumerable attacks, for two main reasons. First, because it was the first time that a leading Jewish public intellectual considered the option of a state that would be common to the Israelis and the Palestinians as a way of resolving the conflict between them. Judt felt that for Israel, the option of withdrawing from occupied Palestinian lands had expired. "The time had passed" when that was still possible, he wrote. Annexing the Occupied Territories without granting national rights to the Palestinians would definitely transform Israel into a segregationist state. And once again expelling Palestinians from their land

would make Israel "an outlaw state, an international pariah."
As a result, Judt proposed to start "thinking the unthinkable":
the existence of a democratic state shared by Jews and Arabs
(and other minorities), and built on the joint territory of Israel
and Palestine. In other words, a political option where Judt
recognized that there would be "no more place for a Jewish
state." At best, such a state would lose a great deal of its sovereignty by becoming part of a federation with the Palestinians
in which the two groups would collectively have equivalent
rights. Judt was just asking the question. But the mere fact
of raising the idea generated furious reactions within and
beyond the American Jewish community.

Today, the idea that a Jewish state might no longer have a
future isn't widely held by American public opinion, but it has
become a legitimate subject for debate. New York University
professor Peter Beinart enlivened that debate with a July 2020
New York Times article with the provocative title "I no longer
believe in a Jewish state."[2] An outspoken progressive Zionist,
Beinart says he long believed in the two-state option, with one
Jewish (Israel), and the other Palestinian. He feels that history
has moved on. "The goal of equality is now more realistic than
the goal of separation," he writes.

Seventeen years earlier, Tony Judt broke with Zionist ideology. Today, Beinart is giving up on the Jewish state to preserve
the possibility of a "Jewish homeland," whether within a state
shared with the Palestinians, or in a joint federation. The challenge he is making to progressives is fundamental. It involves
access to equality, to parity in rights and dignity between the
two peoples inhabiting the common space formed by Israel
and Palestine, regardless of the political form that access to

equality takes. The stance Beinart is taking may be controversial, but unlike Tony Judt in his day, he can't be ostracized.

The second reason that Judt drew so many brickbats was the way he saw Israel. "The very idea of a 'Jewish state'—a state in which Jews and the Jewish religion have exclusive privileges from which non-Jewish citizens are forever excluded—is rooted in another time and place," he wrote. As a historian, he felt that Israel was the result of a kind of outdated, anti-modern nationalism, the kind of ethnocentric nationalism that prevailed in Eastern Europe in the nineteenth century. It was incompatible with the evolution of a "globalized" world (whose unequal tendencies he also criticized), where crossing borders, mixing populations, and being open to the future had become the norm. "The depressing truth is that Israel's current behavior is not just bad for America, though it surely is," he wrote. "It is not even just bad for Israel itself, as many Israelis silently acknowledge. The depressing truth today is that Israel is bad for the Jews." His conclusion: "Israel, in short, is an anachronism, and a dysfunctional anachronism. In the contemporary 'clash of cultures,' between open and pluralist democracies on one side and belligerently intolerant faith-driven ethno states, Israel greatly risks coming down on the wrong side."

When Judt wrote those lines in 2003, he couldn't have imagined that eighteen years later not only was the dysfunctional anachronism of walled-off ethno-nationalism so embedded in the State of Israel that it would be written into its Basic Laws, but that it would be on a vigorous upswing internationally. Nonetheless, his diagnosis of the reactionary character of ethno-national thinking remains more valid than ever.

In Israel's case, the idea put forth by Judt was that this country, created as a refuge for Jews whose lives were persecuted and threatened, had instead become bad for them, turning into a segregationist state that constitutes less a protection for the Jews of the world than a threat to them.

At the time, the idea provoked outraged commentaries. Loyal readers of the *New York Review of Books* threatened to cancel their subscriptions if Judt continued to write for the magazine. *NYRB* editor Robert Silvers refused to back down.

In the United States today, those old polemics seem hopelessly dated, and Judt's proposals exceptionally premonitory. Because a number of Israelis think that Israel in fact has come down on the wrong side, and become an ethnically segregated state through its laws, and especially by its daily practice. Also because a great majority of Israeli Jews unreservedly support the turn Israel has taken in its treatment of the Palestinians as well as the way it views democratic norms within their own country, as this book has tried to show, confirming Judt's prediction about Israel's evolution. As we have seen, more and more Americans, and especially American Jews—some of whom still consider themselves Zionists—also feel that Israel has indeed come down on the wrong side, that its political rightward drift is a calamity, and that the consequences for them could be disastrous. And that explains the anger of those among them who turn their back on Israel.

Why did Israel become "bad for the Jews"? First, by latching on to the emerging power of the new ethnic and authoritarian currents sweeping the planet, by (justly) presenting itself as a precursor and an original theoretician of this move toward separateness, Israel sets the Jews accompanying its destiny on the path to abandoning that which made Judaism's culture and glory in the modern age: the multifaceted engagement in progress, a belief in science over superstition, and a rejection of racism in all its forms.

The relationship to anti-Semitism maintained by Zionism in general and in particular by its extreme right fringe, which has become so influential, is the second reason Israel is bad for diaspora Jews. It denounces anti-Semitism while denying the suffering it itself inflicts on the Palestinians—now an article of faith among Israeli political elites—and, I would add, tries to make the Palestinians into the real instigators of the Holocaust. "The Palestinians are already ignored and their suffering denied," writes Lebanese essayist Dominique Eddé. "Making them invisible has the disastrous effect of pouring fuel on the anti-Semitic fire."[3]

Especially since for Netanyahu, his entourage, and the settler ultranationalists, maintaining an alliance with those countries where anti-Semitism is on the rise is more of a priority than protecting the Jews living there, so long as it helps strengthen the State of Israel. Basically, those Zionists feel that diaspora Jews deserve whatever happens to them. If they wanted to avoid a revival of anti-Semitism, they should have just come to live in Israel. This means that if a wave of anti-Semitism arose tomorrow in the United States, Europe, or elsewhere, and Israel had a close relationship with the regime where that was happening, the Jews there might be abandoned to their fate. This is what happened in Hungary, where, the better to protect Israel's interests, Netanyahu told his ambassador not to get involved when the Jews there were enduring an anti-Semitic campaign.

The Israeli authorities export the Israel-Palestinian conflict wherever they can. Some leaders in the Arab-Muslim space do as well, but at least in the West, Israelis do it with the benefit of a very favorable balance of power. They are trying to drag the world's Jewish communities onto the path of radical Islamophobia while promoting the fraudulent use of the accusation of anti-Semitism and the assimilation of anti-Zionism as the embodiment of modern anti-Semitism. In both cases, the aim is to turn them into weapons to defend the worst policies, and sometimes this is done in ways that are scandalously favorable to the anti-Semites themselves. In short, the Israelis are trying to confine anti-Semitism within the sole Arab-Muslim space, the better to absolve traditional older "white" anti-Semitism. In doing that, Israelis are endangering the Jews who support them, by enlisting them in a racist trend that is sure to turn against them eventually.

Racism isn't divisible. Some people might find the idea politically attractive that a clearly illegitimate racism— anti-Semitism—might exist along with other forms of racism that are more understandable or legitimate (or more cynically useful). But that only leads to disaster. If the Jews who support Israel think that by embracing anti-Arab racism or Islamophobia they are getting on the right side, the winners' side, the side of those who will escape the ill wind brought by this new Western racism, they are wrong. If racism triumphs, they too will be its victims, sooner or later.

It's important to stress that in France these two forms of racism—anti-Semitism on one side, Islamophobia on the other— are minority positions within the two groups concerned, the Jews and the Muslims. But they are clearly on the rise. Muslim anti-Semitism spawns many more serious criminal acts, whereas anti-Arab racism and Islamophobia are more widespread and legitimized in the public space, including unfortunately, in Jewish congregational circles. Perversely, each brand of racism feeds the other, driving people to exclusion and walling themselves in. Frantz Fanon, the French West Indian political philosopher, adopted a line taught him by his philosophy professor: "When you hear people speak ill of the Jews, listen up, they're talking about you"—you, the Blacks. The line still rings true today, and Arabs and Muslims in France would do well to adopt it. But French Jews should also listen up and understand that when people speak ill of Muslims, they're also talking about you. What line did the white supremacist Robert Bowers repost before shooting eleven worshipers at the Pittsburgh synagogue? "Open you [sic] Eyes! It's the filthy EVIL jews Bringing the Filthy EVIL Muslims into the Country!!"[4]

When will the leaders of the French Jewish community and the intellectuals who follow them understand that by opening the doors to the French politicians who rail against the "great replacement" of the white European race, and who make Muslims the principal vector of the fear they feel when contemplating the prospect of an inevitable mixing of white Westerners with other races, they are also helping to spread that old anti-Semite refrain that claims that Jews are the hidden manipulators of a vast plot to degrade the superior race and its culture? When will they understand that if anti-Muslim racism is propagated, it will sooner or later lead to anti-Semitic racism? That is something that young American Jews understand, as they build alliances with the small

U.S. Muslim community, not only because it's seen as a necessity in the fight against racism, but also because it's the best
protection against the spread of anti-Semitism among American Muslims. The reverse is also true. Many American Muslim associations are cultivating connections with Jewish ones.
That is something that French Jewish institutions and their
supporters refuse to even consider. They don't understand
that Islamophobia is an increasingly central component of
the pro-Israeli vulgate and that the Jews that support it are
shooting themselves in the foot.

The divergence between French and American Jews goes
even further. "If French Jews reach the point where they
consider that the Israeli government has to be right, regardless of what it does, where they justify its crimes, then they
are helping to strengthen anti-Semitism," says sociologist
Michel Wieviorka.[5] The sentence may be shocking. But what
do we say of young Muslims in neighborhoods where they
refuse to condemn Islamist crimes because you shouldn't
divide the community, not give weapons to the enemy, et cetera? We would say that they're helping to strengthen Islamophobia, and we would be right. It happens that it's precisely
among those people that you find anti-Semitic Muslims. The
same is true of those congregational Jews who are prepared
to defend Israel's crimes to the bitter end. They are feeding
anti-Semitism, and it's among that group that you mainly
find the Muslim-hating Jews. Israel, by allying itself with the
world's bearers or protectors of racist and xenophobic tendencies, from Trump to Modi by way of Orban, by legitimizing them by the momentary priority of hostility to Muslims,

the latest card to play in the racist game, is doing nothing more than feeding hatred of Jews themselves. Hatred first because Jews will be—and already often are—taken as targets by those ignorant people who conflate Israeli identity with Jewish identity. Hatred also because anti-Muslim racism will inevitably link up with racism in general sooner or later, and with anti-Semitism in particular.

Now we're getting to the third reason why Israel has become bad for the Jews. It's because the fight against anti-Semitism has been discredited by the ideological and interested conjunction between white supremacists in the United States and those nostalgic for the nationalisms of the 1920s and 1930s in Poland, Hungary, Romania, and elsewhere, all of whom historically harbored strong anti-Semitic movements. Who can believe the sincerity of Israeli leaders in fighting anti-Semitism when it takes the form of a miserable manipulation? Supposedly there would be one kind of anti-Semites that you fight (Muslims, Arabs, Iranians, etc.), and another kind that you get along with because you share a common worldview. Meanwhile this utilitarian relationship with anti-Semitism is accompanied by an international effort to make anti-Zionism the contemporary incarnation of anti-Semitism. The aim is to make all international forums adopt the new definition of anti-Semitism propounded by the International Holocaust Remembrance Alliance (IHRA), which, in the guise of banal modifications, has expanded it to include any statement criticizing Israel.

To take just one case, it cites "the refusal of Jews' right to self-determination" as an example of anti-Semitism. Yet it is precisely the right to self-determination of the Jewish people that lies at the heart of Israel's nation-state law. It's a right granted only to Jewish citizens of Israel, and denied to all other citizens, namely those who are Palestinian. In short, it is precisely the subject where you find ethnic segregation between Jewish and Palestinian citizens of the same state. Under the IHRA's definition, rejecting that law would be anti-Semitic. But if anti-Zionism embodies the contemporary form of anti-Semitism, wrote Adam Shatz, "one would be hard pressed to find a Palestinian, or an Arab, or a Muslim, who is not an anti-Semite."[6] That, in fact, is exactly the object of the game.

"Forbidding any criticism of Israeli governments is the objective sought by the IHRA's attempt to have a normative description of anti-Semitism adopted," says Michel Tubiana, president emeritus of Human Rights League of France. "This attempt, sustained by every single member of the organized Jewish communities, along with its desire to criminalize the anti-Zionists' conversation, will do nothing to fight anti-Semitism, but to the contrary will reinforce it. By assimilating a demonstration of intolerable racism to a criticism, however radical, of Israel and its policy, it assimilates all Jews to the latter's misdeeds, and in particular to those it commits against the Palestinian people. If you wanted to draw a line connecting the Jews of France and other countries with the Israeli authorities' racist discourse and dehumanizing practices, you couldn't have done it better."[7]

So Tony Judt's vision was correct. Israel's ethnocentric nature and the policies it pursues, far from forming a barrier to anti-Semitism, can only favor it. When he wrote his article, Judt couldn't anticipate that globalization, led by unchecked financial capitalism, would promote such massive upwellings of identity politics and xenophobia pretty much everywhere, joining the ethnocentric closing-in that Israel had made its own for decades. But that phase will also come to an end, hopefully without our going through a third world war. For a long time, Israel was the beneficiary of a favorable prejudice and a kind of protective impulse, internationally and especially in Western countries. Israel embodied Jewish survival after the Holocaust. But that status is crumbling fast, and the process seems irreversible. To some extent, it's understandable: time passes and the vivid memory of that horrendous crime begins to fade. But the process is also largely fed by the attitude of Israeli leaders and their society, who join in distancing themselves from the Holocaust and denaturing its memory by simply turning it into an instrument of political manipulation.

In an article published in August 2018,[8] sociologist Eva Illouz wrote that she could see two positive results from Israel's damaging self-enclosure and its followers' blindness. First, she hoped that it would gradually make diaspora Jews more independent of Israel. As we have seen, that process is already underway, at least in the United States. Second, it would give Europe a vocation, "that of opposing racism and anti-Semitism in every shape and especially of defending Europe's liberal values for which we, Jews and non-Jews, Zionists and anti-Zionists, have fought so hard. In this fight, alas, Israel is no longer in our side." No, it isn't—if it ever was.

After Gaza

It all began, as it often does, with an Israeli provocation. Emboldened by having their members elected to the Knesset, Kahanists (Jewish religious supremacists), started attacking Palestinians in Jerusalem, yelling, "Death to Arabs!" The police seemed in no hurry to end the fighting. This was spring 2021, during Ramadan. Soon, the police were stopping young Palestinians from entering the area near the Damascus Gate of the Old City, where they had traditionally celebrated the end of their daily fast. The Palestinian mobilization grew. Before long, there were more than three hundred people injured on the Temple Mount and its surroundings.

What followed hewed to a classic scenario. The Palestinians demanded the cancellation of a decision expelling some Palestinian families from an Arab neighborhood of East Jerusalem to make way for Israeli settlers. Hamas then gave Israel twenty-four hours to withdraw its police forces and cancel the families' expulsions. When Israel didn't respond, Hamas hijacked the young Palestinians' revolt by firing missiles into Jerusalem and Tel Aviv. The Israeli army swung into action. Eleven days later, under pressure from the Biden administration, the antagonists signed a cease-fire. Once again, the destruction in Gaza was massive, with twenty times more Palestinians dying than Israelis (232 versus 12). But for Hamas, that was beside the point. In this armed confrontation, Israel appeared to lack any identifiable political purpose beyond the army's goal of asserting its pointless "dissuasion capability." Hamas emerged as the sole representative of Palestinian interests. The Palestinian Authority, missing in action, was discredited in its people's eyes.

More importantly, the confrontation in April and May took on a popular dimension that few observers anticipated. While diplomats and the media were riveted by the images of war, something unique happened. On May 18, a general strike united the Palestinians of the Occupied Territories with those who are citizens of Israel. Successfully led from Jaffa to Ramallah, Nazareth, and Jenin and in innumerable townships, and despite Israeli military and police pressure, the strike gave the day an unprecedented symbolic dimension: Palestinians from the Mediterranean to the Jordan showed that they shared a common destiny. This popular, peaceful mobilization of people enduring a serious crisis of political representation exploded the bet made by Trump, Netanyahu, Mohammed bin Salman, and others, who wanted to believe that the pompous Abraham Accords, the alliance of convenience between Israel and various Arab monarchies, had finally settled the "Palestinian question."

The war pushed Israel into a state of political isolation deeper than ever. True, the White House initially blocked once again any U.N. resolution demanding that Israel stop its bombing. But in the end, after a brief standoff with Netanyahu, Joe Biden imposed a cease-fire on Gaza without Israel's being able to extract the least prior commitment from Hamas. Worse, Israel's image emerged even more tattered in the world's eyes. Here and there, support for Israel began to fissure. In the United States, Biden had to reckon with the surge of support for the Palestinian cause within the Democratic Party that appeared during the crisis. During a visit to Detroit, Biden said to Rashida Tlaib, the Democratic congresswoman of Palestinian origin, "I admire your passion, and I admire your concern for so many other people."[9] In France, Foreign Minister Jean-Yves Le Drian even said "the A-word": apartheid. True, he was merely warning that Israel might run "a strong risk of apartheid" sometime in the future. But the language was unprecedented in French diplomacy.[10]

Diplomats are often slower to evolve than civil society. It's worth remembering here that B'Tselem, the main Israeli human rights association, concluded in January 2021 that Israel was imposing apartheid "from the sea to the Jordan River" (see page 275). In late April, Human Rights Watch published a report that reached exactly the same conclusion.[11] HRW asked the International Criminal Court to open an investigation of Israel for the "crime of apartheid" over its policy of "systematic discrimination against Palestinians." That image now clings to Israel, and the stain will continue to spread as long as the State of Israel pursues its current policy.

From now on, what we can hope for from Jews, whether Israelis or not, is that they stop wearing blindfolds and that they realize that the State of Israel is dragging them into an ethnocentric and monolithic closing-in that, according to Tony Judt, "is rooted in another time."

Acknowledgments

I want to thank sociologist Eva Illouz, who unwittingly gave me the title for this work. On September 19, 2018, she published a long, remarkable article in the Israeli daily *Haaretz* titled "The State of Israel vs. the Jewish People." Both the article's title and the topics it explored corresponded to issues that had been preoccupying me for several years. I don't agree with all of the points of view expressed in the article, but I wholeheartedly subscribe to its central argument: that the kind of nation Israel is becoming and the policy that characterizes it are contrary to the interests of Israeli Jewish citizens and of Jews in general. Eva Illouz not only inspired the book's title, she also granted me an interview at Jerusalem University that proved especially useful.

I also want to thank the following people for their contributions: lawyer Arié Alimi; historian Jean-Christophe Attias (École pratique des hautes études); Yizhar Be'er, president of the Keshev Center for the Protection of Democracy in Israel; sociologist and historian Pierre Birnbaum; Daniel Blatman, professor of Holocaust history at Hebrew University of Jerusalem; senator and historian Esther Benbassa; Jean-Yves Camus, an independent scholar who specializes in the extreme right and French Judaism; astrophysicist Hagai El-Ad, the director of B'Tselem (Jerusalem); film director Anat Even and her husband Roni (Tel Aviv); sociologist Todd Gitlin (Columbia University, New York); journalist J. J. Goldberg, former editor-in-chief of *The Forward* (New York); attorney Sacha Ghozlan, former president of the Union of Jewish Students of France; *Haaretz* journalist Amira Hass (Ramallah); Reform rabbi Delphine Horvilleur; Daniel Kronberg, editor of the *Israel Journal of Mathematics* at Hebrew University of Jerusalem; *Haaretz* journalist Gideon Levy (Tel Aviv); lawyer Eitay Mack (Jerusalem); essayist Michael Massing (New York); Yehudah Mirsky, professor of Judaic studies at Brandeis University (Boston); filmmaker Erez Pery, former director of the Sderot Cinema School; historian Shlomo Sand (Tel Aviv); Pierre Saragoussi, founding president of the Fondation pour la mémoire de la Shoah; essayist and journalist Adam Shatz (New York); Yehuda Shaul, cofounder of Breaking the Silence (Tel Aviv); Harry Siegman, emeritus president of the U.S./Middle East Project; mathematician Kobi Snitz at the Weitzmann Institute of Science (Rehovot); attorney Leah Tsemel, Israeli defender of Palestinian rights (Jerusalem); journalist and historian Dominique Vidal; philosopher and political theorist Michael Walzer at the Institute for Advanced Study (Princeton); anticolonialism activist Michel Warschawski (Jerusalem); Dov Waxman, professor of Israel studies at the University of California, Los Angeles; sociologist Michel Wieviorka (EHESS, Paris); and psychologist Kim Yuval of Tel Aviv University.

As with two of my earlier works, this book owes a great deal to the exceptional welcome afforded me in the United States by Judith and Victor Gurewich. In taking me in, they provided the warmth, calm, and tranquility—and intellectual stimulation—that allowed me to give shape to my ideas. Finally, I want salute the wonderful work done by translator William Rodarmor, whose dedication and good humor made the translation project a pleasure.

—*Sylvain Cypel*

Notes

Preface to the 2024 edition

1. *The State of Israel vs. the Jews* was first published in 2021. This new introduction for the paperback edition was written on January 4, 2024, three months after Hamas's October 7, 2023 attack near the Gaza Strip and the war launched by the Israeli army in response. It was updated in March 2024.

2. "Moshe Dayan's Eulogy for Roi Rutenberg – April 19, 1956." https://www.jewishvirtuallibrary.org/moshe-dayan-s-eulogy-for-roi -rutenberg-april-19-1956. Retrieved February 2, 2024.

3. Hilo Glazer, "The scope of Hamas's campaign of rape against Israeli women is revealed, testimony after testimony," *Haaretz*, November 30, 2023.

4. Brian Finucane, "Is Washington responsible for what Israel does with American weapons?" *Foreign Affairs*, November 17, 2023.

5. Yuval Abraham, "A mass assassination factory: Inside Israel's calculated bombing of Gaza," *+972 Magazine* and *Local Call*, November

30, 2023. The quotes in this and the next paragraph are from that article.

6. "Israel warns Hezbollah war would invite destruction," Reuters and *Yedioth Ahronoth*, October 3, 2008.

7. Abraham, "Mass assassination."

8. "Israel completes 'iron wall' barrier on Gaza border," Agence France-Presse, December 7, 2021.

9. "Netanyahu to Germany's Scholz: 'Hamas the new Nazis,'" Jewish News Syndicate, October 17, 2023.

10. Tovah Lazaroff, "Netanyahu: 'Hamas's Yahya Sinwar is like a little Hitler in his bunker,'" Reuters, November 5, 2023.

11. Mike Godwin is an American attorney and author who created the Internet adage Godwin's law and the notion of an Internet meme.

12. Nir Hasson and Liza Rozovsky, "Hamas committed documented atrocities. But a few false stories feed the deniers," *Haaretz*, December 4, 2023.

13. Hasson and Rozovsky, "Hamas committed documented atrocities."

14. See Cédric Mathiot, Florian Gouthière, and Jacques Pezet, "Un massacre et des mystifications," *Libération*, December 11, 2023.

15. Ben Samuels, "Israel's repulsive embrace of Elon Musk is a betrayal of Jews, dead and alive," *Haaretz*, November 27, 2023.

16. Samuels, "Israel's repulsive embrace."

17. See Jean-Pierre Filiu, *Main basse sur Israël. Nétanyahou et la fin du rêve sioniste*, La Découverte, 2019. The quotes that follow, and that are cited by Filiu, are from two works by Benjamin Netanyahu published by the Jonathan Institute: *International Terrorism: Challenge and Response* (1981) and *Terrorism: How the West Can Win* (1986).

18. Avi Shlaim, "All that remains," *Prospect*, December 6, 2023.

19. Adam Raz, "A brief history of the Netanyahu-Hamas alliance," *Haaretz*, October 20, 2023.

20. Dmitry Shumsky, "Why did Netanyahu want to strengthen Hamas?" *Haaretz*, October 11, 2023.

21. Gideon Levy, "Israel is fostering the next generation of hatred against itself," *Haaretz*, December 7, 2023.

22. Amira Hass, "Huge craters, dead children, collapsed homes: In southern Gaza, there is nowhere to flee," *Haaretz*, December 8, 2023.

23. Yossi Verter, "Israel: A country in trauma, bereft of government," *Haaretz*, October 13, 2023.

24. Haggai Mattar, "How October 7 has changed us all," *+972 Magazine*, November 8, 2023.

25. "Far-right minister: Nuking Gaza is an option, population should 'go to Ireland or deserts,'" *Times of Israel*, November 5, 2023.

26. Quoted in Gideon Levy, "Giora Eiland's monstrous Gaza proposal is evil in plain sight," *Haaretz*, November 23, 2023.

27. "Right now, one goal, Nakba! A Nakba that will overshadow the Nakba of '48," *Middle East Monitor*, October 9, 2023.

28. Ami Spiro, "You want to support Gaza, I'll put you on a bus there," *Times of Israel*, October 18, 2023.

29. Samah Salaime, "For Israeli leaders, every Palestinian citizen has a seat on the bus to Gaza," *+972 Magazine*, October 13, 2023.

30. Rogel Alpher, "The Israelis who no longer buy into 'Having no other country,'" *Haaretz*, November 6, 2023.

31. Maria Fantappie and Vali Nasr, "The war that remade the Middle East," *Foreign Affairs*, November 20, 2023.

32. Nahal Toosi, "U.S. diplomats slam Israel policy in leaked memo," *Politico*, November 6, 2023.

33. Toosi, "U.S. diplomats slam Israel."

34. See the text of the International Convention on the Suppression and Punishment of the Crime of Apartheid, adopted by the United Nations General Assembly on November 30, 1973.

35. Anshel Pfeffer, "Israel isn't committing a genocide, but it has genocidaires," *Haaretz,* January 5, 2024.

36. "Netanyahu defends Israel's unparalleled 'morality' in Gaza war," *Al-Monitor*, December 31, 2023.

37. Emanuel Fabian, "Defense minister announces 'complete siege' of Gaza: no power, food or fuel," *Times of Israel*, October 9, 2023.

38. Chris McGreal, "U.S. opinion divided amid battle for narrative over Hamas attack on Israel," *The Guardian*, October 10, 2023.

39. Mari Cohen, "Progressive Zionists choose a side," *Jewish Currents*, November 11, 2023.

40. Cohen, "Progressive Zionists."

41. Alex Kane, "Building the case of U.S. complicity," *Jewish Currents*, December 5, 2023.

42. "Violent threats across the country disrupt Muslim groups raising support for Palestinians," *PBS NewsHour*, October 20, 2023.

43. Trita Parsi, "Biden can't save America from Trump if he alienates young voters over Gaza," *New Republic*, November 27, 2023.

44. Parsi, "Biden can't save America from Trump."

45. Brian Banco, Nahal Toosi, Alexander Ward, and Matt Berg, *Politico – National Security Daily*, December 14, 2023.

46. Thomas L. Friedman, "The debate that Israel needs over the war," *New York Times*, December 1, 2023.

47. Joost Hiltermann, "No exit from Gaza," *Foreign Affairs*, November 22, 2023.

48. Palestinian Center for Policy and Survey Research, Public Opinion Poll No. (90), December 13, 2023.

49. "The war in Gaza must end." Statement by Martin Griffiths, Under-Secretary-General for Humanitarian Affairs and Emergency Relief Coordinator, January 5, 2024.

50. Amira Hass, "A personal plea from a friend in Gaza," *Haaretz*, December 4, 2023.

Introduction: An unbridgeable hiatus

1. Sylvain Cypel, *Walled: Israeli Society at an Impasse* (New York: Other Press, 2007).

2. Carmi Gillon, interviewed by Sylvain Cypel, "La notion de pressions modérées est sérieuse, pas hypocrite" [The notion of moderate pressures is serious, not hypocritical], *Le Monde*, June 29, 2004.

3. Statement by Netanyahu during a ceremony at the Shimon Peres Negev Nuclear Research Center, Twitter, @IsraeliPM, August 29, 2018. https://twitter.com/israelipm/status/1034849446952091648.

4. Raoul Wootliff, "'Parts of Gaza sent back to Stone Age': Gantz videos laud his IDF bona fides," *Times of Israel*, January 20, 2019.

5. One especially symbolic aspect of this doctrine has been little noted. It explains why massive destruction of civilian neighborhoods is essential to success. It justifies its point of view by the fact that Shia Hezbollah militia moved about like fish in water. But this hides the critical fact that Israel's 2006 war against Lebanon was a political and military failure. Military analysts conceded this at the time, while the general staff did all it could to deny it.

6. Daniel Halbfinger and Isabel Kerchner, "Golan Heights recognition by US sets precedent for annexation, Netanyahu says," *New York Times*, March 26, 2019.

7. "Diplomatic terrorism," *Middle East Monitor*, February 17, 2014.

8. Chemi Shalev, "Pew poll proves Israel's isolation as adoring Trumpland," *Haaretz*, October 2, 2018.

9. Tovah Lazaroff, "There are no innocents in Gaza, says Israeli defense minister," *Jerusalem Post*, April 8, 2018.

10. Thomas Friedman, "Biden made sure 'Trump is not going to be president for four more years,'" *New York Times*, December 3, 2020.

Chapter 1: Imposing Fear, Teaching Contempt

1. ABC News, October 2, 2000.

2. Netta Ahituv, "Endless trip to hell: Israel jails hundreds of Palestinian boys a year," *Haaretz*, March 16, 2019.

3. Ahituv.

4. Gideon Levy, "Die, suffer, you kahba," *Haaretz*, June 4, 2017.

5. Amira Hass, "An apology to Elor Azaria," *Haaretz*, April 15, 2019.

6. Author interview, January 7, 2019.

7. Author interview, January 3, 2019.

8. Breaking the Silence (BtS) is covered in Chapter 6, "BtS, the enemy within."

9. Author interview, January 6, 2019. The quotes in this paragraph and the next two are from Yehuda Shaul.

10. The quotes in this paragraph are from the article "Israeli capriciousness as I witnessed it at the Bethlehem checkpoint," *Haaretz*, November 25, 2018.

11. Amira Hass, "Rosa Luxemburg's specter in a Palestinian refugee camp," *Haaretz*, June 4, 2019.

12. Amira Hass, "Everyone knows settlers cut down Palestinian olive trees. But Israel doesn't care," *Haaretz*, November 5, 2018.

13. Michael Sfard, "The flourishing of the Jewish KKK," *Haaretz*, December 25, 2018.

14. Gush Emunim (Bloc of the Faithful) was formed by a group of rabbis and youth leaders from the religious-Zionist party after Israel's June 1967 conquest of the West Bank, Gaza, and the Golan Heights. It pushed for the annexation and settlement of Palestinian territory in the name of Greater Israel. That is based on the idea that the sanctified Land of Israel was given by God to his Chosen People. Gush Emunim was formally organized in 1974. It no longer exists officially, but its leaders are active in the right-wing settler movement.

15. Statements like these are unfortunately all too common. Among the most notorious are those by the Lubavitcher rabbi Yitzchak Ginsburgh. In a long interview published in the Hebrew-language *Maariv* on October 20, 2000, he declared that "The Arab has very little intelligence, and an animal nature."

16. Shabtay Bendet, "I was a settler. I know how settlers become killers," *Haaretz*, January 30, 2019.

17. Bendet.

18. Audrey Duperron, "Pourquoi Israël est un modèle en matière de lutte contre le terrorisme" [Why Israel is a model in the war on terrorism], *L'Express*, July 18, 2016.

19. David Shulman, "Israel's Irrational Rationality," *New York Review of Books*, June 22, 2017.

20. Amira Hass, "Israel conducts mass psychological experiment on Gaza," *Haaretz*, August 15, 2018.

Chapter 2: Pissing in the Pool from the Diving Board

1. Anat Even, *Disappearances*, Rouge Productions, 2017.

2. Yotam Berger, "Declassified: Israel made sure Arabs couldn't return to their villages," *Haaretz*, May 27, 2019.

3. Author interview, January 7, 2019.

4. Interview with Elor Azaria, *Times of Israel*, August 29, 2018: "I did the right thing."

5. Author interview, January 6, 2019.

6. Gideon Levy, "Israeli soldiers who beat detained Palestinians are part of a bigger evil," *Haaretz*, March 12, 2019.

7. Shlomi Eldar, "Israeli activists call out military academy for messianic teachings," *Al-Monitor*, October 22, 2018.

8. Eldar.

9. Author interview, January 7, 2019.

10. Amira Hass, "Miracle in Judeostan," *Haaretz*, July 10, 2018.

11. Hass.

12. Chen Shalita, "Carmi Gillon: the occupation is destroying us and you can see that in short clips," *Globes*, April 18, 2015. In Hebrew.

13. Abi Kaufman, "'She just wants chocolate! What is she, an Arab?,'" *+972 Magazine*, February 22, 1015, https://www.972mag.com/she-just-wants-chocolate-what-is-she-an-arab/103037/.

14. David Shulman, "Israel's irrational rationality," *New York Review of Books,* June 22, 2017.

15. Shai Stern, "Cease-fire in East Jerusalem," uploaded July 15, 2014, YouTube video, 5:14, https://www.youtube.com/watch?v=VF4V2huxDqM. In Hebrew.

16. "Settlement fires school's Israeli Arab cleaning staff after threats from parents," *Times of Israel*, February 16, 2019.

17. Avner Faingulernt and Macabit Abramson, *War Matador*, JMT Films, 2011.

18. "Israeli soldier, prison guard acquitted in death of asylum-seekers they mistook for terrorist," *Haaretz*, July 20, 2020.

19. "Arab MK ejected for insulting police chief," *Times of Israel*, July 14, 2014.

20. Kach is the Hebrew acronym of *Kahane chai,* which means "Kahane lives."

21. Piotr Smolar, "Le sombre pacte de Nétanyahou avec l'extrême droite" [Netanyahu's dark pact with the extreme right], *Le Monde,* March 3, 2019.

22. "Why Is Israel's Justice Minister in an Ad for 'Fascism' Perfume?" *New York Times,* March 19, 2019, https://www.nytimes.com/2019/03/19/world/middleeast/ayelet-shaked-perfume-ad.html.

23. Josh Nathan-Kazis, "Sheldon Adelson's dismissal of Israeli democracy draws silence from groups he backs," *The Forward,* November 12, 2014.

24. *Jerusalem Post,* "'Cut the bullshit,' Israeli Culture minister Miri Regev tells liberals," uploaded March 6, 2016, YouTube video, 0:24, https://www.youtube.com/watch?v=SNg5v8BqTdw.

25. "Israel's minister of incitement," *Haaretz,* November 20, 2012.

26. Harriet Sherwood, "Israeli minister inflames racial tensions," *The Guardian,* May 31, 2012.

27. Gilad Sharon, "A decisive conclusion is necessary," *Jerusalem Post,* November 18, 2012.

28. "Smotrich: Peretz enduring 'lynch' over remarks in support of conversion therapy," *Times of Israel,* July 14, 2019.

29. For details of the Duma firebombing, see Chapter 1, "The flourishing of a Jewish Ku Klux Klan."

30. Ravit Hecht, "The face of Israel's far right wants to 'abort' Palestinian hope," *Haaretz,* December 3, 2016.

Chapter 3: But What's Your Blood?

1. "Benjamin Netanyahu says Israel 'Is not the state of all its citizens,'" *The Guardian,* March 10, 2019.

2. In 2000, an Israeli Palestinian couple named Kaadan tried to buy a lot in the new town of Katzir. When the city hall turned them down, they appealed, eventually to the Supreme Court, whose ruling said, "The Court examined whether the State may allocate land directly to its citizens on the basis of religion or nationality. The answer is no. As a general rule, the principle of equality prohibits the State from distinguishing between its citizens on the basis of religion or nationality."

3. Revital Hovel, "Justice minister: Israel must keep Jewish majority, even at the expense of human rights," *Haaretz*, February 13, 2018.

4. Revital Hovel, "Justice minister slams Israel's top court. Says it disregards Zionism and upholding Jewish majority," *Haaretz*, August 29, 2017.

5. "Rivlin: 'Nation-state law is bad for Israel,'" *Ynet*, September 5, 2018. Also: "Rivlin says Jewish Nation-state law 'bad for Israel and the Jewish people,'" *Times of Israel*, September 6, 2018. In an open letter concerning the most controversial paragraph of the law, which authorized a community to refuse to allow a non-Jew to live among them, Israel's president wrote that this law "could harm the Jewish people worldwide and in Israel, and would be used as a weapon by our enemies." From Jonathan Lis, "'Could Harm Jews': Israeli president warns Jewish-only communities undermine Zionist vision," *Haaretz*, October 7, 2018.

6. Gideon Levy, "A law that tells the truth about Israel," *Haaretz*, July 12, 2018.

7. David Shulman, "The last of the Tzaddiks," *New York Review of Books*, June 28, 2018.

8. Philippe Sands, *East West Street: On the Origins of "Genocide" and "Crimes against Humanity"* (New York: Alfred A. Knopf, 2016).

9. Amira Hass, "Shin Bet holds German at Israeli border: 'Your Blood isn't German, it's Palestinian,'" *Haaretz*, August 26, 2018.

10. Revital Hovel, "Israeli hospitals admit to segregating Jewish and Arab women in maternity wards," *Haaretz*, April 27, 2019.

11. Hovel.

12. Noa Shpigel, "Hundreds of Israelis demonstrate against home sale to Arab family," *Haaretz*, June 13, 2018.

13. Judy Maltz, "More Israelis are coming out as anti-Arab, activists warn, with politicians setting the tone," *Haaretz*, June 22, 2018.

14. Maltz.

15. Maltz.

16. Maltz.

17. Almog Ben Zikri, "Israeli plan against 'illegal and hostile Bedouins constructions' falsifies data," *Haaretz*, June 6, 2018.

18. Judy Maltz, "More Israelis are coming out as anti-Arab, activists warn, with politicians setting the tone," *Haaretz*, June 22, 2018.

19. Sylvain Cypel, "J'entre au gouvernement pour qu'Ariel Sharon ne s'arrête pas au milieu du gué" [I am joining the government so Ariel Sharon doesn't stop midstream], *Le Monde*, April 7, 2002.

20. Dina Kraft, "Haaretz poll: 42% of Israelis back West Bank annexation, including two-state supporters," *Haaretz*, March 25, 2019.

21. Following the 1993 Oslo Accords and subsequent agreements between the Israeli government and the Palestine Liberation Organization, the territory of the West Bank was divided into three categories. This has produced a confusing patchwork of lands, where adjoining properties might be under two different administrations. The three categories are:

- Zone A, under sole Palestinian control (13 percent of the West Bank land area)
- Zone B, under civilian Palestinian authority, but Israeli security (24 percent)
- Zone C, under sole Israeli control (63 percent)

Some 90 percent of Palestinians live in Zones A and B. Only 10 percent remain in Zone C.

22. Efrat Forsher, "Right-wing officials commit to plan to settle 2 million Jews in Judea and Samaria," *Israel Hayom*, February 5, 2019.

23. Carolina Landsmann, "How Israeli right-wing thinkers envision the annexation of the West Bank," *Haaretz*, 18 August 2018. The following four paragraphs are based on that article.

24. Jack Khoury, "Israeli minister: Arabs are guests here. For now," *Haaretz*, October 4, 2019.

25. Author interview, January 7, 2019.

26. Hagar Shezaf: "Israel's High Court strikes down West Bank land-grab law as 'unconstitutional,'" *Haaretz*, June 9, 2020.

27. Shezaf.

28. Author interview, January 3, 2019.

Chapter 4: This Country Belongs to the White Man

1. Interview with Eli Yichai, *Maariv*, June 4, 2012.

2. It is estimated that besides the 40,000 undocumented African refugees in Israel (they once numbered as many as 65,000, before a third were expelled from the country), there were 40,000 immigrants with visas—mainly Eastern Europeans, but also Filipinos, Thais, Chinese, and Turks. There was also another 90,000, mostly Europeans, who overstayed their visas but were not being pursued; and finally 20,000 West Bank Palestinians married to Israeli Palestinian citizens, for whom Israeli citizenship was denied, and who were therefore living illegally in Israel.

3. Gershom Gorenberg, "Is Israel betraying its history by expelling African asylum-seekers?" *Washington Post*, January 29, 2018.

4. Harriet Sherwood, "Israel PM: Illegal African immigrants threaten identity of the Jewish state," *The Guardian*, May 20, 2012.

5. "Israeli MP Miri Regev says African migrants 'are a cancer in our body' at Tel Aviv protest," *Huffington Post*, May 25, 2012.

6. Tomer Zarchin and Ilan Lior, "Hundreds demonstrate in south Tel Aviv against illegal migrants," *Haaretz*, May 23, 2012.

7. Brian Goldstone, "No shelter in the land of last refuge," *New Republic*, June 26, 2018.

8. Isabel Kershner, "Israel offers African migrants a choice: ticket out or jail," *The New York Times*, January 4, 2018.

9. Hagai Amit, "As Israel deports asylum-seekers, it imports thousands of foreign workers," *Haaretz*, February 5, 2018.

10. Michael Sfard, interviewed by David B. Green, "For an Israeli lawyer fighting for Palestinian rights, winning is a double-edged sword," *Haaretz*, January 28, 2018.

11. Stephen Miller's racism was so notorious that the Anti-Defamation League, the main American association in the fight against anti-Semitism, and the Union for Reform Judaism, the largest Jewish movement in North America, once asked Trump to bar a man whom they said "promoted hate speech spewed from neo-Nazis, bigots, and white supremacists" from his White House team. "Jewish groups join letter demanding ouster of Stephen Miller for white supremacist views," *Jewish Telegraphic Agency*, November 20, 2019.

12. "Richard Spencer compares his white supremacy to Zionism," *Jewish Telegraphic Agency*, August 17, 2017.

13. Amir Tibon, "Trump envoy Greenblatt condemns Israeli rabbis' remarks that endorsed racism, Hitler," *Haaretz*, May 1, 2019.

14. Nathan Thrall, "How the battle over Israel and anti-Semitism is fracturing American politics," *New York Times Magazine*, March 28, 2019.

15. Sara Yael Hirschhorn, *City on a Hilltop: American Jews and the Israeli Settler Movement* (Cambridge: Harvard University Press, 2017).

16. Barak Ravid, "Netanyahu: 'We'll surround Israel with fences to defend ourselves against wild beasts,'" *Haaretz*, February 9, 2016.

17. Gil Stern Hoffman and Shuly Wasserstrom, "MKs slam Netanyahu over his son dating a non-Jewish Norwegian woman," *Jerusalem Post*, January 26, 2014.

18. Salman Masalha, "Outcry over Israeli-Arab intermarriage exposes the racist truth about Israel," *Haaretz*, October 19, 2018.

19. Harry Ostrer, *Legacy: A Genetic History of the Jewish People* (Oxford: Oxford University Press, 2012).

20. Richard Lewontin, "Is there a Jewish gene?" *New York Review of Books*, December 6, 2012.

21. Sylvain Cypel, "A la poursuite du 'gène juif'" [In search of the "Jewish gene"], *Revue XXI*, April 2015.

22. Eva Jablonka and Marion J. Lamb, *Evolution in Four Dimensions: Genetic, Epigenetic, Behavioral, and Symbolic Variation in the History of Life* (Cambridge: MIT Press, 2005).

23. Author interview, October 17, 2014.

24. Noah Slepkov, "Israel's rabbis think genetic testing can 'prove' Jewishness. They're wrong," *Haaretz*, April 29, 2019.

Chapter 5: Locate. Track. Manipulate.

1. "Israel's dirty arms deals with Myanmar," *Haaretz*, August 29, 2018.

2. John Brown, "Rights groups demand Israel stop arming neo-Nazis in Ukraine," *Haaretz*, July 9, 2018.

3. Stockholm International Peace Research Institute report, March 11, 2019.

4. According to the Statistical Abstract of Israel, 2019, more than 6.7 million Palestinians were living in Mandatory Palestine territory in 2018: 3 million in the West Bank, more than 1.9 million in Israel proper, and more than 1.8 million in the Gaza Strip. (In 2019, the Jewish population was 6.8 million.)

5. Actually, three million Palestinians live in the West Bank. See previous note.

6. Yuval Noah Harari, interviewed by Piotr Smolar, "On pourra bientôt pirater les êtres humains" [Soon we'll be able to hack human beings], *Le Monde*, September 19, 2018.

7. Hagar Shezaf and Jonathan Jacobson, "Revealed: Israel's cyber-spy industry helps world dictators hunt dissidents and gays," *Haaretz*, October 20, 2018.

8. Thomas Brewster, "Everything we know about NSO Group, the professional spies who hacked iPhones with a single text," *Forbes*, August 25, 2016.

9. Hagar Shezaf and Jonathan Jacobson, "Revealed: Israel's cyber-spy industry helps world dictators hunt dissidents and gays," *Haaretz*, October 20, 2018.

10. Chaim Levinson, "With Israel's encouragement, NSO sold spyware to UAE and other Gulf states," *Haaretz*, August 23, 2020.

11. Shezaf and Jacobson.

12. Shezaf and Jacobson.

13. Shezaf and Jacobson.

14. "Israel claims 200 attacks predicted, prevented with data tech," the Associated Press, June 12, 2018.

15. BDS activities are detailed in Chapter 6, "BDS, the strategic threat."

16. Amitai Ziv, "Top secret Israeli cyberattack firm, revealed," *Haaretz*, January 4, 2019.

17. Isaac Zack was one of NSO's first partners. He also sits on the boards of several Israeli cybersecurity companies, including Cy-oT and Orchestra.

18. Author interview, January 8, 2019. Unless otherwise noted, the quotes in this and the next two paragraphs are from that interview.

19. Hagar Shezaf and Jonathan Jacobson, "Revealed: Israel's cyber-spy industry helps world dictators hunt dissidents and gays," *Haaretz*, October 20, 2018.

20. Andrew Ferguson, a professor at University of the District of Columbia David A. Clarke School of Law, is the author of *The Rise of Big Data Policing: Surveillance, Race, and the Future of Law Enforcement* (New York: New York University Press, 2017). He writes that Israel has been able to lead the way in developing population surveillance largely because other countries face resistance from organizations that defend public freedoms, whereas Israel's state apparatus faces far fewer constraints.

21. Gur Megiddo, "'His Highness asks': Did Saudis try to enlist former Israeli PM Barak to buy cyberattack technology?" *Haaretz*, November 28, 2018.

22. Amos Harel, Chaim Levinson, and Yaniv Kubovicvh, "Israeli cyber firm negotiated advanced attack capabilities sale with Saudis," *Haaretz*, November 25, 2018.

23. Harel, Levinson, and Kubovicvh.

24. "Israeli tech helped Saudis kill journalist, Snowden tells Tel Aviv confab," *Times of Israel*, November 7, 2018.

25. Adam Entous and Ronan Farrow, "Private Mossad for hire," *The New Yorker*, February 18 and 25, 2019.

26. Psy-Group stopped its operations when special prosecutor Robert Mueller included the company in his investigation into possible manipulation of the 2016 presidential election.

27. Gur Megiddo, "Black Cube CEO suspected of running crime organization. Revealed: the Romania interrogation," *Haaretz*, October 26, 2020.

28. Adam Entous and Ronan Farrow, "Private Mossad for hire," *The New Yorker*, February 18 and 25, 2019.

29. See Barak Ravid, "Israeli ministry trying to compile a database of citizens who support BDS," *Haaretz*, March 3, 2017.

30. Uri Blau, "Inside the clandestine world of Israel's 'BDS-busting' ministry," *Haaretz*, March 26, 2017.

31. Blau.

32. Blau.

33. Jeff Halper, "Europe must not buy what Israel is selling to combat terror," *Haaretz*, August 20, 2017.

Chapter 6: The Shin Bet State Is Here

1. Lahav Harkov, "Israeli minister: 'Belgians who continue to eat chocolate and enjoy life can't fight terror,'" *The Jerusalem Post*, March 23, 2016.

2. Jeff Halper, "Europe must not buy what Israel is selling to combat terror," *Haaretz*, August 20, 2017.

3. Guy Laron, *The Six-Day War: The Breaking of the Middle East* (New Haven: Yale University Press, 2017).

4. Quoted by Gideon Levy, "It's even allowed to hate Israel," *Haaretz*, October 7, 2018.

5. Editorial, "The Shin Bet state is here," *Haaretz*, August 8, 2018.

6. B'Tselem, "Hagai El-Ad's address at the United Nations Security Council," October 18, 2018.

7. Editorial, "In Israel, it's loyalty or culture," *Haaretz*, October 21, 2018.

8. "Book nixed for 'intermarriage' fears flies off the shelves," *Times of Israel*, December 31, 2015. Am Oved published the book in Hebrew as

Gader Chaya [Living fence] in May 2014. It has been adapted into a play at the Cameri Theater in Tel Aviv.

9. Jonathan Lis, "Ministers to discuss bill granting immunity for actions taken during security operations," *Haaretz*, November 15, 2018.

10. Entsar Abu Jahal, "Palestinians outraged at Israeli bill to ban filming of IDF," *Al-Monitor*, June 5, 2018.

11. Author interview, January 7, 2019.

12. Breaking the Silence, *Our Harsh Logic: Israeli Soldiers' Testimonies from the Occupied Territories, 2000–2010* (New York: Metropolitan Books, 2011).

13. Author interview, January 6, 2019.

14. Author interview, January 6, 2019.

15. Peter Beaumont, "Israel sunk in 'incremental tyranny,' say former Shin Bet chiefs," *The Guardian*, April 6, 2017.

16. U.N. Resolution 3068, November 30, 1973. International Criminal Court, Rome Status, 17 July 1998, in force on 1 July 2002, United Nations, Treaty Series, vol. 2187, No. 38544, article 7-h.

17. Reuters, "Pompeo says to mark settlement goods as 'Made in Israel,'" November 20, 2020.

18. BBC News, "Airbnb reverses ban on West Bank settlement listings," April 10, 2019, https://www.bbc.com/news/world-middle-east-47881163.

19. Chaim Levinson and Barak Ravid, "Israel secretly using U.S. law firm to fight BDS activists in Europe, North America," *Haaretz*, October 25, 2017.

20. Anshel Pfeffer, "Israel's ministry of silly affairs," *Haaretz*, October 11, 2018.

21. Nathan Thrall, "BDS: How a controversial non-violent movement has transformed the Israeli-Palestinian debate," *The Guardian*, August 14, 2018.

22. Thrall.

23. Toward the end of his life, David Kimche (1928–2010) became a strong proponent of returning the Occupied Territories. After being an apostle for and a major player in Israeli power for decades, in 2003 he supported the Geneva Accord. This informal text suggested ways for Israel to withdraw from practically all of the Occupied Territories, leaving two states with capitals both in Jerusalem. Too late, Kimche aligned himself with such former intelligence chiefs as ex–Shin Bet director Ami Ayalon, who saw the light after leaving the service.

24. Gideon Levy, "Hurray for Airbnb," *Haaretz*, November 22, 2018.

25. "Israel to expel human rights director for 'actively supporting' BDS," *Times of Israel*, May 9, 2018.

26. "'You won't see your kids for a long time.' Reza Aslan reveals he was detained by Shin Bet at Israeli border," *Haaretz*, August 14, 2018.

27. On May 31, 2016, the IDF intervened to prevent a flotilla of eight ships carrying nearly seven hundred passengers, humanitarian aid, and construction material from reaching Gaza from the sea. Land access to the territory had long been blocked by Israel and Egypt.

28. Yotam Berger, "For second time in a month, Shin Bet detained left-wing activist at Ben-Gurion Airport," *Haaretz*, June 10, 2018.

29. For details on the emptying of Khan al-Ahmar, see Chapter 2, "The meaning of the Azaria affair."

30. Judy Maltz, "Saved from deportation, Jewish-American activist approved for Israeli citizenship," *Haaretz*, November 18, 2018.

31. Noa Landau, "U.S. member of the Jewish-Arab NGO questioned, separated from luggage at Israel's airport," *Haaretz*, April 16, 2019.

32. Laudau.

33. Peter Beinart, "I was detained at Ben-Gurion Airport because of my beliefs," *The Forward*, August 13, 2018.

34. Jonathan Lis, "Israel's travel ban: Knesset bars entry to foreigners who call for boycott of Israel or settlements," *Haaretz*, March 7, 2017.

35. Lis.

36. Noa Landau, "Ex–Shin Bet chief on questioning of foreigners at Israel's borders: Shin Bet becoming a problem," *Haaretz*, October 5, 2018.

Chapter 7: A Species on the Verge of Extinction

1. Chemi Shalev, "Is Israel's anti-BDS detention policy stupid, evil—or both?" *Haaretz*, October 14, 2018.

2. Wikipedia: "A court of cassation is a high-instance court that exists in some judicial systems. Courts of cassation do not reexamine the facts of the case; they only interpret the relevant law…[They] differ from systems which have a supreme court which can rule on both the facts of the case and the relevant law. The term derives from the Latin *cassare*, 'to reverse/overturn.'"

3. Since 1967, some 100,000 Palestinians in the Occupied Territories have experienced administrative detentions. In contrast, the number of Jews interned administratively in all of Israel's history can be counted on the fingers of two hands. The most recent case is that of Mordechai Mayer, a settler arrested in August 2015 and suspected of setting fire to the house of a Palestinian couple, killing them and their baby. Mayer and three of his accomplices were released five months later. The true killers were other settlers, who were found shortly thereafter. One of them, Amiram Ben-Uliel, was convicted of murder on May 18, 2020.

4. *TOI* staff and Susan Surkes, "High court rejects petition against evacuation of 700 East Jerusalem residents," *Times of Israel*, August 22, 2018. The full decision is at https://supremedecisions.court.gov.il/, November 21, 2018.

5. "Greenlighting East-Jerusalem eviction attests to revolution in Israel's Supreme Court," *Haaretz*, November 22, 2018.

6. Israel does not have a written constitution, and is ruled by fourteen Basic Laws. See the Knesset, "Basic Laws," https://main.knesset.gov.il/en/activity/pages/basiclaws.aspx.

7. Michael Sfard, *The Wall and the Gate: Israel, Palestine, and the Legal Battle for Human Rights* (New York: Metropolitan Books, 2018).

8. See for example the interview with Michael Sfard in "The law is what keeps the edifice of occupation from crashing down," *+972 Magazine*, June 22, 2018. "The occupation is built on three cornerstones: the gun, the settlement, and the law. The law is what props up the edifice of occupation and prevents it from crashing down. It allows it to confront problems that would weaken it, and to a certain degree it prevents it from going mad."

9. Starting in 1991, Israel began annexing land belonging to Bil'in, a Palestinian village next to the Green Line, the 1967 borders. In 2006 the villagers launched nonviolent demonstrations against the land seizures and the Israeli "security wall" built on their land. The struggle became emblematic, and a number of Israeli pacifists joined it. In 2007 the Supreme Court ordered the IMF to change the route of the wall to avoid some of the expropriations.

10. In 2002, Israel began to build a wall around the West Bank, calling it a "security" or "separation" barrier—"the apartheid wall," to Palestinians—that cuts across Palestinian territory, enclosing Palestinians and their townships. In 2003, the United Nations condemned the wall's route by a vote of 144 to 4. In 2004, the International Court of Justice declared it "contrary to international law."

11. B'tselem, *Fake Justice: The Responsibility Israel's High Court Justices Bear for the Demolition of Palestinian Homes and the Dispossession of Palestinians*, February 6, 2019.

12. B'tselem.

13. Mordechai Kremnitzer, "Shin Bet harassment of left-wing activists serves political interests — and not for the first time," *Haaretz*, August 16, 2018.

14. Kremnitzer.

15. Versa, Opinions of the Supreme Court of Israel, HCJ 5239/11, *Avneri v. Knesset*, April 15, 2015.

16. Lara Friedman, "A defeat for Israel, a victory for settlers and BDS," *Haaretz*, April 19, 2015.

17. Nir Hassan, "Israel's AG: Absentee properties in East Jerusalem can be confiscated," *Haaretz*, June 5, 2013.

18. Mordechai Kremnitzer, "Israeli Arab poet's sentencing proves Israel has separate laws for Arabs and Jews," *Haaretz*, August 1, 2018.

19. Amira Hass, "A question for Leah Tsemel," *Haaretz*, July 16, 2019.

20. Sfard, 62.

21. Ravit Hecht, "The Israeli lawyer who defends the most violent fighters against the occupation," *Haaretz*, May 25, 2019.

22. David Shulman, "The last of the Tzaddiks," *New York Review of Books*, June 28, 2018.

23. Nir Hasson, "Hasidic Jews attack Palestinian teens in Jerusalem; police arrest Arab who called for help," *Haaretz*, October 11, 2018.

24. Author interview, January 6, 2019.

25. Author interview, January 3, 2019.

26. Author interview, January 3, 2019.

27. Author interview, January 3, 2019.

28. Statement at the iRcMMO conference, "Democracy and Freedoms in Israel," the Senate, Paris, June 17, 2019.

29. "Don't fire the teacher. Jail him," Arutz Sheva, September 2, 2015.

30. Yarden Skop, "Controversial teacher Adam Verete fired due to budget cuts," *Haaretz*, May 6, 2014.

31. Author interview, January 4, 2019.

32. Tibi first used the expression in 2000, and has often repeated it since. On CNN, for example: "Ahmed Tibi: Israel is democratic toward Jews and Jewish toward Arabs," CNN live, December 1, 2014.

33. Statement made on the ITC network, October 5, 2019.

34. Shraga Blum, "Doudou Elharar: 'Juguler l'antisionisme des artistes'" [Dudu Elharar: Curbing artists' anti-Zionism], Juif.org, March 10, 2010.

35. Gideon Levy, "It's not Netanyahu, it's the nation," *Haaretz*, April 5, 2018.

36. Levy.

37. Author interview, January 6, 2019.

38. Author interview, January 4, 2019.

39. Yaniv Sagee, "To protest loudly," *Times of Israel*, August 8, 2018.

40. Jacques Mandelbaum, "Nadav Lapid, le cinéma pour patrie" [Nadav Lapid, cinema is his country], *Le Monde*, March 27, 2019.

41. *Le Monde*, March 17, 2015.

42. Itay Tiran, "BDS is a legitimate form of resistance," *Haaretz*, September 5, 2018. Tiran's quotes in the following paragraphs come from this article.

Chapter 8: Hitler Didn't Want to Exterminate the Jews

1. Nicholas Fandos and Mark Landler, "Sean Spicer raises outcry with talk of Hitler, Assad and poison gas," *New York Times*, April 11, 2017.

2. "Netanyahu says Muslim leader convinced Hitler to kill Jewish people," Reuters, October 21, 2015.

3. "Netanyahu: Hitler didn't want to exterminate the Jews," *Haaretz*, October 21, 2015.

4. In *The Destruction of the European Jews* (New York: Holmes & Meier, 1985), Raul Hilberg estimates the number at 1.4 million.

5. Christopher Browning, "A lesson for Netanyahu from a real Holocaust historian," *Foreign Policy*, October 22, 2015. Browning is the author of *Ordinary Men: Reserve Police Battalion 101 and the Final Solution in Poland* (New York: HarperCollins, 1992).

6. "Top analyses and opinions about Netanyahu's controversial claims about Hitler and the Mufti," *Haaretz*, October 22, 2015.

7. Anshel Pfeffer, "The Mufti speech reveals Netanyahu's twisted view of Zionism," *Haaretz*, October 22, 2015.

8. Browning.

9. Anwar Sadat was a republican army officer hostile to the monarchy and Britain's occupation of Egypt. Driven by anti-British nationalism, he occasionally worked as an agent for German intelligence services.

10. Reported by Aryeh Naor, Menachem Begin's private secretary at the time, the line has been repeated in many publications. See, for example, Avraham Burg, *The Holocaust Is Over; We Must Rise from Its Ashes* (New York: St. Martin's Press, 2008), 57.

11. Gideon Levy, "On this Holocaust Remembrance Day, let us forget," *Haaretz*, May 2, 2019.

12. Levy.

13. Kapos, some of whom were Jewish, assisted SS guards in the death camps. Nearly all of them were killed along with the others.

14. Mazal Mualem, "Israel's tribal wars veer out of control," *Al-Monitor*, January 26, 2018.

15. Menachem Rosensaft, "Israeli settlers use Nazi imagery against Jews," *Tablet*, February 18, 2015.

16. See *Walled: Israeli Society at an Impasse,* by Sylvain Cypel (New York: Other Press, 2007), in particular Chapter 15, "The hidden plot of our lives," 411–44.

17. Author interview, January 3, 2019. Erez Pery is the director of *The Interrogation* (2016), a film based on the interrogation of Auschwitz commandant Rudolph Höss that was conducted by Poland's Supreme National Tribune, as well as the memoir Höss wrote. He was executed by hanging in 1947.

18. Benjamin Netanyahu, *A Durable Peace: Israel and Its Place Among the Nations* (New York: Warner Books, 1995).

19. The "common target" line is quoted by Chemi Shalev in his article "Is Israel's anti-BDS detention policy stupid, evil—or both?" *Haaretz,* October 14, 2018.

20. Shalev.

21. Among many reports, see David Jackson, "Post Pittsburgh shooting: Trump blames media for 'anger,' singles out CNN as 'fake news.'" *USA Today,* October 29, 2018.

22. Quoted by Peter Beinart in "How Trumpian nativism leads to anti-Semitism," *The Atlantic,* November 2, 2018.

23. See, for example, "Torch-wielding white nationalists clash with counterprotesters at UVA," *Daily Beast,* August 12, 2017.

24. "Echoing Trump, Israeli ambassador Dermer blames 'both sides' for anti-Semitism," *Haaretz,* October 29, 2018.

25. Sylvain Cypel, "Les tribulations des chrétiens américains en Israël" [American Christians' tribulations in Israel], *Le Monde,* December 16, 2002.

26. Joshua Cohen, "Israel's season of discontent," *New Republic* special edition on American Judaism, "A diaspora divided," September 6, 2018.

27. Nathan Thrall, "How the battle over Israel and anti-Semitism is fracturing American politics," *New York Times Magazine,* March 28, 2019.

28. Following his trial in Jerusalem, Eichmann was condemned to death and executed on May 31, 1962.

29. Ofer Aderet, "Ex-Mossad agent who helped capture Eichmann backs far right German party as 'great hope,'" *Haaretz*, February 3, 2018.

30. The national poets are those who were already publishing at the time of the 1948 War of Independence.

31. See Dan Tamir, *Hebrew Fascism in Palestine, 1922–1942* (London: Palgrave Macmillan, 2018).

32. Tom Heneghan, "Europe far-right courts Israel in anti-Islam drive," Reuters, December 20, 2010.

33. Author interview, January 4, 2019.

34. Claire Gatinois, "Brézil: les fantômes du nazisme hantent le gouvernement de Bolsonaro" [Brazil: Nazi ghosts haunt Bolsonaro's government], *Le Monde*, February 4, 2019.

35. "Duterte, qui s'était comparé à Hitler, visite le mémorial de la Shoah" [Duterte, who had compared himself to Hitler, visits the Holocaust memorial], *Le Figaro*, September 3, 2018.

36. Francesca Trivellato, *The Promise and Peril of Credit: What a Forgotten Legend about Jews and Finance Tells Us about the Making of European Commercial Society* (Princeton: Princeton University Press, 2019).

37. See Jacob Soll, "The making of an anti-Semitic myth," *New Republic*, April 10, 2019.

38. AFP, July 9, 2017. See also Barak Ravid, "Israel urges Hungarian prime minister to take down Soros campaign with anti-Semitic overtones," *Haaretz*, July 9, 2017.

39. Barak Ravid, "On Netanyahu's order, Israel's foreign ministry retracts criticism of anti-Semitism in Hungary and slams George Soros," *Haaretz*, July 10, 2017.

40. Matti Friedman, "What happens when a Holocaust memorial plays host to autocrats," *New York Times Magazine*, December 8, 2018.

41. Author interview, January 4, 2019.

42. See Jewish Telegraphic Agency, "Holocaust scholar Yehuda Bauer slams Israel's détente with Poland," July 4, 2018. See also Ofer Aderet, "Top Holocaust historian: Netanyahu's deal on Poland's Holocaust law 'a betrayal' that 'hurts the Jewish people,'" *Haaretz*, July 30, 2018.

43. Anshel Pfeffer, "With Poland, Netanyahu discovers the limits of playing with history," *Haaretz*, February 18, 2019.

44. Alex Eichler, "Was Glenn Beck's George Soros takedown anti-Semitic?" *The Atlantic*, November 12, 2010.

45. Larry Cohler-Esses, "George Soros described by Hungary as 'Satan' seeking to destroy 'Christian Europe,'" *The Forward*, October 11, 2017. See also Emily Tamkin, "Who's afraid of George Soros?" *Foreign Policy*, October 10, 2017. The article gives a good summary of the rumors, fake news, and accusations made against Soros by Eastern European authorities.

46. Dana Milbank, "Anti-Semitism is no longer an undertone of Trump's campaign. It's the melody," *Washington Post*, November 17, 2016.

47. Peter Beinart, "How Trumpian nativism leads to anti-Semitism," *The Atlantic*, November 2, 2018.

48. Tim Hains, "Trump to Republican Jewish Coalition: 'You're not going to support me because I don't need your money,'" *Real Clear Politics*, December 3, 2015.

49. "Donald Trump tells U.S. Jews: Netanyahu is your prime minister," YouTube, April 7, 2019 (https://www.youtube.com/watch?v=PPTQaOVbR9k)

50. Author interview, May 24, 2019.

51. *Anti-Semitism Monitor*, February 21, 2019. See also Etan Nechin, "Netanyahu now endorses Jewish fascism. U.S. Jews, cut your ties with him!" *Haaretz*, February 21, 2019.

Chapter 9: It's Not Necessary or Healthy to Keep Quiet

1. Counting the American Jewish population is difficult. See Emily Guskin, "How many Jews live in the U.S.? That depends on how you define 'Jewish,'" *Washington Post*, February 23, 2018.

2. David Rothkopf, "Israel is becoming an illiberal thugocracy, and I'm running out of ways to defend it," *Haaretz*, January 8, 2018.

3. Daniel Sokatch, "Israel's nation-state bill is tribalism at its worst; betrays human dignity and equality," New Israel Fund press release, July 18, 2018.

4. Yair Ettinger, "Anti-Semitism, assimilation, and the paradox of Jewish survival—an interview with David Myers, new president of the NIF," *Haaretz*, November 18, 2018.

5. Ettinger.

6. Daniel Sokatch, "Netanyahu won the election. Will he now dismantle Israel's democracy?" *Haaretz*, April 10, 2019.

7. "UJR president Rabbi Rick Jacobs statement on Israel's nation-state law," Union for Reform Judaism, July 18, 2018, https://urj.org/press-room/urj-president-rabbi-rick-jacobs-statement-israels-nation-state-law.

8. The name IfNotNow is derived from a saying by the first-century Jewish sage Hillel the Elder: "If I am not for myself, who will be for me? And being for myself, what am 'I'? If not now, when?"

9. Judy Maltz, "Sharp decline in number of American Jews on Birthright trips," *Haaretz*, December 11, 2018. Numbers are down as much as 50 percent in some cases.

10. Lornet Turnbull, "Why young Jews are detouring from Israel to Palestine," *Yes! Magazine*, May 8, 2019.

11. Azad Essa, "The new faces of Jewish-American resistance to Israel," *Middle East Eye*, March 18, 2019.

12. Essa.

13. Essa.

14. J. J. Goldberg, *Jewish Power: Inside the American Jewish Establishment* (New York: Perseus Books, 1996).

15. Author interview, May 6, 2015.

16. Dov Waxman, *Trouble in the Tribe: The American Jewish Conflict over Israel* (Princeton: Princeton University Press, Princeton, 2016). I interviewed him on May 24, 2019, when Waxman was still at Northeastern University. He now teaches at UCLA.

17. Author interview, May 16, 2019.

18. Author interview, May 14, 2019.

19. Author interview, May 16, 2019.

20. Author interview, May 19, 2019.

21. "But I gave them Jerusalem! What more do they want?" Trump apparently complained in private. Anshel Pfeffer, "Donald Trump thinks the Jews aren't grateful enough," *Haaretz*, September 20, 2018.

22. See Chapter 3, "'Vital space' for the Jewish people."

23. Author interview, May 19, 2019.

24. Danielle Ziri, "Jewish groups and synagogues to shelter immigrants during ICE raids," *Haaretz*, July 14, 2019.

25. Ronald Lauder, "Israel: this is not what we are," *New York Times*, August 13, 2018.

26. Allison Kaplan Sommer and Bar Peleg, "'Racist and discriminatory': U.S. Jewish leaders warn Israel against passage of nation-state law," *Haaretz*, July 15, 2018.

27. Josefin Dolstein, "Natalie Portman slams Israel's nation-state law as 'racist,'" *Times of Israel*, December 14, 2018.

28. "Progressive Jews blast new nation-state law as danger to Israel's future," *Haaretz*, July 19, 2018.

29. Amir Tibon, "Antithesis of American values: pro-Israel Democratic senators slam Netanyahu's deal with Kahanists," *Haaretz*, March 3, 2019.

30. David Friedman, "Read Peter Beinart and you'll vote Donald Trump," Arutz Sheva, https://www.israelnationalnews.com/Articles/Article.aspx/18828. Wrote Friedman: "Are J Street supporters really as bad as kapos? The answer, actually, is no. They are far worse than kapos—Jews who turned in their fellow Jews in the Nazi death camps. The kapos faced extraordinary cruelty, and who knows what any of us would've done under those circumstances to save a loved one? But J Street? They are just smug advocates of Israel's destruction delivered from the comfort of their secure American sofas—it's hard to imagine anyone worse."

31. Nathan Thrall, "How the battle over Israel and anti-Semitism is fracturing American politics," *New York Times Magazine*, March 28, 2019.

32. Thrall.

33. "Rashida Tlaib endorses BDS movement," *Middle East Eye*, December 3, 2018. See also, "Rashida Tlaib to head congressional delegation to West Bank, endorses BDS," *Haaretz*, December 4, 2018.

34. "Trump repeats claims that Democrats are 'anti-Israel' and 'anti-Jewish' ahead of Netanyahu's visit," *Washington Post*, March 22, 2019.

35. See the article by former senior AIPAC executive M. J. Rosenberg, "This is how AIPAC really works," *The Nation*, February 14, 2019, and the one by Ady Barkan, "What Ilhan Omar said about AIPAC was right," *Haaretz*, February 12, 2019.

36. Angelo Fichera, "Doctored quote tied to Rep. Omar," FactCheckOrg, April 11, 2019.

37. Thrall.

38. Editorial, "Curbing speech in the name of helping Israel," *New York Times*, December 18, 2018.

39. Michelle Alexander, "Time to break the silence on Palestine," *New York Times*, January 19, 2019.

40. See Chapter 6, "Israel extends its net from Palestinians to deviant Jews."

41. Taly Krupkin, "Israel's travel ban backlash: over 100 Jewish studies scholars threaten to not visit Israel in protest," *Haaretz*, March 10, 2017.

42. Krupkin.

43. Krupkin.

44. Krupkin.

45. This may be costing Israel as much as 100 million shekels (about $29 million) a year. The official figure is secret. Why? "We are working on foreign soil, and have to be very cautious," said Sima Vaknin-Gil, the director general of the Strategic Affairs Ministry, which is in charge of the worldwide fight against BDS. See Uri Blau, "Inside the clandestine world of Israel's 'BDS-busting' ministry," *Haaretz*, March 26, 2017. Also, Amir Tibon, "We are working on foreign soil and have to be very cautious," *Haaretz*, October 23, 2018.

46. Author interview, May 16, 2019.

47. "Revealed: Secret ADL memo slammed anti-BDS laws," *The Forward*, December 14, 2018.

48. Author interview, May 24, 2019.

49. Joshua Shanes, "Liberal Zionists faced a critical test with Airbnb. We flunked it," *Haaretz*, November 26, 2018.

50. Shanes.

Chapter 10: "No! No! You can't quote me on that!"

1. Author interview, February 20, 2019.

2. Pierre Mendès-France, for example, who led the government in 1954–55, bears the addition of "France" to his name (Mendes de França) to distinguish him from the branches of his family that emigrated to Germany and Holland.

3. Doris Bensimon-Donath, *L'intégration des Juifs nord-africains en*

France [The integration of North African Jews in France] (Paris and the Hague: Mouton et Co., 1971).

4. Author interview, June 16, 2020. Enderlin is the author of *Les Juifs de France entre République et sionisme* [French Jews between Republic and Zionism] (Paris: Le Seuil, 2020).

5. Pierre Birnbaum, *Les Deux Maisons: Essai sur la citoyenneté des juifs (en France et aux Etats-Unis)* [The two houses: an essay on Jews' citizenship in France and the United States] (Paris: Gallimard, 2012).

6. Birnbaum, 25.

7. Pierre Birnbaum, *Les désarrois d'un fou de l'Etat* [The distress of an admirer of the State], conversations with Jean Baumgarten and Yves Déloye (Paris: Albin Michel, 2015), 203.

8. Birnbaum, *Les Deux Maisons*, 15.

9. Birnbaum, *Les Deux Maisons*, 23.

10. Charles Enderlin, *Les Juifs de France entre République et sionisme* [French Jews between Republic and Zionism] (Paris: Le Seuil, 2020), 58.

11. Pierre Birnbaum, *Les désarrois d'un fou de l'Etat*, 185.

12. *La France juive* [Jewish France] was a hugely successful anti-Semitic tract published by Édouard Drumont. A work of 1,200 pages, it ran to 140 printings during the two years following its initial publication in 1886.

13. Quoted in Enderlin, *Les Juifs de France entre République et sionisme*, 318.

14. Author interview, June 16, 2020.

15. Emmanuel Brenner, *Les Territoires perdus de la République* [The Republic's lost territories] (Paris: Éditions Mille et une nuits, 2002). Quoted in Enderlin, 392.

16. Author interview, February 20, 2019

17. For details on Shakir's expulsion, see Chapter 6, "The security state in action."

18. "Stop Boycott. Comprendre l'expulsion d'Omar Shakir d'Israël en cinq questions" [Stop boycott: understanding Omar Shakir's expulsion from Israel in five questions], *La Lettre du CRIF,* November 6, 2019, http://www.crif.org/fr/actualites/novembre-2019-stop-boycott-comprendre-lexpulsion-domar-shakir-disrael-en-5-questions.

19. The Fondation pour la Mémoire de la Shoah supports projects in Holocaust history and research, education and transmission, memory, solidarity and Jewish culture. It was formed in 2000 with money and other property taken from French Jews during World War II.

20. *Aliyah,* Hebrew for "going up," has been used from the start of the Zionist movement to refer to Jewish immigration to Palestine, then to Israel.

21. Author interview, July 16, 2019.

22. Author interview, July 26, 2019.

23. Author interview, July 12, 2019.

24. Author interview, July 12, 2019.

25. Author interview, July 10, 2019.

26. Author interview, July 17, 2019.

27. At the end of March 2019, the United Nations reported that the total for one year stood at 195 killed and 29,000 wounded, of whom 7,000 were hit with bullets.

28. "Ambassador to France criticized over censorship attempt," *YNet,* https://www.ynetnews.com/articles/0,7340,L-5372294,00.html.

29. Meyer Habib, "'Envoyé spécial' sur 'Les estropiés de Gaza': halte à la haine!" [Envoyé special on "Gaza's crippled youth": stop the hatred!), *Tribune juive,* October 11, 2018.

30. France's 1990 Gayssot Law makes it an offense "to question the existence or size of the category of crimes against humanity as defined in the London Charter of 1945, on the basis of which Nazi leaders were convicted by the International Military Tribunal at Nuremberg in 1945–46" (Wikipedia).

31. Author interview, April 30, 2019.

32. Author interview, September 14, 2019.

33. Author interview, July 10, 2019.

34. Author interview, July 12, 2019.

35. Nathan Thrall, "How the battle over Israel and anti-Semitism is fracturing American politics," *New York Times Magazine*, March 28, 2019.

36. Author interview, July 22, 2019.

37. Pierre Vidal-Naquet's books include *Assassins of Memory*, about fanatics who deny the existence of the Holocaust, translated by Jeffrey Mehlman (New York: Columbia University Press, 1993), and *The Jews: History, Memory, and the Present*, which explores the myths and ideologies that have become entangled with Jewish history over the centuries, translated by David Ames Curtis (New York: Columbia University Press, 1996).

38. See Jérôme Fourquet's studies of the Jewish vote in the 2007 and 2012 French presidential elections, and the shift to the candidate of the conservative right, Nicolas Sarkozy.

39. Richard Marienstras (1928–2011), a great Shakespeare specialist and engagé progressive intellectual, was active in France's Jewish press between 1970 and 1990.

40. Author interview, April 9, 2019.

41. Simone Veil (1927–2017) was a French lawyer and an important politician.

42. French ethno-nationalist websites include Riposte laïque and Europe-Israël News, which repeats practically verbatim the rants on

Fdesouche, which stands for "Français de souche," meaning the real, native-born French.

43. Author interview, July 26, 2019.

44. Author interview, July 17, 2019.

45. Bat Ye'or is the pen name of Gisèle Littman (1933–), an Egyptian-born British author whose writings focus on the history of religious minorities in the Muslim world. A *dhimmi* is a person living in a region overrun by Muslim conquest who was accorded a protected status and allowed to retain his or her original faith.

46. Hebrew acronym for the Israel Defense Forces.

47. Author interview, July 17, 2019.

48. Author interview, September 14, 2019.

49. Author interview, July 26, 2019.

50. On March 13, 2012, Mohammed Merah shot three soldiers at Montauban. On March 19 at the Ozar Hathora Jewish day school in Toulouse, he killed a rabbi and three children, and wounded four other children.

51. Benbassa interview, July 26, 2019.

52. According to a March 2018 CRIF study by historian Marc Knobel, more than 55,000 French Jews emigrated to Israel between 2000 and 2017. But the figure is open to question. First, because some estimates say that half of those people came back, unable to settle happily in their new country. But also because some percentage—hard to estimate, but significant—make *aliyah*, get an Israeli passport, and buy an apartment in Israel, but only live there occasionally while continuing to work in France.

After 2000, there was an increase in the number of French Jews emigrating to Israel. But that figure has been dropping sharply. It went from 8,000 in 2015 to 800 in the first six months of 2019, according to Jewish Agency figures (*Haaretz*, August 1, 2019).

53. "Un pays face à la terreur" [A country facing terror], *Libération*, January 11, 2015.

Chapter 11: I Am Exhausted by Israel

1. Yotam Berger and Noa Landau, "At West Bank event, Netanyahu promises no more settlers, Arabs will be evicted," *Haaretz*, July 10, 2019.

2. David Shulman, "Israel's irrational rationality," *New York Review of Books*, June 22, 2017.

3. Author interview, July 7, 2019.

4. Author interview, July 7, 2019.

5. Author interview, January 6, 2019.

6. Author interview, January 6, 2019.

7. Author interview, January 6, 2019.

8. Author interview, January 6, 2019.

9. Gideon Levy, "Netanyahu's Israel will declare an apartheid state. Will the West do nothing?" *Haaretz*, April 30, 2019.

10. Author interview, January 3, 2019.

11. Bertrand Badie, *L'Impuissance de la puissance* [The impotence of power] (Paris: Fayard, 2004).

12. General Yitzhak Brick, interviewed by Amos Harel, "Israelis are living on the *Titanic*—no one wants to hear bad news about the Army," *Haaretz*, January 16, 2019.

13. Historian Benny Morris, interviewed by Ofer Aderet, "Israel will decline, and the Jews will be a persecuted minority. Those who can will flee to America," *Haaretz*, January 18, 2019.

14. Morris, interviewed by Aderet.

15. Haim Gouri died on January 31, 2018.

16. Gili Izikovich, "Poet and Palmach icon Haim Gouri turns down 'Zionist work of art' prize," *Haaretz*, January 4, 2016.

17. Author interview, early January, 2006.

18. Author interview, January 7, 2019.

19. Isy Morgensztern, "Isaac Bashevis Singer—Sur un dieu caché" [Isaac Bashevis Singer—on a hidden god], *Un siècle d'écrivains* no. 92 (October 2, 1996).

20. Simon Schama, *The Story of the Jews: Belonging, 1492–1900* (London: The Bodley Head, 2017).

21. Yuri Slezkine, *The Jewish Century* (Princeton: Princeton University Press, 2004).

22. Author interview, May 17, 2019.

23. Author interview, May 24, 2019.

24. According to Eric Duffin in "Denominational affiliation of Jews in the U.S.," *Statista*, January 2017, the 60 percent of U.S. households who belong to a synagogue define themselves this way: 28 percent Reform, 14 percent Conservative, 10 percent Orthodox, 2 percent Reconstructionist, 9 percent other, and 37 percent as "just Jewish."

25. *Tikkun olam* should be seen as the proper state of mind when drafting this text: "It is every Jew's duty to leave the world in better condition than it was when they were born."

26. The Pittsburgh Platform is a pivotal 1885 document in the history of the American Reform Movement in Judaism. It called for Jews to adopt a modern approach to the practice of their faith. The founding document of "Classical Reform," it rejected laws that have only a ritual, rather than an ethical or moral, basis. These include Jewish dietary laws.

27. Yehuda Kurtzer, "The deep sources of a great divide," *New Republic*, September 6, 2018.

28. Jacob Bacharach, "A homeland in America," *New Republic*, September 6, 2018.

29. Well-known representatives of this diaspora renewal include Rabbi Aryeh Cohen, who teaches rabbinical literature at American

Jewish University in Los Angeles, and playwright Tony Kushner, who wrote *Angels in America* and the screenplays for Steven Spielberg's movies *Munich* and *Lincoln*.

30. Daniel Boyarin, *Border Lines: The Partition of Judaeo-Christianity* (Philadelphia: University of Pennsylvania Press, 2006), xiv.

31. Boyarin, xiv.

32. Author interview, June 13, 2019.

33. Author interview, May 14, 2019.

34. Jonathan Weisman, "American Jews and Israeli Jews are headed for a messy breakup," *New York Times*, January 4, 2019.

35. Quoted in Weisman.

36. Quoted in Weisman.

37. Chemi Shalev, "Israel's irreconcilable differences with U.S. Jews and the Democratic Party may soon lead to final divorce," *Haaretz*, September 17, 2018.

38. "Judaism adjusting to multiracial congregations in Bay Area," *Religion Watch* 33, no.11 (September 2018).

39. Weisman.

40. Author interview, January 9, 2019. The quotes in the next three paragraphs are from this interview.

41. Author interview, April 30, 2019.

42. Author interview, February 20, 2019.

Chapter 12: The Last Goddamn Thing We Need

1. B'Tselem, *A Regime of Jewish Supremacy from the Sea to the Jordan River: This Is Apartheid*, January 12, 2021. https://www.btselem.org/publications/fulltext/202101_this_is_apartheid

2. The agreement to limit Iran's military nuclear arsenal, the Joint Comprehensive Plan of Action (JCPoA), was an accord made part

of international law by United Nations Security Council Resolution 2231.

3. William J. Burns, *The Back Channel: A Memoir of American Diplomacy and the Case for Its Renewal* (New York: Random House, 2019), 427.

4. Judy Maltz, "For Israel, Biden's Team Is Full of Familiar Faces," *Haaretz*, January 21, 2021.

5. *A Regime of Jewish Supremacy.*

6. Interview with Michael Ben-Yaïr: "Non à l'apartheid, pour sauver le sionisme" [Reject apartheid to save Zionism], *Le Monde*, February 9, 2002.

7. Jimmy Carter, *Palestine: Peace Not Apartheid* (New York: Simon & Schuster, 2006).

8. *A Regime of Jewish Supremacy.*

9. Evan Osnos, *Joe Biden: The Life, the Run, and What Matters Now* (New York: Simon & Schuster, 2020), 144.

10. "Biden's State pick backs two-state solution, says US embassy stays in Jerusalem," *The Times of Israel*–AFP, January 19, 2021.

11. Steve Kendricks and Shira Rubin, "Netanyahu approves hundreds of new homes for West Bank settlers on the eve of Biden's presidency," *The Washington Post*, January 11, 2021.

12. Thomas L. Friedman, "Biden Made Sure 'Trump Is Not Going to Be the President for Four More Years,'" *The New York Times*, December 2, 2020.

13. "Netanyahu urges no return to Iran nuclear deal," Reuters, November 22, 2020.

14. Amos Harel, "Assassination of Iranian nuclear scientist a tactical success that risks a strategic escalation," *Haaretz*, November 29, 2020.

15. Amos Harel, "Backing Netanyahu on Iran, Israel's military chief strikes defiant tone against Biden," *Haaretz*, January 27, 2021.

16. Friedman.

17. See Chapter 8, "Soros, Trump, and anti-Semitism."

18. Amos Harel, "The Americans will sign a deal with Iran with or without Israel," *Haaretz*, January 29, 2021.

19. Harel.

Conclusion

1. Tony Judt, "Israel: The Alternative," *New York Review of Books*, October 23, 2003. Tony Robert Judt (1948–2010) was an English-American historian, essayist, and New York University professor in European history. His many books include *Reappraisals: Reflections on the Forgotten Twentieth Century* (2008), *Postwar: A History of Europe since 1945* (2005), and *A Grand Illusion? An Essay on Europe.* (1996).

2. Peter Beinart, "I no longer believe in a Jewish State," *New York Times*, July 8, 2020. Beinart also published a more detailed article defending the same argument: "Yavne: A Jewish case for equality in Israel-Palestine" in *Jewish Currents*, July 7, 2020.

3. Dominique Eddé, ajout à la "Lettre à Alain Finkielkraut" [supplement to her "Letter to Alain Finkielkraut"] (*L'Orient–Le Jour*, March 10, 2019), Mediapart, March 11, 2019.

4. Lois Beckett, "Pittsburgh shooting: suspect railed against Jews and Muslims on site used by 'alt-right,'" *The Guardian*, October 27, 2018.

5. Author interview, April 9, 2019.

6. Adam Shatz, "Trump's America, Netanyahu's Israel," *London Review of Books*, April 8, 2019.

7. Michel Tubiana, "Du bon usage de l'antisémitisme en politique" [On the proper use of anti-Semitism in politics], Mediapart, February 18, 2019.

8. Eva Illouz, "Orbán, Trump, et Netanyahou semblent affection-ner barrières et murs" [Orban, Trump, and Netanyahu seem to like bar-riers and walls], *Le Monde,* August 8, 2018.

9. "Rep. Tlaib Pushes Biden to Protect At-risk Palestinians in Mid-dle East Conflict," National Public Radio, May 18, 2021.

10. "Paris met en garde contre un 'risque d'apartheid en Israel,'" 23 mai 2021 [Paris warns against a "risk of apartheid in Israel"], Radio France Internationale, May 23, 2021.

11. *A Threshold Crossed: Israeli Authorities and the Crimes of Apartheid and Persecution,* Human Rights Watch, April 27, 2021.

Index

Jews of Pittsburgh, 183, 199, 272

journalists, 14, 56, 118, 147; Omar
Abdulaziz, 124–25; Lucy Aharish,
103; Michelle Alexander, 220–21;
Uri Avnery, 171; Adam Entous,
125; Ronan Farrow, 125; Matti
Friedman, 194; Thomas L. Fried-
man, 284; Caroline Glick, 87;
Gershom Gorenberg, 94; Julia
Ioffe, 201; Evan Osnos, 282; Adam
Shatz, 245; Meir Weintrater, 243;
Jonathan Weisman, 269. *See also
under individual names*

J Street U National Board, 185, 209,
337n30

Judaism. *See* American Judaism;
French Judaism; Reform Judaism;
Union for Reform Judaism

Judt, Tony Robert, 291–294, 300–301,
302, 347n1

K

Kaczynski, Jaroslaw, 195, 202

Kahanist party, 62, 214, 226, 302

Katz, Israel, 131, 196

Khashoggi, Jamal, 123–24

Kimche, David, 149, 326n23

Klein, Morton, 175, 200

Knesset, the, 71–72, 88, 137, 139, 152,
205, 214, 221; and Palestinians, 135,
252; Bezalel Smotrich and, 69, 154;
and Supreme Court decisions, 167

Knesset members, 62, 65, 71, 107,
137, 142, 154; Arab, 62, 252; Anat
Berko, 202; Black Ethiopian, 93;
and BtS, 142; Benny Elon, 186;
Oded Forer, 252; Oren Hazan, 67,
103; Zvi Hendel, 178–79; Robert
Ilatov, 137; Yair Lipid, 103; Salman
Masalha, 103; Shuli Mualem-

Refaeli, 137; Miri Regev, 61, 62,
65–66; Ahmed Tibi, 170; and Julie
Weinberg-Connors, 152; Nissim
Ze'ev, 102; Haneen Zoabi, 66, 150

Kremnitzer, Mordechai, 142, 162,
164–65

Kronberg, Daniel, 28, 90, 152, 168

Ku Klux Klan 34–35, 37, 38, 68, 188,
200

L

Le Drian, Jean-Yves, 304

Leibowitz, Yeshayahu, 133, 139, 268

Le Monde, 67, 185

Levin, Hanoch, 251, 257

Levy, Gideon, 27, 53, 75–76, 150, 171,
179, 256

L'Express weekly magazine, 41, 43

LGBT community, 119, 183

Liberal Zionists, 215, 223, 224

Lieberman, Avigdor, 15, 16, 66, 67,
90, 255

Likud Party, 65–66, 74, 79, 85, 102;
founder of, 75, 128; members, 61,
86, 95, 103, 178, 202, 254

M

Maariv, 91, 314n15

Mack, Eitay, 121–23

Maghreb Jews, 5, 227, 228, 231,
233, 234

Mandatory Palestine, 51, 88, 322n4

Marienstras, Richard, 246, 273,
342n39

MBS. *See* bin Salman, Mohammed
(MBS)

Merah, Mohammed, 249, 343n50

Miller, Stephen, 99, 185, 320n11

Modi, Narendra, 13–14, 19, 45, 110,
116, 123

Morawiecki, Mateusz, 195, 196
Morris, Benny, 257, 258–59, 260,
  344n13
Mossad, 126–27, 148, 149, 188, 286
Myanmar, 18, 110, 122
Myers, David, 206, 208

N

nation-state law, 82, 173, 206, 213;
  debated, 71, 80; of the Jewish
  people, 72, 75, 98, 209, 300;
  opposed, 128, 207, 248; passage of,
  76–77, 280; and segregation, 166,
  225, 244, 252
Nazi Germany, 180, 193
Nazis, 193, 195, 341n30; Einsatzgruppen, 2, 177; Facebook
  and, 199; and Jews, 197, 337n30
Nazism, 178, 181–82
Negev desert, 93, 97
neo-Nazis, 111, 184, 188, 202, 320n11
Netanyahu, Benjamin, 14, 63, 79, 89,
  101, 157, 191, 192, 206, 283; and
  anti-Semitism, 18, 194, 295; and
  asylum seekers, 94, 95, 96, 97; and
  Azaria, 51–52, 53; and BDS, 144;
  and Beinart's interrogation, 154;
  and Biden, 286; and Blinken, 283;
  and Bolsonaro, 116; Dermer and,
  184; family of, 102, 189; a hero in
  France, 249; and Holocaust fake
  history, 176–77, 181–82; and Iran,
  285, 286, 288; and Kahanists, 214,
  226; Lieberman and, 66; and
  nationalists, 62, 72, 180, 264; and
  Obama, 212, 286; and Orban, 193,
  194; and Palestinians, 252–53, 277;
  and Polish regime, 195, 196; return
  to power of, 11, 191, 216; Strategic
  Affairs Ministry under, 127;

supporters in America, 184, 200;
  and Trump, 9, 17, 56, 176, 183, 303
Neve Sha'anan, Tel Aviv, 93, 97
New Israel Fund (NIF), 206, 207
New Republic, 95, 266
news agencies, 36, 41
New Yorker, 125, 126, 282
New York Review of Books, 43, 294
New York Times, 37, 201, 219, 220,
  221, 284, 292
NGOs, 45, 95, 136, 138, 155, 162, 171;
  B'Tselem, 28, 240, 279; El-Haq,
  240; Military Court Watch, 26;
  Monitor website, 142; Opponents
  of the Palestinian occupation,
  167; Yesh Din, 36
Nicaragua, 111, 115
Nigeria, 115, 118
NSO Group, 116–20, 124–25, 323n17

O

OAS (Organisation Armée Secrète,
  Secret Army Organization), 232,
  233
Obama, Barack, 7, 200, 212, 283, 286,
  287; advisor to, 214–15
Occupied Territories, 28, 64, 151,
  255, 276, 326n23; abuses in, 32,
  52, 140, 327n3; annexing of, 83,
  291; apartheid imposed on, 72,
  132–33, 279; B'Tselem and, 27,
  280; BDS and, 143–45, 149; boycotting goods from, 134–35, 163, 219,
  220, 224; colonization of, 160–61
Odeh, Ayman, 75, 88
Omar, Ilhan, 155, 184, 216, 217–18
Orban, Viktor, 14, 45, 123, 193, 194,
  202, 212
Oslo Accord, 35, 50, 148, 180, 278,
  281, 282, 318n21

Vidal-Naquet, Pierre, 245, 273, 342n37
Vietnam, 115, 220–21

W

Walzer, Michael, 212, 222, 262, 269
Waxman, Dov, 202, 211, 223, 262, 265, 336n16
Weintrater, Meir, 238, 243
Weisman, Jonathan, 269, 270
white supremacists, 98, 99, 185, 202; in America, 100, 200, 212–13, 299
Wieviorka, Michel, 245, 273
World Jewish Congress, 213, 248
writers: Susan Abulhawa, 151; Reza Aslan, 152; Jacob Bacharach, 266–67; and BDS, 145, 221; loyalty law and, 66; Nobel Prize in literature, 262; Dorit Rabinyan, 136; Moriel Rothman-Zecher, 152; Henry Siegman, 212; Isaac Bashevis Singer, 262; singer-song-, 170; Shai Stern, 59–60; Bat Ye'or (pen name of Gisèle Littman), 342n45

X

xenophobia, 13, 95, 183, 202, 213, 218, 219, 301

Y

Yad Vashem Holocaust Center, 110, 177, 192, 194
Ye'or, Bat, 247, 248
Yemen, 21, 239
Yesh Din. *See under* human rights
yeshivot, 54, 85
Yishai, Eli, 91, 92
YouTube, 59, 164, 180

Z

Zack, Isaac, 120, 323n17
Zahalka, Jamal, 61, 62
Zimmerman, Simone, 152, 208
Zionism, 3, 4, 8, 65, 168, 173, 206; and anti-Semitism, 18, 295; changing, 6, 74, 191, 260; and ethnicity, 48, 76, 92, 104; history of, 134, 190; and the Jewish diaspora, 184, 188, 262–64, 266, 295; national epic, 48, 50; and Palestinians, 11, 48, 341n20; religious, 35, 39, 254, 314n14; Twentieth Zionist Congress, 48; Zionist Strategic Center (ZSC), 142; Zionist Work of Art Prize, 260. *See also* Liberal Zionists
Zionist Organization of America (ZOA), 175, 184, 186
Zoabi, Haneen, 66, 150

Sylvain Cypel is a writer for *Le 1*, the magazine *America*, and the online news website Orient XXI. He is a former senior editor at *Le Monde*, which he joined in 1998 as deputy head of the international section, following a five-year tenure as editor in chief of *Courrier International*. From 2007 to 2013 he was *Le Monde*'s permanent US correspondent in New York. Cypel holds degrees in sociology, contemporary history, and international relations, the last of which he earned at the University of Jerusalem. He lived in Israel for twelve years and is now based in Paris. His book *Walled: Israeli Society at an Impasse* was published by Other Press in 2007.

William Rodarmor has translated some forty-five books and screenplays in genres ranging from serious fiction to espionage and fantasy novels, and won the 1996 Lewis Galantière Award from the American Translators Association. His recent translations include *And Their Children After Them* by Nicolas Mathieu (2020) and *Article 353* by Tanguy Viel (2019). He lives in Berkeley, California.